Asset Freezing at the International Criminal Court and the United Nations Security Council

Asset Freezing at the International Criminal Court and the United Nations Security Council

A Legal Protection Perspective

Daley J. Birkett

eleven international publishing

Published, sold and distributed by Eleven International Publishing
P.O. Box 85576
2508 CG The Hague
The Netherlands
Tel.: +31 70 33 070 33
Fax: +31 70 33 070 30
email: sales@elevenpub.nl
www.elevenpub.com

Sold and distributed in USA and Canada
Independent Publishers Group
814 N. Franklin Street
Chicago, IL 60610, USA
Order Placement: +1 800 888 4741
Fax: +1 312 337 5985
orders@ipgbook.com
www.ipgbook.com

Eleven International Publishing is an imprint of Boom uitgevers Den Haag.

ISBN 978-94-6236-185-0
ISBN 978-90-8974-486-9 (e-book)

Table of Contents

Table of Instruments		**ix**
Table of Cases		**xv**
1	**Introduction**	**1**
1.1	Framing the issue	1
1.2	Developing the research question	1
1.3	Methodology	3
1.4	Roadmap	5
2	**Asset Freezing: Theory, Objects and Purposes**	**9**
2.1	Introduction	9
2.2	Asset Freezing and Confiscation	9
2.2.1	Defining the Parameters	10
2.2.1.1	Conviction-based confiscation	12
2.2.1.2	Non-conviction-based confiscation	15
2.2.2	Justifying the Confiscation and Freezing of Assets	16
2.2.2.1	Punitive	17
2.2.2.2	Preventive	18
2.2.2.3	Restorative	19
2.2.2.4	Other	19
2.3	Situating ICC- and UNSC-Requested Asset Freezing Measures	20
2.4	Conclusion	24
3	**Coexistent but Uncoordinated – Asset Freezing Measures at the ICC and the UNSC**	**25**
3.1	Introduction	25
3.2	Modalities	26
3.3	Shared Goals?	28
3.4	Strengthening Cooperation	32
3.5	In Search of Coordination	36
3.5.1	Libya: Coexistent and Coordinated?	37
3.5.2	Coexistent but Uncoordinated	40
3.5.2.1	Democratic Republic of the Congo	40
3.5.2.2	Côte d'Ivoire	51

3.5.2.3 Sudan 55
3.5.2.4 Central African Republic 57
3.5.2.5 Mali 61
3.5.3 Neither Coexistent nor Coordinated 63
3.5.3.1 Uganda 63
3.5.3.2 Kenya 64
3.6 Conclusion 65

4 Recovering Assets at ICTs – Fines, Forfeiture and Orders for Reparations 67
4.1 Introduction 67
4.2 The Post-World War II Military Tribunals 67
4.3 The *Ad Hoc* International Criminal Tribunals 71
4.4 The Rome Statute System 73
4.4.1 Fine and Forfeiture Measures 73
4.4.2 Orders for Reparations 77
4.5 ICTs Established after the Adoption of the Rome Statute 79
4.5.1 The Special Court for Sierra Leone 79
4.5.2 The Special Panels for Serious Crimes 81
4.5.3 The Iraqi High Tribunal 82
4.5.4 The Extraordinary Chambers in the Courts of Cambodia 82
4.5.5 The Special Tribunal for Lebanon 83
4.5.6 The Extraordinary African Chambers 84
4.5.7 The Kosovo Specialist Chambers 85
4.6 Some Suggested Reasons behind ICTs' Failure to Order Asset Recovery Measures 87
4.6.1 Theoretical Basis 87
4.6.2 Dearth of Assets 88
4.6.3 Other Reparations Paradigms 88
4.7 Conclusion 89

5 Pre-Trial 'Protective Measures for the Purpose of Forfeiture' at the ICC – Protecting and Balancing Competing Rights and Interests 91
5.1 Introduction 91
5.2 Protective measures at the ICC 92
5.2.1 The evidentiary threshold 93
5.2.2 Prior notification and modification 94
5.2.3 The right to appeal 95

5.2.4 The 'rights of the parties concerned' and 'the ultimate benefit of victims' 96
5.2.4.1 Accused persons 96
5.2.4.1 The Prosecutor 98
5.2.4.3 Victims 99
5.2.4.4 Bona fide third parties 99
5.3 The ICC practice 100
5.3.1 The purpose of protective measures and the range of assets susceptible thereto 101
5.3.2 Balancing competing rights and interests in the protective measures process 106
5.4 Concluding remarks 112

6 UNSC-Requested Asset Freezes and the Legal Protection of Individuals 115
6.1 Introduction 115
6.2 The Evolution of UNSC Sanctions: From General to Targeted Measures 115
6.3 Identifying (Quasi-)Legal Protections 118
6.3.1 Exemptions 118
6.3.2 The Focal Point for de-Listing 120
6.3.3 Other (Quasi-)Legal Protections 122
6.4 Conclusion 128

7 Asset Freezing at the European and Inter-American Courts of Human Rights – Lessons for the ICC, the UNSC and States 129
7.1 Introduction 129
7.2 Asset Freezing in the Law and Practice of the Strasbourg and San José Courts 131
7.2.1 Protection of property 135
7.2.1.1 Džinić v Croatia 136
7.2.1.2 Chaparro Álvarez and Lapo Íñiguez v. Ecuador 144
7.2.2 Right to respect for private and family life 147
7.2.2.1 Nada v Switzerland 148
7.2.2.2 The need for clear reasoning at the ICC 150
7.3 Conclusion 153

8	**Managing the Frozen Assets of Accused Persons at the ICC – The Fallout of the Bemba Acquittal**	**155**
8.1	Introduction	155
8.2	The *Bemba* Case	158
8.2.1	(Un)freezing Bemba's Assets	158
8.2.2	Bemba's Claim for Compensation and Damages	164
8.3	Domestic Approaches	169
8.3.1	Third party management of seized or frozen assets	170
8.3.2	Use or Sale of Frozen Assets	172
8.4	International Responses	175
8.4.1	Utilising Article 96(3) of the ICC Statute	175
8.4.2	Lessons from Article 106 of the ICC Statute	176
8.4.3	Amending Article 85(3) of the ICC Statute?	177
8.5	Conclusion	179
9	**Conclusion**	**181**
Bibliography		**189**

Table of Instruments

Treaties

African Charter on Human and Peoples' Rights (adopted 27 June 1981, entered into force 21 October 1986) 1520 UNTS 217 (Banjul Charter)

Agreement Between the United Nations and the Royal Government of Cambodia Concerning the Prosecution under Cambodian Law of Crimes Committed During the Period of Democratic Kampuchea (adopted 6 June 2003, entered into force 29 April 2005) 2329 UNTS 117 (ECCC Agreement)

American Convention on Human Rights: "Pact of San José, Costa Rica" (adopted 22 November 1969, entered into force 18 July 1978) 1144 UNTS 123 (ACHR)

Arab Charter on Human Rights (adopted 15 September 1994) reprinted in (2005) 12 International Human Rights Reports 893 (Arab Charter)

Charter of the International Military Tribunal (adopted 8 August 1945, entered into force 8 August 1945) 82 UNTS 279 (IMT Charter)

Charter of the United Nations (adopted 26 June 1945, entered into force 24 October 1945) 1 UNTS XVI (UN Charter)

Convention for the Protection of Human Rights and Fundamental Freedoms (adopted 4 November 1950, entered into force 3 September 1953) 213 UNTS 262 (ECHR)

International Covenant on Civil and Political Rights (adopted 16 December 1966, entered into force 23 March 1976) 999 UNTS 171 (ICCPR)

Relationship Agreement between the International Criminal Court and the United Nations, (adopted 4 October 2004, entered into force 4 October 2004) 2283 UNTS 195 (ICC-UN Relationship Agreement)

Rome Statute of the International Criminal Court (adopted 17 July 1998, entered into force 1 July 2002) 2187 UNTS 90 (Rome Statute, ICC Statute)

United Nations Convention Against Corruption (adopted 31 October 2003, entered into force 14 December 2005) 2349 UNTS 41 (UNCAC)

United Nations Convention against Illicit Traffic in Narcotic Drugs and Psychotropic Substances (adopted 20 December 1988, entered into force 11 November 1990) 1582 UNTS 95 (UN Drug Trafficking Convention)

United Nations Convention against Transnational Organized Crime (adopted 15 November 2000, entered into force 29 September 2003) 2225 UNTS 209 (UNTOC)

Other International Instruments

Charter of the International Military Tribunal for the Far East (adopted 19 January 1946, entered into force 19 January 1946) TIAS No 1589 (IMTFE Charter)

Control Council Law No. 10 (adopted 20 December 1945, entered into force 20 December 1945) 3 Official Gazette Control Council for Germany 50-55 (Control Council Law No 10)

Law of the Supreme Iraqi Criminal Tribunal (adopted 18 October 2005, entered into force 18 October 2005) Official Gazette of the Republic of Iraq, No 4006, 18 October 2005 (IHT Statute)

Law on Specialist Chambers and Specialist Prosecutor's Office (adopted 3 August 2015, entered into force 15 September 2015) Official Gazette of the Republic of Kosova, No 27, 31 August 2015 (KSC Law)

Law on the Establishment of Extraordinary Chambers in the Courts of Cambodia for the Prosecution of Crimes Committed during the Period of Democratic Kampuchea, with inclusion of amendments as promulgated on 27 October 2004, NS/RKM/1004/006 (ECCC Law)

Protocol to the Convention for the Protection of Human Rights and Fundamental Freedoms (adopted 20 March 1952, entered into force 18 May 1954) 213 UNTS 262 (Protocol 1)

Regulation No. 2000/15 on the Establishment of Panels with Exclusive Jurisdiction over Serious Criminal Offences (6 June 2008) UN Doc UNTAET/REG/2000/15 (Regulation 2000/15)

Regulations of the Trust Fund for Victims (3 December 2005) ICC-ASP/4/Res.3 (TFV Regulations)

Statut des Chambres africaines extraordinaires au sein des juridictions sénégalaises pour la poursuite des crimes internationaux commis au Tchad durant la période du 7 juin 1982 au 1er décembre 1990 (Statute of the Extraordinary African Chambers within the courts of Senegal created to prosecute international crimes committed in Chad between 7 June 1982 and 1 December 1990) (adopted 30 January 2013, entered into force 8 February 2013) (2013) 52 ILM 1028 (EAC Statute)

Statute of the International Residual Mechanism for Criminal Tribunals, UNSC Res 1966 (22 December 2010) UN Doc S/RES/1966, Annex 1 (MICT Statute)

Statute of the International Tribunal for Rwanda, UNSC Res 955 (8 November 1994) UN Doc S/RES/1995, Annex (ICTR Statute)

Statute of the International Tribunal, UN Doc S/25704, Annex (ICTY Statute)

Statute of the Special Court for Sierra Leone (adopted 16 January 2002, entered into force on 12 April 2002) 2178 UNTS 138 (SCSL Statute)

Statute of the Special Tribunal for Lebanon, UNSC Res 1757 (30 May 2007) UN Doc S/RES/1757, Annex (STL Statute)

Universal Declaration of Human Rights (adopted 10 December 1948) UNGA Res 217 A(III) (UDHR)

Rules of Procedure and Evidence

ICC, Rules of Procedure and Evidence (adopted 9 September 2002, entered into force 9 September 2002) ICC-ASP/1/3 (ICC RPE)

ICTR, Rules of Procedure and Evidence, as amended on 13 May 2015 (adopted 29 June 1995, entered into force 29 June 1995) UN Doc ITR/3/Rev.23 (ICTR RPE)

ICTY, Rules of Procedure and Evidence, as amended on 8 July 2015 (adopted 11 February 1994, entered into force 14 March 1994) UN Doc IT/32/Rev. 50 (ICTY RPE)

MICT, Rules of Procedure and Evidence, as amended on 26 September 2016 (adopted 8 June 2012, entered into force 8 June 2012) UN Doc MICT/1/Rev/2 (MICT RPE)

SCSL, Rules of Procedure and Evidence, as amended on 31 May 2012 (adopted 16 January 2002, entered into force 12 April 2002) (SCSL RPE)

STL, Rules of Procedure and Evidence as amended on 3 April 2017 (adopted 20 March 2009, entered into force 20 March 2009) STL-BD-2009-01-Rev.8 (STL RPE)

Domestic Legislation

Australia

International Criminal Court Act 2002

Proceeds of Crime Act 2002

Canada

Seized Property Management Act 1993

Germany

Bundesergänzungsgesetz zur Entschädigung für Opfer der nationalsozialistischen Verfolgung (BEG) vom 18. September 1953 (Federal Supplementary Law for the Compensation of Victims of National Socialist Persecution of 18 September 1953)

Kenya

International Crimes Act 2008

New Zealand

Criminal Proceeds (Recovery) Act 2009

International Crimes and International Criminal Court Act 2000

Netherlands

Wetboek van Strafvordering (Code of Criminal Procedure)

Republic of Ireland

International Criminal Court Act 2006

Senegal

Code de Procédure Pénale Sénégalais (Senegalese Code of Criminal Procedure)

Switzerland

Ordonnance instituant des mesures à l'encontre de personnes et entités liées à Oussama ben Laden, au groupe «Al-Qaïda» ou aux Taliban (Ordinance on Measures against Persons and Organisations with Ties to Osama Bin Laden, the "Al-Qaida" Group or the Taliban)

United Kingdom

International Criminal Court Act 2001

Proceeds of Crime Act 2002

Table of Cases

Extraordinary African Chambers (EAC)

Ministère Public c Hissein Habré (Jugement) (30 May 2016)

Le Procureur Général c Hissein Habré (Arrêt) (27 April 2017)

European Court of Human Rights (ECtHR)

Džinić v Croatia App no 38359/13 (ECtHR, 17 May 2016).

Huvig v France App no 11105/84 (ECtHR, 24 April 1990)

Nada v Switzerland App no 10593/0856 (ECtHR, 12 September 2012)

Extraordinary Chambers in the Courts of Cambodia (ECCC)

Co-Prosecutors v KAING Guek Eav alias Duch (Inquiry into income and assets of the Accused) 001/18-07-2007/ECCC/TC (15 October 2009)

Co-Prosecutors v KAING Guek Eav alias Duch (Judgement) 001/18-07-2007/ECCC/TC (26 July 2010)

Inter-American Court of Human Rights (IACtHR)

Case of Chaparro Álvarez and Lapo Íñiguez v. Ecuador (Judgment of November 21, 2007) IACtHR Series C No 170 (21 November 2007)

International Criminal Court (ICC)

Situation in Darfur, Sudan

Prosecutor v Abdallah Banda Abakaer Nourain and Saleh Mohammed Jerbo Jamus

Prosecutor v Banda and Jerbo (Summons to Appear for Saleh Mohammed Jerbo Jamus) ICC-02/05-03/09-2-RSC (27 August 2009)

Prosecutor v Banda and Jerbo (Summons to Appear for Abdallah Banda Abakaer Nourain) ICC-02/05-03/09-3 (27 August 2009)

Prosecutor v Abdel Raheem Muhammad Hussein

Prosecutor v Hussein (Warrant of Arrest for Abdel Raheem Muhammad Hussein) ICC-02/05-01/12-2 (1 March 2012)

Prosecutor v Ahmad Muhammad Harun ("Ahmad Harun") and Ali Muhammad Ali Abd-Al-Rahman ("Ali Kushayb")

Prosecutor v Harun and Kushayb (Warrant of Arrest for Ahmad Harun) ICC-02/05-01/07-2 (27 April 2007)

Prosecutor v Harun and Kushayb (Warrant of Arrest for Ali Kushayb) ICC-02/05-01/07-3, (27 April 2007)

Prosecutor v Bahr Idriss Abu Garda

Prosecutor v Abu Garda (Summons to Appear for Bahr Idriss Abu Garda) ICC-02/05-02/09-2 (7 May 2009)

Prosecutor v Omar Hassan Ahmad Al Bashir ("Omar Al Bashir")

Prosecutor v Al Bashir (Warrant of Arrest for Omar Hassan Ahmad Al Bashir) ICC-02/05-01/09-1 (4 March 2009)

Prosecutor v Al Bashir (Second Warrant of Arrest for Omar Hassan Ahmad Al Bashir) ICC-02/05-01/09-95 (12 July 2010)

Situation in the Republic of Côte d'Ivoire

Situation in the Republic of Côte d'Ivoire (Request for authorisation of an investigation pursuant to article 15) ICC-02/11-3 (23 June 2011)

Situation in the Republic of Côte d'Ivoire (Corrigendum to "Decision Pursuant to Article 15 of the Rome Statute on the Authorisation of an Investigation into the Situation in the Republic of Côte d'Ivoire") ICC-02/11-14-Corr (15 November 2011)

Prosecutor v Charles Blé Goudé

Prosecutor v Blé Goudé (Warrant Of Arrest For Charles Blé Goudé) ICC-02/11-02/11-1 (21 December 2011)

Prosecutor v Charles Blé Goudé and Laurent Gbagbo

Prosecutor v Gbagbo and Blé Goudé (Transcript) ICC-02/11-01/15-T-232-FRA (15 January 2019)

Prosecutor v Gbagbo and Blé Goudé (Reasons for oral decision of 15 January 2019 on the *Requête de la Défense de Laurent Gbagbo afin qu'un jugement d'acquittement portant sur toutes les charges soit prononcé en faveur de Laurent Gbagbo et que sa mise en liberté immédiate soit ordonnée*, and on the Blé Goudé Defence no case to answer motion) ICC-02/11-01/15-1263 (16 July 2019)

Prosecutor v Laurent Gbagbo

Prosecutor v Gbagbo (Warrant Of Arrest For Laurent Koudou Gbagbo) ICC-02/11-01/11-1 (23 November 2011)

Prosecutor v Gbagbo (Declaration Accepting the Jurisdiction of the International Criminal Court dated 18 April 2003) ICC-02/11-01/11-129-Anx16-tENG (6 September 2012)

Prosecutor v Gbagbo (Letter from Alassane Ouattara to the President of the ICC dated 14 December 2010) ICC-02/11-01/11-129-Anx14-tENG (9 October 2012)

Prosecutor v Gbagbo (Letter from Alassane Ouattara to the Prosecutor of the ICC dated 3 May 2011) ICC-02/11-01/11-129-Anx15-tENG (10 October 2012)

Prosecutor v Simone Gbagbo

Prosecutor v Simone Gbagbo (Warrant of Arrest for Simone Gbagbo) ICC-02/11-01/12-1 (29 February 2012)

Situation in the Central African Republic

Situation in the Central African Republic (Decision Assigning Situation in the Central African Republic to PTC III) ICC-01/05-1 (19 January 2005)

Situation in the Central African Republic (Prosecutor's Application for Warrant of Arrest under Article 58) ICC-01/05-01/08-26-Red (9 May 2008)

Situation in the Central African Republic (Final decision on the reparations proceedings) ICC-01/05-01/08-3653 (3 August 2018)

Situation in the Central African Republic (Public Redacted Version of "Preliminary application for reclassification of filings, disclosure, accounts and partial unfreezing of Mr. Bemba's assets") ICC-01/05-01/08-3654-Red (30 October 2018)

Situation in the Central African Republic (Public Redacted version of "Response to Redacted version of the Registry's Observations on Mr. Bemba's Request for Reclassification of Information relating to Mr Jean-Pierre Bemba Gombo's Assets") ICC-01/05-01/08-3657-Red (30 October 2018)

Situation in the Central African Republic (Public Redacted version of "Mr. Bemba's response to the "Redacted version of Registry's Submissions in relation to Protective Measures imposed on Mr Bemba's Assets"") ICC-01/05-01/08-3659-Red (30 October 2018)

Situation in the Central African Republic (Public redacted version of "Decision on the Defence's preliminary application for reclassification of filings, disclosure, accounts and partial unfreezing of Mr Bemba's assets", 24 August 2018) ICC-01/05-01/08-3655-Red (16 November 2018)

Situation in the Central African Republic (Public redacted version of "Decision on Mr Bemba's preliminary application for reclassification of filings, disclosure, accounts, and partial unfreezing of Mr Bemba's assets and the Registry's Request for guidance", 18 October 2018) ICC-01/05-01/08-3660-Red2 (20 November 2018)

Situation in the Central African Republic (Public Redacted Version of "Registry's Observations on the Defence Request for Reclassification of Information relating to Mr Jean-Pierre Bemba Gombo's Assets", 3 September 2018) ICC-01/05-01/08-3656-Red2 (7 December 2018)

Situation in the Central African Republic (Public Redacted Version of "Registry's Submissions in relation to Protective Measures imposed on Mr Bemba's Assets", 21 September 2018) ICC-01/05-01/08-3658-Red2 (7 December 2018)

Situation in the Central African Republic (Public Redacted Version of "Urgent request for partial reconsideration and associated orders") ICC-01/05-01/08-3663-Red (10 December 2018)

Situation in the Central African Republic (Public Redacted Version of "Mr. Bemba's claim for compensation and damages") ICC-01/05-01/08-3673-Red (11 March 2019)

Situation in the Central African Republic (Order on the conduct of the proceedings related to "Mr Bemba's claim for compensation and damages") ICC-01/05-01/08-3675 (14 March 2019)

Situation in the Central African Republic (Public redacted version of "Prosecution's response to Mr Bemba's claim for compensation and damages", 6 May 2019) ICC-01/05-01/08-3680-Red (6 May 2019)

Situation in the Central African Republic (Public Redacted Version of the "Registry's Observations on the Defence Compensation Claim) ICC-01/05-01/08-3681-Red3 (6 May 2019)

Situation in the Central African Republic (Hearing on Mr Bemba's claim for compensation) ICC-01/05-01/08-T-376-ENG (9 May 2019)

Situation in the Central African Republic (Public Redacted Version of "Mr. Bemba's reply to the Prosecution Response to and Registry Submissions on "Mr. Bemba's claim for compensation and damages"") ICC-01/05-01/08-3687-Red (20 June 2019)

Situation in the Central African Republic (Public redacted version of "Prosecution's response to Mr Bemba's reply on compensation and damages", 26 June 2019) ICC-01/05-01/08-3690-Red (28 June 2019)

Situation in the Central African Republic (Public Redacted Version of the "Registry's Observations on Mr Jean-Pierre Bemba Gombo's Lawyers' Reply ICC-01/05-01/08-3687-Conf") ICC-01/05-01/08- 3689-Red3 (25 July 2019)

Situation in the Central African Republic (Decision on Mr Bemba's claim for compensation and damages) ICC-01/05-01/08-3694 (18 May 2020)

Situation in the Central African Republic (Request for leave to appeal the 'Decision on Mr Bemba's claim for compensation and damages') ICC-01/05-01/08-3695 (25 May 2020)

Situation in the Central African Republic (Prosecution response to Mr Bemba's request for leave to appeal the 'Decision on Mr Bemba's claim for compensation and damages') ICC-01/05-01/08-3696 (1 June 2020)

Prosecutor v Jean-Pierre Bemba Gombo

Prosecutor v Bemba Gombo (Warrant of Arrest for Jean-Pierre Bemba Gombo) ICC-01/05-01/08-1-tENG (23 May 2008)

Prosecutor v Bemba Gombo (Decision to Unseal the Warrant of Arrest for Mr Jean - Pierre Bemba Gombo) ICC-01/05-01/08-5-tENG (24 May 2008)

Prosecutor v Bemba Gombo (Decision et demande en vue d'obtenir l'identification, la localisation, le gel et la saisie des biens et avoirs adressées a la Republique portugaise) ICC-01/05-01/08-8 (27 May 2008)

Prosecutor v Bemba Gombo (Warrant of arrest for Jean-Pierre Bemba Gombo replacing the warrant of arrest issued on 23 May 2008) ICC-01/05-01/08-15-tENG (10 June 2008)

Prosecutor v Bemba Gombo (Registrar's Decision on the Application for Legal Assistance paid by the Court Filed by Mr Jean- Pierre Bemba Gombo) ICC-01/05-01/08-76-tENG (25 August 2008)

Prosecutor v Bemba Gombo (Requête en mainlevée de saisie (Application for Lifting the Seizure) ICC-01/05-01/08-81-Conf-tENG (26 August 2008)

Prosecutor v Bemba Gombo (Decision on the Defence's Application for Lifting the Seizure of Assets and Request for Cooperation to the Competent Authorities of Portugal) ICC-01/05-01/08-251-Anx (10 October 2008)

Prosecutor v Bemba Gombo (Decision on the Second Defence's Application for Lifting the Seizure of Assets and Request for Cooperation to the Competent Authorities of the Republic of Portugal) ICC-01/05-01/08-249 (14 November 2008)

Prosecutor v Bemba Gombo (Reasons for the decision on the Applications for judicial review of Mr Jean-Pierre Bemba Gombo of 10 and 11 November 2008) ICC-01/05-01/08-310 (5 December 2008)

Prosecutor v Bemba Gombo (Redacted version of "Decision on legal assistance for the accused") ICC-01/05-01/08-567-Red (26 November 2009)

Prosecutor v Bemba Gombo (Redacted Version of Decision on the Defence Application for Review of the Registrar's Decision of 15 October 2010 on the Application for Adjustment of the Expenses and Fees of the Defence (ICC-01/05-01/08-1007-Conf)) ICC-01/05-01/08-1007-Red (7 December 2010)

Prosecutor v Bemba Gombo (Judgment pursuant to Article 74 of the Statute) ICC-01/05-01/08-3343 (21 March 2016)

Prosecutor v Bemba Gombo (Decision on Sentence pursuant to Article 76 of the Statute) ICC-01/05-01/08-3399 (21 Junc 2016)

Prosecutor v Bemba Gombo (Judgment on the appeal of Mr Jean-Pierre Bemba Gombo against Trial Chamber III's "Judgment pursuant to Article 74 of the Statute") ICC-01/05-01/08-3636-Red (8 June 2018)

Prosecutor v Bemba Gombo (Decision on the appeals of the Prosecutor and Mr Jean-Pierre Bemba Gombo against the decision of Trial Chamber III of 21 June 2016 entitled "Decision on Sentence pursuant to Article 76 of the Statute") ICC-01/05-01/08-3637 (8 June 2018)

Prosecutor v Bemba Gombo (Order in relation to advanced legal assistance fees) ICC-01/05-01/08-3651-Red (17 July 2018)

Prosecutor v Jean-Pierre Bemba Gombo and others

Prosecutor v Bemba Gombo and others (Warrant of arrest for Jean-Pierre Bemba Gombo, Aimé Kilolo Musamba, Jean-Jacques Mangenda Kabongo, Fidèle Babala Wandu and Narcisse Arido) ICC-01/05-01/13-1-tENG (20 November 2013)

Prosecutor v Bemba Gombo and others (Decision on "Narcisse Arido's regulation 35 motion to extend time for initial appearance to March 24, 2014 to allow attorney, Abbe Jolles, to travel from Washington DC, USA" dated 18 March 2014) ICC-01/05-01/13-274 (19 March 2014)

Prosecutor v Bemba Gombo and others (Decision on Mr Kilolo's "Notice of appeal against the decision of the Single Judge ICC-01/05-01/13-743-Conf-Exp" dated 10 November 2014 and on the urgent request for the partial lifting of the seizure on Mr Kilolo's assets dated 24 November 2014) ICC-01/05-01/13-773 (1 December 2014)

Prosecutor v Bemba Gombo and others (Addendum à la "Requête de la défense aux fins de levée du gel des avoirs de Monsieur Aimé Kilolo Musamba") ICC-01/05-01/13-1014-Conf-Exp (28 July 2015)

Prosecutor v Bemba Gombo and others (Decision on Kilolo Defence Motion for Inadmissibility of Material) ICC-01/05-01/13-1257 (16 September 2015)

Prosecutor v Bemba Gombo and others (Decision on the 'Requête de la défense aux fins de levée du gel des avoirs de Monsieur Aimé Kilolo Musamba') ICC-01/05-01/13-1485-Red (17 November 2015)

Prosecutor v Bemba Gombo and others (Decision on Sentence pursuant to Article 76 of the Statute) ICC-01/05-01/13-2123-Corr (22 March 2017)

Prosecutor v Bemba Gombo and others (Judgment on the appeals of the Prosecutor, Mr Jean-Pierre Bemba Gombo, Mr Fidèle Babala Wandu and Mr Narcisse Arido against the decision of Trial Chamber VII entitled "Decision on Sentence pursuant to Article 76 of the Statute") ICC-01/05-01/13-2276-Red (8 March 2018)

Prosecutor v Bemba Gombo and others (Decision Re-sentencing Mr Jean-Pierre Bemba Gombo, Mr Aimé Kilolo Musamba and Mr Jean-Jacques Mangenda Kabongo) ICC-01/05-01/13-2312 (17 September 2018)

Situation in the Central African Republic II

Situation in the Central African Republic II (Decision Assigning the Situation in the Central African Republic II to PTC II) ICC-01/14-1 (18 June 2014)

<u>Prosecutor v Alfred Yekatom</u>

Prosecutor v Yekatom (Public Redacted Version of "Warrant of Arrest for Alfred Yekatom", ICC-01/14-01/18-1-US-Exp, 11 November 2018) ICC-01/14-01/18-1-Red (17 November 2018)

Prosecutor v Patrice-Edouard Ngaïssona

Prosecutor v Ngaïssona (Public Redacted Version of "Warrant of Arrest for Patrice-Edouard Ngaïssona") ICC-01/14-01/18-89-Red (13 December 2018)

Situation in the Democratic Republic of the Congo

Situation in the Democratic Republic of the Congo (Decision assigning the situation in the Democratic Republic of Congo to Pre-Trial Chamber I) ICC-01/04-1 (5 July 2005)

Prosecutor v Bosco Ntaganda

Prosecutor v Ntaganda (Warrant of Arrest) ICC-01/04-02/06-2-Anx-tEN (22 August 2006)

Prosecutor v Ntaganda (Decision on the Prosecution Application for a Warrant of Arrest) ICC-01/04-02/06-1-Red-tENG (6 March 2007)

Prosecutor v Callixte Mbarushimana

Prosecutor v Mbarushimana (Warrant of Arrest for Callixte Mbarushimana) ICC-01/04-01/10-2-tENG (28 September 2010)

Prosecutor v Mbarushimana (Decision on the Prosecutor's Application for a Warrant of Arrest for Callixte Mbarushimana) ICC - 01/04 - 01/10-7 (28 September 2010)

Prosecutor v Mbarushimana (Decision on the confirmation of charges) ICC-01/04-01/10-465-Red (16 December 2011)

Prosecutor v Mbarushimana (Judgment on the appeal of the Prosecutor against the decision of Pre-Trial Chamber I of 16 December 2011 entitled "Decision on the confirmation of charges") ICC-01/04-01/10-514 (30 May 2012)

Prosecutor v Mathieu Ngudjolo Chui

Prosecutor v Ngudjolo Chui (Warrant of Arrest for Mathieu Ngudjolo Chui) ICC-01/04-01/07-260-tENG (6 July 2007)

Prosecutor v Ngudjolo Chui (Demande adressée à la république démocratique du Congo en vue d'obtenir l'identification, la localisation, le gel et la saisie des biens et avoirs de Mathieu Ngudjolo Chui) ICC-01/04-01/07-266 (14 November 2007)

Prosecutor v Ngudjolo Chui (Version Publique Expurgée de l' « Ordonnance relative à l'exécution du mandat d'arrêt à l'encontre de Mathieu Ngudjolo Chui » rendue le 6 juillet 2007) ICC-01/04-01/07-294 (21 February 2008)

Prosecutor v Ngudjolo Chui (Judgment Pursuant to Article 74 of the Statute) ICC-01/04-02/12-3-tENG (18 December 2012)

Prosecutor v Ngudjolo Chui (Decision on the "Requête en indemnisation en application des dispositions de l'article 85(1) et (3) du Statut de Rome") ICC-01/04-02/12-301-tENG (16 December 2015)

Prosecutor v Sylvestre Mudacumura

Prosecutor v Mudacumura (Decision on the Prosecutor's Application under Article 58) ICC-01/04-01/12-1-Red (13 July 2012)

Prosecutor v Thomas Lubanga Dyilo

Prosecutor v Lubanga Dyilo (Decision on the Prosecutor's Application for a warrant of arrest, Article 58) ICC-01/04-01/06-1-Corr-Red (10 February 2006)

Prosecutor v Lubanga Dyilo (Warrant of Arrest) ICC-01/04-01/06-2-tEN (10 February 2006)

Prosecutor v Lubanga Dyilo (Request to the Democratic Republic of the Congo for the purpose of obtaining the identification, tracing, freezing and seizure of property and assets belonging to Mr. Thomas Lubanga Dyilo) ICC-01/04-01/06-22-tEN (9 March 2006)

Prosecutor v Lubanga Dyilo (Request to States Parties to the Rome Statute for the Identification, Tracing and Freezing or Seizure of the Property and Assets of Mr Thomas Lubanga Dyilo) ICC-01/04-01/06-62-tEN (31 March 2006)

Prosecutor v Lubanga Dyilo (Decision on the procedures to be adopted for *ex parte* proceedings) ICC-01/04-01/06-1058 (6 December 2007)

Prosecutor v Lubanga Dyilo (Decision Establishing the Principles and Procedures to be Applied to Reparations) ICC-01/04-01/06-2904 (7 August 2012)

Prosecutor v Lubanga Dyilo (Judgment on the appeals against the "Decision establishing the principles and procedures to be applied to reparations" of 7 August 2012 with AMENDED order for reparations (Annex A) and public annexes 1 and 2) ICC-01/04-01/06-3129 (3 March 2015)

Prosecutor v Lubanga Dyilo (Order for Reparations) ICC-01/04-01/06-3129-AnxA (3 March 2015)

Prosecutor v Lubanga Dyilo (Corrected version of the "Decision Setting the Size of the Reparations Award for which Thomas Lubanga Dyilo is Liable") ICC-01/04-01/06-3379-Red-Corr-tENG (21 December 2017)

Prosecutor v Lubanga Dyilo (Judgment on the appeals against Trial Chamber II's 'Decision Setting the Size of the Reparations Award for which Thomas Lubanga Dyilo is Liable') ICC-01/04-01/06-3466-Red (18 July 2019)

<u>Prosecutor v Germain Katanga</u>

Prosecutor v Katanga (Warrant of Arrest for Germain Katanga) ICC-01/04-01/07-1-tENG (2 July 2007)

Prosecutor v Katanga (Request to the Democratic Republic of the Congo for the purpose of obtaining the identification, tracing, freezing and seizure of the property and assets of Germain Katanga) ICC-01/04-01/07-7-tENG (6 July 2007)

Prosecutor v Katanga (Order on the execution of the warrant of arrest against Germain Katanga) ICC-01/04-01/07-54-tENG (5 November 2007)

Prosecutor v Katanga (Order for Reparations pursuant to Article 75 of the Statute) ICC-01/04-01/07-3728-tENG (24 March 2017)

Prosecutor v Katanga (Public redacted Judgment on the appeals against the order of Trial Chamber II of 24 March 2017 entitled "Order for Reparations pursuant to Article 75 of the Statute") ICC-01/04-01/07-3778-Red (9 March 2018)

Situation in the Republic of Kenya

Situation in the Republic of Kenya (Decision Assigning the Situation in the Republic of Kenya to Pre-Trial Chamber II) ICC-01/09-1 (6 November 2009)

Situation in the Republic of Kenya (Request for authorisation of an investigation pursuant to Article 15) ICC-01/09-3 (26 November 2009)

Situation in the Republic of Kenya (Corrigendum of the Decision Pursuant to Article 15 of the Rome Statute on the Authorization of an Investigation into the Situation in the Republic of Kenya) ICC-01/09-19-Corr (30 March 2011)

Prosecutor v Francis Kirimi Muthaura, Uhuru Muigai Kenyatta and Mohammed Hussein Ali

Prosecutor v Muthaura, Kenyatta and Ali (Decision on the Prosecutor's Application for Summonses to Appear for Francis Kirimi Muthaura, Uhuru Muigai Kenyatta and Mohammed Hussein Ali) ICC-01/09-02/11-01 (8 March 2011)

Prosecutor v Muthaura, Kenyatta and Ali (Decision Ordering the Registrar to Prepare and Transmit a Request for Cooperation to the Republic of Kenya for the Purpose of Securing the Identification, Tracing and Freezing or Seizure of Property and Assets of Francis Kirimi Muthaura, Uhuru Muigai Kenyatta and Mohammed Hussein Ali) ICC-01/09-02/11-42 (5 April 2011)

Prosecutor v Paul Gicheru and Philip Kipkoech Bett

Prosecutor v Gicheru and Bett (Decision on the "Prosecution's Application under Article 58(1) of the Rome Statute") ICC-01/09-01/15-1-Red (10 March 2015)

Prosecutor v Uhuru Muigai Kenyatta

Prosecutor v Kenyatta (Submissions of the Government of the Republic of Kenya pursuant to the 'Order for Submissions on the Implementation of the Request regarding the Freezing of Assets') ICC-01/09-02/11-923-Conf-Corr (28 May 2014)

Prosecutor v Kenyatta (Decision on the implementation of the request to freeze assets) ICC-01/09-02/11-931 (8 July 2014)

Prosecutor v Kenyatta (Dissenting Opinion of Judge Henderson) ICC-0l/09-02/11-931-Anx (8 July 2014)

Prosecutor v Kenyatta (Order concerning the public disclosure of confidential information) ICC-01/09-02/11-967 (21 October 2014)

Prosecutor v Walter Osapiri Barasa

Prosecutor v Barasa (Warrant of arrest for Walter Osapiri Barasa) ICC-01/09-01/13-1-Red2 (2 August 2013)

Prosecutor v William Samoei Ruto, Henry Kiprono Kosgey and Joshua Arap Sang

Prosecutor v Ruto, Kosgey and Sang (Decision on the Prosecutor's Application for Summons to Appear for William Samoei Ruto, Henry Kiprono Kosgey and Joshua Arap Sang) ICC-01/09-01/11-1 (8 March 2011)

Situation in the Libyan Arab Jamahiriya

Situation in the Libyan Arab Jamahiriya (Warrant of Arrest for Muammar Mohammed Abu Minyar Gaddafi) ICC-01/11-01/11-2 (27 June 2011)

Situation in the Libyan Arab Jamahiriya (Warrant of Arrest for Saif Al-Islam Gaddafi) ICC-01/11-01/11-3 (27 June 2011)

Situation in the Libyan Arab Jamahiriya (Warrant of Arrest for Abdullah Al-Senussi) ICC-01/11-01/11-4 (27 June 2011)

Prosecutor v Mahmoud Mustafa Busayf Al-Werfalli

Prosecutor v Al-Werfalli (Warrant of Arrest) ICC-01/11-01/17-2 (15 August 2017)

Prosecutor v Al-Werfalli (Second Warrant of Arrest) ICC-01/11-01/17-13 (4 July 2018)

Prosecutor v Al-Tuhamy Mohamed Khaled

Prosecutor v Khaled (Warrant of Arrest for Al-Tuhamy Mohamed Khaled with under seal and *ex parte* Annex) ICC-01/11-01/13-1 (18 April 2013)

Situation in the Republic of Mali

Situation in the Republic of Mali (Decision assigning the situation in the Republic of Mali to Pre-Trial Chamber II) ICC-01/12-1 (19 July 2012)

Prosecutor v Al Hassan Ag Abdoul Aziz Ag Mohamed Ag Mahmoud

Prosecutor v Al Hassan (Warrant of Arrest for Al Hassan Ag Abdoul Aziz Ag Mohamed Ag Mahmoud) ICC-01/12-01/18-2-tENG (27 March 2018)

Prosecutor v Ahmad Al Faqi Al Mahdi

Prosecutor v Al Mahdi (Mandat d'arrêt à l'encontre d'Ahmad Al Faqi Al Mahdi) ICC-01/12-01/15-1-Red (18 September 2015)

Prosecutor v Al Mahdi (Reparations Order) ICC-01/12-01/15-236 (17 August 2017)

Prosecutor v Al Mahdi (Public redacted Judgment on the appeal of the victims against the "Reparations Order") ICC-01/12-01/15-259-Red2 (8 March 2018)

Situation in Uganda

Situation in Uganda (Decision Assigning Situation in Uganda to PTC II) ICC-02/04-1 (5 July 2004)

Situation in Uganda (Warrant of Arrest for Vincent Otti) ICC-02/04-01/05-54 (8 July 2005)

Situation in Uganda (Warrant of Arrest for Raska Lukwiya) ICC-02/04-01/05-55 (8 July 2005)

Situation in Uganda (Warrant of Arrest for Okot Odhiambo) ICC-02/04-01/05-56 (8 July 2005)

Situation in Uganda (Warrant of Arrest for Dominic Ongwen) ICC-02/04-01/05-57 (8 July 2005)

Situation in Uganda (Warrant of Arrest for Joseph Kony Issued on 8 July 2005 as Amended on 27 September 2005) ICC-02/04-01/05-53 (27 September 2005)

Redacted

Prosecutor v [Redacted] (Judgment on the appeal of the Prosecutor against the decision of [REDACTED]) ICC-ACRed-01/16 (15 February 2016)

International Criminal Tribunal for the former Yugoslavia (ICTY)

Prosecutor v Milošević and others (Decision on Review of Indictment and Application for Consequential Orders) ICTY-02-54 (24 May 1999)

Prosecutor v Tadić (Decision on the Defence Motion for Interlocutory Appeal on Jurisdiction) ICTY-94-1 (2 October 1995)

International Criminal Tribunal for Rwanda (ICTR)

Miscellaneous–Kabuga Family (Appeal of the Family of Felicien Kabuga against Decisions of the Prosecutor and President of the Tribunal) ICTR-01-A (22 November 2002)

Prosecutor v Musema (Decision on an Application by African Concern for Leave to Appear as Amicus Curiae) ICTR-96-13-T (17 March 1999)

Prosecutor v Bagosora and others (Decision on Amicus Curiae Request by African Concern) ICTR-98-41-T (23 March 2004)

International Military Tribunal (IMT)

Judgment of the Nuremberg International Military Tribunal 1946 (1947) 41 American Journal of International Law 172

U.S. Military Tribunals

Judgment of 31 July 1948, in *Trials of War Criminals Before the Nuremberg Military Tribunals under Control Council Law No. 10*, vol IX (United States Government Printing Office 1950)

Special Court for Sierra Leone (SCSL)

Prosecutor v Norman and others (Norman – Decision on *Inter Partes* Motion by Prosecution to Freeze the Account of the Accused Sam Hinga Norman at Union Trust Bank (Sl) Limited or at Any Other Bank in Sierra Leone) SCSL-04-14-PT (19 April 2004)

Prosecutor v Sesay and others (Judgement) SCSL-04-15-T (2 March 2009)

Prosecutor v Taylor (Principal Defender's Determination of Mr. Charles Ghankay Taylor's Indigence) SCSL-03-01-I-85 (3 April 2006)

Domestic Courts

England and Wales

R v Waterfield (17 February 1975)

Italy

Corte di Appello di Roma (19 July 2012) Ordinanza N 4/12 RGIE

United States of America

Kaley v United States 134 S Ct 1090 (2014)

1 Introduction

1.1 Framing the issue

The International Criminal Court (ICC, Court) and the United Nations Security Council (UNSC) are both authorised to request States to take coercive measures with respect to individuals' assets. In pursuing its mandate to bring an end to impunity, the Court is not only empowered to request States to arrest accused persons, but also to identify, trace, freeze and seize their assets.[1] Similarly, the UNSC is equipped with the power to request States to freeze individuals' assets by Chapter VII of the UN Charter in furtherance of its primary responsibility for the maintenance of international peace and security. The UNSC has employed these procedures in a number of situations in which the Court has also been engaged.[2] Individuals' assets can therefore be targeted by both bodies.

Regardless of duration, freezing individuals' assets infringes on their rights. But the longer assets are frozen, the more likely and/or more severe these infringements become. Asset freezing measures implemented at the behest of the Court and the UNSC are rarely short in duration, with the former capable of enduring from the issuance of a warrant of arrest until the accused person is acquitted or convicted and the latter continuing until the UNSC no longer needs to act to maintain or restore international peace and security. The focus of this book rests on the two bodies' use of these asset freezing mechanisms, with a particular emphasis on the legal protections available to those individuals at the receiving end of the coercive measures at the disposal of the ICC and the UNSC, respectively.

1.2 Developing the research question

Although the ICC's constituent instrument (Rome Statute, ICC Statute) obliges its States Parties to assist the Court in identifying, tracing, freezing and/or seizing assets when so requested,[3] it provides little guidance as to how this ought to be done. Nor is much guidance provided in the ICC Statute regarding how the rights of the individuals against whom asset freezing measures are imposed at the Court's request are, or ought to be, protected. The academic literature offers limited further insights, with Carla Ferstman constituting a rare

1 For States Parties, see Rome Statute, art 93(1); for other States, see Rome Statute, art 87(5)(a).
2 Democratic Republic of the Congo, Côte d'Ivoire, Sudan, Libya, Central African Republic and Mali. See Chapter 3.
3 See Rome Statute, art 86.

example of a scholar having critically engaged with this sphere of the Court's operations, albeit from the perspective of victims of the alleged crimes.[4]

Moreover, despite practical overlap between their activities, and though the ICC and the UN have explicitly acknowledged a relationship between their respective responsibilities, particularly with regard to peace and security,[5] the interaction between ICC asset freezing procedures and asset freezing under the auspices of the UNSC has also been subjected to limited academic scrutiny. Larissa van den Herik[6] and Marina Mancini[7] are two scholars who have engaged with this interplay in detail, while others have discussed it in passing.[8] To respond to the lacuna in the practice of the ICC and the UNSC as well as in the pertinent academic literature, this study is designed to answer the following research question:

> 'Are the asset freezing measures executed at the request of the ICC and UNSC consistent with the rights of the individuals against whom they are imposed?'

The question necessitates an examination of two related issues: (i) how ICC- and UNSC-requested asset freezing measures infringe upon the rights of individuals; and (ii) in what way individuals can enforce the rights with which these measures interfere. The rights of several individuals beyond the immediate target of the measures might be affected by the freezing of assets. In the Rome Statute system, these could include alleged victims of the crimes of which the object of the asset freezing measures is accused. But the focus of the present book rests on the individuals whose rights are necessarily infringed whether their assets are frozen by the ICC or the UNSC, namely those against whom the restrictions are imposed. For related reasons, though the UNSC is also empowered to ask States to apply other coercive measures, including travel bans, in discharging its responsibilities under the UN Charter, this study is limited to analysing asset freezing measures, a tool also in the arsenal of the Court. In a similar vein, the European Union (EU) also implements

4 Carla Ferstman, 'Cooperation and the International Criminal Court: The Freezing, Seizing and Transfer of Assets for the Purpose of Reparations' in Olympia Bekou and Daley J Birkett (eds), *Cooperation and the International Criminal Court: Perspectives from Theory and Practice* (Brill Nijhoff 2016).

5 ICC-UN Relationship Agreement, preamble.

6 Larissa van den Herik, 'The Individualisation of Enforcement in International Law: Exploring the Interplay between United Nations Targeted Sanctions and International Criminal Proceedings' in Tiyanjana Maluwa, Max du Plessis and Dire Tladi (eds), *The Pursuit of a Brave New World in International Law: Essays in Honour of John Dugard* (Brill Nijhoff 2017) 234-263.

7 Marina Mancini, 'UN Sanctions Targeting Individuals and ICC Proceedings: How to Achieve a Mutually Reinforcing Interaction' in Natalino Ronzitti (ed), *Coercive Diplomacy, Sanctions and International Law* (Brill Nijhoff 2016) 228–245.

8 See eg Paul Bentall, 'United Nations targeted sanctions and other policy tools: diplomacy, legal, use of force', in Thomas J Biersteker, Sue E Eckert and Marcos Tourinho (eds), *Targeted Sanctions: The Impacts and Effectiveness of United Nations Action* (CUP 2016) 96-99.

UNSC- requested asset freezes on a supranational plane, with its Member States responsible for giving domestic effect to the pertinent EU legislation. In this way, the EU can reasonably be said to act as an intermediary. However, because this only applies to a limited number of States with respect to asset freezes imposed at the behest of the UNSC, the study will not focus on EU law and will instead pursue a global approach, to be discussed in greater detail in the following section. Notwithstanding, to the extent that the rights of individuals other than the person subjected to the asset freeze, the general legal protections developed in the context of UNSC-ordered travel bans and the implementation of UNSC-requested asset freezing measures at the EU level are relevant in providing an answer to the research question, the study takes these issues into consideration.

1.3 Methodology

The study employs a doctrinal research methodology, 'a two-part process of locating "the law" or doctrine and then analysing the texts',[9] a methodology claimed to be 'suited to research projects that seek to systematise legal norms, and to understand the relationships between different bodies of legal norms'.[10] Although it is recognised that the issues under examination in this book are not confined to the field of (international) law, with politics a particularly prevalent consideration when discussing the operations of the ICC and the UNSC, the study does not explicitly engage with non-legal fields or their methodologies. Nor does it utilise empirical legal research. Because the present study aims to discern the legal protections available to individuals subjected to ICC- and UNSC-issued asset freezing requests across multiple bodies of legal rules, the doctrinal research methodology is more apposite than other methods in order to answer the foregoing research question.[11]

As for the law, or doctrine, to be identified in order to conduct this doctrinal research, the study probes several bodies of legal rules capable of protecting individuals' rights during the asset freeing process. Freezing assets at the ICC's request takes place during the pre-trial phase of proceedings,[12] but persists until the person against whom the measures are applied is acquitted or convicted. Accordingly, in terms of the Court-related body of legal rules,

9 Terry Hutchinson and Nigel Duncan, 'Defining and Describing What We Do: Doctrinal Legal Research' (2012) 17 Deakin Law Review 83, 116.

10 Tamara Hervey, Robert Cryer and Bal Sokhi-Bulley, *Research Methodologies in EU and International Law* (Hart Publishing 2011) 38.

11 Discussing the employment of the doctrinal research method in international criminal law scholarship, see Elies van Sliedregt, 'Editorial – International Criminal Law: Over-studied and Underachieving?' (2016) 29 Leiden Journal of International Law 1, 5 ff. See in particular fn 20 ('The doctrinal research method comes intuitively to lawyers. This makes it difficult for legal scholars to explain to "outsiders" what they do.')

12 Rome Statute, art 57(3)(e).

the study analyses the sources of law applied at the ICC,[13] with the first port of call being the Rome Statute itself, together with its Rules of Procedure and Evidence (RPE) and its case law. As the first and only permanent international criminal tribunal, the focus of the study rests on the ICC, but, in order to better understand the Court's approach to freezing individuals' assets, where necessary the study analyses the law and practice of other international(ised) criminal tribunals (ICTs)[14] established before and subsequent to the adoption of the ICC Statute. With respect to the decisions of the Court, many ICC filings pertaining to asset freezing remain confidential. However, increasingly, there is a practice of de-classifying documents when the need for their confidentiality ceases. Consequently, albeit with some delay, the ICC's approach to the freezing of assets and other related issues is becoming more apparent.[15]

As for the UNSC-associated body of legal norms, the starting point of the analysis is the constituent instrument of the UN, the UN Charter, and the document governing relations between the UN and the Court, namely the ICC-UN Relationship Agreement. In addition, because UNSC-requested asset freezing measures are managed by sanctions committees, subsidiary organs of the UNSC, the book also scrutinises relevant documents issued by these bodies. To the extent that such documents serve the purpose of contributing towards answering the research question, documents issued by other organs of the UN, including the UN General Assembly, will also be critically evaluated.

Another body of legal rules to be examined with a view to identifying the available legal protections for individuals exposed to the ICC's asset freezing capabilities is international human rights law, with which the Court's application and interpretation of its sources of applicable law must be consistent.[16] This requirement renders 'internationally recognized human rights'[17] of paramount importance to answering the research question. In addition, because human rights not only underpin measures taken pursuant to the Rome Statute but also the UN Charter,[18] the study will examine the law and practice of international human rights bodies. Because of the depth of their pertinent case law on which the ICC

---

13 Rome Statute, art 21.

14 According to Sarah Williams, there are no universally-agreed definitions of international(ised) or hybrid criminal tribunals, but such institutions share a number of critical features. See Sarah Williams, *Hybrid and Internationalised Criminal Tribunals: Selected Jurisdictional Issues* (Hart Publishing 2012) 249-252. For the purpose of the present research, it is sufficient that such tribunals have the capacity to exercise jurisdiction over one or more international crimes. See also Sarah MH Nouwen, 'Hybrid Courts: The Hybrid Category of a New Type of International Crimes Courts' (2006) 2 Utrecht Law Review 190, 208.

15 Indeed, in November 2017, the Court published a 'booklet' on the subjects of asset recovery and financial investigations. ICC, 'Financial investigations and recovery of assets' (ICC 2017).

16 Rome Statute, art 21(3).

17 ibid.

18 See Chapter 7.

has relied in developing its jurisprudence on the application and interpretation of the Rome Statute 'consistent with internationally recognized human rights',[19] the book focuses upon cases decided by the European Court of Human Rights (ECtHR) and the Inter-American Court of Human Rights (IACtHR). Such an examination aims to illuminate the multiple human rights implicated by both asset freezing processes.

Domestic legislation is also analysed in the study. This is because State action is required to implement asset freezing measures requested by the ICC and UNSC. In other words, such measures are not self-executing in States' national legal orders. Though comparative research into the law and practice of all States that implement ICC- and UNSC-requested asset freezing measures might lead to a more thorough outcome, within the constraints of this study, certain domestic laws are examined to the extent that they relate to the research question. Finally, throughout the book, in analysing the legal texts identified, scholarly books, reports and articles will be consulted in order to respond to the research question, as will relevant documents from international and non-governmental organisations beyond those instituted in accordance with the Rome Statute and UN Charter.

1.4 Roadmap

Chapter 2 demarcates the types of asset freezing measures employed in domestic systems, including their respective objectives and modalities, before situating the ICC Statute and UN Charter regimes in a particular category or categories of such procedures. Examining measures used within and outside the criminal law context, this chapter seeks to act as a theoretical framework through which the subsequent chapters can be viewed.

Chapter 3 demonstrates that the UNSC and the ICC are frequently engaged in the same situations (primarily those involving armed conflict), the former in pursuit of its primary responsibility under the UN Charter for maintaining and restoring international peace and security and the latter pursuant to its commitment to bringing an end to impunity. The chapter also examines whether measures taken by UNSC-appointed sanctions committees to freeze individuals' assets under Chapter VII of the UN Charter could strengthen the Rome Statute framework for the freezing of accused persons' assets. It does so by analysing eight situations where the two bodies' activities (could) have overlapped, with a particular focus on the parallel implementation of asset freezing measures. The chapter shows that, even though the two bodies' respective activities in this area might have coincided on several occasions, they have scarcely been coordinated. This leads the

19 Rome Statute, art 21(3).

author to conclude that closer, formalised cooperation between the two bodies is aspirational but unlikely.

Chapter 4 evaluates the powers afforded to ICTs to order fines, forfeiture and reparations. This evaluation is key because the ICC's asset freezing powers are primarily used with a view to ordering the application of one or more of these tools in the event of a conviction. Chapter 4 therefore examines the development of the fine, asset forfeiture and reparation procedures in the constituent instruments and case law of a number of ICTs, with a focus on the powers granted to the Court under the ICC Statute. The chapter demonstrates that, although many ICTs have been granted the power to impose fines and forfeiture measures since the modern inception of international criminal law in Nuremberg, these procedures have been underutilised in practice even though a number of perpetrators of international crimes have, in fact, been solvent.

Chapter 5 addresses the legal measures designed to protect the rights of individuals against whom asset freezing measures are imposed at the request of the Court in the Rome Statute. Specifically, the authorisation given to the ICC under its constituent instrument to request its States Parties to identify, trace, freeze or seize assets '[w]here a warrant of arrest or a summons has been issued ... having due regard to the strength of the evidence and the rights of the parties concerned'[20] is examined. This chapter critically evaluates the ICC's approach to requesting such protective measures during the pre-trial phase of proceedings before the Court, with a focus on how the rights and interests of the primary stakeholders implicated by this process: (i) accused persons, (ii) the Prosecutor, (iii) victims and (iv) bona fide third parties, are safeguarded and balanced.

The focus of Chapter 6 rests entirely on the UNSC, which, like the Court, is vested with the capacity to request States to freeze individuals' assets. This chapter traces the evolution of UNSC-requested sanctions from general to targeted measures, with asset freezes falling into the latter category, before turning to examine the (quasi-)legal protections available to individuals (and entities) against whom UNSC-requested asset freezing measures are imposed. This chapter concludes that the safeguards not only fall short of judicial review, but also vary widely depending on the sanctions regime pursuant to which those targeted are listed.

Chapter 7 examines the human rights implicated by the asset freezing processes available to the Court and the UNSC. It does so through the lens of the jurisprudence of the ECtHR and the IACtHR, from whose case law, although not uniform, a number of principles can

20 Rome Statute, art 57(3)(e).

be distilled. By scrutinising a series of cases decided under the European Convention on Human Rights and American Convention on Human Rights, Chapter 7 demonstrates that the rights to the peaceful enjoyment of one's property and to respect for one's private and family life, home and correspondence are necessarily implicated by the execution of asset freezing measures in both contexts. The chapter concludes that, considering the multiple human rights constraints placed on the exercise of their powers, both the ICC and UNSC, as well as States acting at their request, must pay attention to this case law with a view to respecting the human rights of those to whom asset freezing measures are applied.

Chapter 8 examines a second aspect of the legal protections available to individuals under the Rome Statute system, namely the management of assets frozen at the Court's request. On 8 June 2018, more than ten years after his arrest, the ICC's Appeals Chamber reversed Jean-Pierre Bemba Gombo's conviction by the Court's Trial Chamber for crimes against humanity and war crimes, acquitting him of all charges. Shortly after the start of his time in detention in The Hague, States froze assets belonging to Mr Bemba across a number of jurisdictions at the request of the ICC. Many of these assets remain frozen, more than 18 months after his acquittal. Chapter 8 scrutinises the effects of prolonged asset freezes by the ICC through the lens of the Bemba case, demonstrating the existence of gaps in legal framework applicable to the management of frozen assets under the Rome Statute system and proposing possible responses thereto at the domestic and international levels.

Chapter 9 concludes the study and proposes a series of recommendations that might assist the ICC and UNSC in protecting the rights of the individuals against whom asset freezing measures are imposed at the request of the two bodies.

2 Asset Freezing: Theory, Objects and Purposes

2.1 Introduction

This chapter aims to unpack what is meant by the term asset freezing for the purposes of this study. To achieve this goal, it first examines the role played by asset freezing as a tool within the broader system of asset recovery. In so doing, it distinguishes the concept from the related processes of identification, tracing and seizure before scrutinising the multiple forms of and, importantly, justifications behind the confiscation of assets, of which freezing constitutes but one step. The chapter then places Rome Statute and UN Charter asset freezing procedures in this wider context before concluding that, in both legal frameworks, the freezing of assets is best characterised as a preventive measure, which can serve an additional restitutive function in the event of their eventual confiscation.

2.2 Asset Freezing and Confiscation

It is worth expressly noting at the outset that the way in which States have chosen to legislate in this area is by no means uniform. Moreover, because a large part of the legislation pertinent to this analysis came into being in response to the challenges posed by 'transnational crime',[1] the chapter draws upon legislation and literature from the field of transnational criminal law, which Neil Boister defines as 'the indirect suppression by international law through domestic penal law of criminal activities that have actual or potential trans-boundary effects.'[2]

1 According to Gerhard Mueller, '[t]he then United Nations (UN) Crime Prevention and Criminal Justice Branch coined the term in order to identify certain criminal phenomena transcending international borders, transgressing the laws of several states or having an impact on another country'. Gerhard OW Mueller, 'Transnational Crime: Definitions and Concepts' in Phil Williams and Dimitri Vlassis (eds), *Combating Transnational Crime: Concepts, Activities and Responses* (Frank Cass 2001) 13.

2 Neil Boister, 'Transnational Criminal Law?' (2003) 14 European Journal of International Law 953, 955. As for transnational crime, '[a]t its simplest, ... transnational crime describes conduct that has actual or potential trans-boundary effects of national and international concern.' ibid 954.

Asset freezing, like the identification, tracing and seizing of assets, constitutes a preliminary step in a wider process of asset recovery, which generally, but not always,[3] culminates in the confiscation of the object(s) of the measures. This is not to say that asset freezing will always be required before confiscation; instead, this is dependent on the modalities of the applicable law.[4] Boister categorises the identification, tracing, freezing and seizure of assets as 'interim legal steps … necessary prior to confiscation'.[5] As an interim step in the in the confiscation process, it seems reasonable to argue that the purposes underpinning asset freezing are closely tied with those behind the confiscation. Before addressing this issue, however, it is necessary to examine what exactly is meant by the freezing of assets. And how does this measure differ from the other interim, or preliminary, measures usually executed before confiscation?

2.2.1 Defining the Parameters

Identification and tracing entail locating the assets through, for example, conducting financial investigations.[6] As Guillermo Jorge notes, these processes can be facilitated by equipping the responsible (law enforcement, administrative and judicial) bodies with the power to monitor assets that may be ultimately confiscated.[7] This can be realised by, for example, 'giving them access to existing banking, legal persons, real estate, vehicles, and other registered movables' databases',[8] without which the competent national authorities might be unable to successfully execute this step.[9] Turning to freezing and seizure of assets, three UN conventions, that is to say the Convention against Illicit Traffic in Narcotic Drugs and Psychotropic Substances, the Convention against Transnational Organized Crime and the Convention against Corruption (or the 'suppression conventions')[10] define the terms 'freezing' and 'seizure' together in the same provision, as follows:

---

3 Neil Boister, *An Introduction to Transnational Criminal Law* (2nd edn, OUP 2018) 335 ('Confiscation of the asset is not … inevitable, and a provisional measure may be used as a tactic on its own simply to immobilize the property while further investigation is undertaken.')

4 ibid.

5 ibid.

6 ibid 336.

7 Guillermo Jorge, 'Article 31: Freezing, Seizure, and Confiscation' in Cecily Rose, Michael Kubiciel and Oliver Landwehr (eds), *The United Nations Convention Against Corruption: A Commentary* (OUP 2019) 322.

8 ibid.

9 ibid. As Neil Boister explains, this step also 'commonly runs into problems of access to the assets and banking confidentiality, and the removal of bank secrecy plays a key role in making these steps possible.' Boister, *An Introduction to Transnational Criminal Law* (n 3) 336.

10 Boister, 'Transnational Criminal Law?' (n 2) 955.

> 'Freezing' or 'seizure' shall mean temporarily prohibiting the transfer, conversion, disposition or movement of property or temporarily assuming custody or control of property on the basis of an order issued by a court or other competent authority[.][11]

As for the difference between freezing and seizure, though no explicit distinction is drawn in the foregoing provision,[12] it is intangible assets, such as deposits held by financial institutions[13] (or, in more recent times, cryptocurrency stored in 'blockchain wallets'),[14] that are susceptible to asset freezing, which 'involves the stopping of all movement of funds held in an account'.[15] On the other hand, seizure is applicable to tangible assets, including hard cash (ie banknotes and coins),[16] vehicles,[17] property,[18] and financial and commercial documents.[19] But freezing and seizure also share one important feature: both are temporary. As Cornelia Spörl contends, the word '"temporarily" shows that freezing and seizure are, in contrast to confiscation, non- permanent but preliminary measures'.[20] Indeed, according to the same abovementioned UN treaties, confiscation 'which includes forfeiture where applicable, shall mean the permanent deprivation of property by order of a court or other competent authority'.[21]

Confiscation procedures have historically been tied to criminal proceedings and, crucially, a criminal conviction. In other words, 'the deprivation of property (crime instrumentalities and proceeds) follows a conviction for a specific crime'.[22] However, States have adopted variants of this form of confiscation as well as procedures beyond the 'traditional'[23] approach, one of which does not have its legal basis in the criminal law. As Michele

---

11 UN Drug Trafficking Convention, art 1(l); UNTOC, art 2(f); UNCAC, art 2(f).

12 Cornelia Spörl. 'Article 2: Use of Terms' in Cecily Rose, Michael Kubiciel and Oliver Landwehr (eds), *The United Nations Convention Against Corruption: A Commentary* (OUP 2019) 30.

13 ibid; Boister, *An Introduction to Transnational Criminal Law* (n 3) 336. Other examples of intangible assets could include stocks, shares and other securities.

14 See eg Fergal O'Brien, 'High Court freezes €52m worth of Bitcoin seized by CAB' *Raidió Teilifís Éireann* (19 February 2020) <https://www.rte.ie/news/courts/2020/0219/1116299-bit-coin-clifton-collins/> accessed 31 August 2020.

15 Boister, *An Introduction to Transnational Criminal Law* (n 3) 336.

16 ibid.

17 ibid.

18 ibid.

19 Spörl (n 12) 30.

20 ibid.

21 UN Drug Trafficking Convention, art 1(f); UNTOC, art 2(g); UNCAC, art 2(g).

22 Michele Simonato, 'Confiscation and fundamental rights across criminal and non-criminal domains' (2017) 18 ERA Forum 365, 366. See also Boister, *An Introduction to Transnational Criminal Law* (n 3) 337 ('Most national legal systems provide for the confiscation on conviction of instruments acquired legally but then used in a crime.')

23 Jorge (n 7) 321; Simonato, 'Confiscation and fundamental rights' (n 22) 366.

Simonato succinctly puts it, 'This development has a manifold rationale: punitive, preventive, and restorative reasons coexist in order to shape the various strategies against "dirty money".'[24] As for the alternative forms of confiscation, writing elsewhere, Simonato provides the following neat summary:

> Assets may be confiscated even if they are not proceeds of the crime for which the offender has been convicted (extended confiscation), if they belong to persons other than the offender (third party confiscation), or if they are the proceeds of an offence which has not been proven at trial (non-conviction based confiscation); in some cases, even if criminal proceedings against the suspect have not started at all (civil asset forfeiture).[25]

Each of these variants will now be briefly examined in turn before turning to the justifications behind confiscating and, as an interim, or preliminary, step to this end, freezing assets.

2.2.1.1 Conviction-based confiscation

Conviction-based confiscation is a centuries-old[26] criminal law instrument. Its character is in personam, meaning that there is a nexus between the measure and the convicted person (and, therefore, the crime committed).[27] Boister describes the tool as 'a two-stage process. First, it depends upon criminal conviction of the holder of the property, and second, upon proof of a link between that property and the criminal activity for which the holder was convicted.'[28] It therefore forms part of the sentencing process, though the same cannot be said of freezing. A process that finds its legal basis in the criminal law is, of course, accompanied by all attendant substantive and procedural safeguards. These would usually include the application of a more onerous standard of proof than that applicable

24 Michele Simonato, 'Extended Confiscation of Criminal Assets: Limits and Pitfalls of Minimum Harmonisation in the EU' (2016) 41 European Law Review 727, 727. See also Jorge (n 7) 320, stating 'the variety of rationales behind national confiscation regimes, which range from deterrence, to restitution (for victims), to prevention (of the accumulation of operational capital in criminal enterprises).'

25 Simonato, 'Confiscation and fundamental rights' (n 22) 366.

26 David J Fried, 'Rationalizing Criminal Forfeiture' (1988-1989) 79 Journal of Criminal Law & Criminology 328, 329 ('For centuries "forfeiture of estate," a form of criminal forfeiture, was a mandatory incident of all common law and most statutory felony convictions. Forfeiture of estate was the taking by the Crown of all of the felon's real and personal property.')

27 See Kai Ambos, *Treatise on International Criminal Law*, vol III (OUP 2016) 655. As Boister puts it: 'It is *in personam* because it is based on the authority of the court over the person and thus by extension permits steps to be taken against his property.' Boister, *An Introduction to Transnational Criminal Law* (n 3) fn 15.

28 Boister, *An Introduction to Transnational Criminal Law* (n 3) 337.

to civil proceedings[29] and the guarantee of fair trial rights.[30] Certain States have sought to avoid the difficulties associated with meeting this standard of proof when securing a conviction and establishing a nexus between the crime and the targeted assets by granting wider powers of confiscation to their competent authorities.

Extended confiscation

Extended, or value, confiscation is one such broader power. In short, this form of confiscation allows the responsible national authorities to recover assets of a value equivalent to the actual proceeds of the crime(s) as opposed to the latter themselves.[31] As Johan Boucht has detailed, removing this causal link can also be accompanied 'by watering down some of the traditional criminal procedural safeguards, for instance by reversing the burden of proof or lowering the standard of proof (or both)'.[32] But why is this beneficial for State authorities? For Simonato, the answer is clear: 'efficiency'.[33] Extended confiscation is efficient because there is no need for the prosecution to establish, in addition to the guilt of the accused person, a nexus between particular assets and the crime(s). Indeed, States are expressly asked to make use of this form of confiscation alongside traditional, conviction-based confiscation of the proceeds of crimes in the three abovementioned UN treaties.[34] Taking the Convention against Corruption as an example, Article 31(1)(a) thereof provides as follows:

> 1. Each State Party shall take, to the greatest extent possible within its domestic legal system, such measures as may be necessary to enable confiscation of:
>
> (a) Proceeds of crime derived from offences established in accordance with this Convention or property the value of which corresponds to that of such proceeds[.][35]

---

29 In England and Wales, among other jurisdictions, the criminal standard of proof ('beyond reasonable doubt') is more onerous than the civil standard ('on the balance of probabilities').

30 Johan Boucht, 'Extended Confiscation and the Proposed Directive on Freezing and Confiscation of Criminal Proceeds in the EU: On Striking a Balance between Efficiency, Fairness and Legal Certainty' (2013) 21 European Journal of Crime, Criminal Law and Criminal Justice 127, 128; Boister, *An Introduction to Transnational Criminal Law* (n 3) 337.

31 Boister, *An Introduction to Transnational Criminal Law* (n 3) 338; Simonato, 'Extended Confiscation' (n 24) 738.

32 Boucht (n 30) 129. See also Jorge (n 7) 325; Simonato, 'Extended Confiscation' (n 24) 738.

33 Simonato, 'Extended Confiscation' (n 24) 738.

34 UN Drug Trafficking Convention, art 5(1)(a); UNTOC, art 12(1)(a); UNCAC, art 31(1)(a).

35 UNCAC, art 31(1)(a).

But extended confiscation is not unproblematic from a human rights perspective. Indeed, the right to a fair trial (particularly the right to be presumed innocent until proven guilty) and the right to the peaceful enjoyment of one's possessions could be violated by its use. It is beyond the scope of this chapter to scrutinise this issue in detail, but it is worth noting that the use of this form of confiscation has led to legal challenges before domestic courts and the European Court of Human Rights.[36]

Third party confiscation

A second broader power that some States have afforded to their competent authorities is that to confiscate assets (that is to say the actual proceeds of crime or property of equivalent value thereto) transferred by an accused or convicted person to certain, in Jorge's words, 'mala fide third parties that are helping the defendant to avoid confiscation'.[37] The European Union has adopted legislation obliging its Member States to provide for this method of confiscation in their respective domestic legal orders,[38] but only with respect to assets

> transferred by a suspected or accused person to third parties, or which were acquired by third parties from a suspected or accused person, at least if those third parties knew or ought to have known that the purpose of the transfer or acquisition was to avoid confiscation, on the basis of concrete facts and circumstances, including that the transfer or acquisition was carried out free of charge or in exchange for an amount significantly lower than the market value.[39]

According to the same legislation, assets in the hands of third parties (as defined in the above provision) should also be subject to freezing with a view to their potential confiscation.[40] As with extended confiscation, third party confiscation is also premised on a criminal conviction. But it is not only the criminal law that States have utilised for the purposes of confiscation.

---

36 For analysis, see Simonato, 'Extended Confiscation' (n 24) 735-39. See also Boister, *An Introduction to Transnational Criminal Law* (n 3) 339.

37 Jorge (n 7) 326. Jorge continues that distinguishing between such third parties and bona fide third parties 'has proven to be one of the most difficult issues in the area of confiscation.' All three UN conventions discussed in this chapter provide that their respective provisions on freezing, seizure and confiscation shall not be interpreted in such a manner as to prejudice the rights of bona fide third parties. UN Drug Trafficking Convention, art 5(8); UNTOC, art 12(8); UNCAC, art 31(9).

38 Directive 2014/42/EU of the European Parliament and of the Council of 3 April 2014 on the freezing and confiscation of instrumentalities and proceeds of crime in the European Union [2014] OJ L127/39.

39 ibid art 6.

40 ibid art 7.

2.2.1.2 Non-conviction-based confiscation

Non-conviction-based confiscation, also known as civil (asset) confiscation,[41] is another tool in the arsenal of several domestic law enforcement authorities.[42] Although not uniform across jurisdictions,[43] this form of confiscation is generally characterised by two core features. First, (certain) assets can be confiscated outside of criminal proceedings, that is to say a conviction is not required and, second, the (less onerous) civil standard of proof is employed.[44] Like its criminal law, conviction-based counterpart, non-conviction-based confiscation has a lengthy history, at least in certain jurisdictions.[45] However, unlike conviction-based confiscation, this alternative form of confiscation possesses an in rem character. Paul Schiff Berman concisely summarises the 'legal fiction'[46] behind non-conviction-based forfeiture: 'the government is acting against the property itself, rather than against the owner.'[47] This can prove particularly beneficial if, for example, the person in possession of the assets is deceased or located outside the jurisdiction of the State seeking to effect confiscation thereof.[48] But why else have certain States resorted to non-criminal law-based procedures for the purpose of confiscation? Simply put, the criminal law is not particularly effective at dealing with organised crime. As Hendry and

41 Jon Petter Rui, 'Introduction' in Jon Petter Rui and Ulrich Sieber (eds), *Non-Conviction-Based Confiscation in Europe: Possibilities and Limitations on Rules Enabling Confiscation without a Criminal Conviction* (Duncker & Humblot 2016) 3.

42 Including the United States and many European States (Italy, Ireland, the United Kingdom, Germany, Norway, Denmark, Sweden, Switzerland, Bulgaria, Liechtenstein and Slovenia). ibid 3-6.

43 ibid. For a specific example, Italy employs a distinct form of confiscation, labelled 'preventive confiscation', which operates 'outside of the criminal justice system, albeit not having a strict civil nature.' Michele Panzavolta and Roberto Flor, 'A Necessary Evil? The Italian "Non-Criminal System" of Asset Forfeiture' in Jon Petter Rui and Ulrich Sieber (eds), *Non-Conviction-Based Confiscation in Europe: Possibilities and Limitations on Rules Enabling Confiscation without a Criminal Conviction* (Duncker & Humblot 2016) 113.

44 Jennifer Hendry and Colin King, 'How far is too far? Theorising non-conviction-based asset forfeiture' (2015) 11 International Journal of Law in Context 398, 399. Discussing the Proceeds of Crime Act 2002, a national law that allows for non-conviction-based confiscation in the United Kingdom, the authors continue as follows: 'a civil procedure, the rules of criminal evidence do not apply here; this opens the door to admission of different types of evidence that would not be admissible at a criminal trial, including inferences from silence, previous behaviour, illegally obtained evidence and abuse of process, and hearsay evidence.'

45 Stefan D Cassella, *Asset Forfeiture Law in the United States* (JurisNet 2007) 29 (discussing how the origins of this 'ancient tradition' can be traced to the English common law and that, in the United States, this method was first employed with respect to customs offences, piracy and slave trafficking).

46 Paul Schiff Berman, 'An Anthropological Approach to Modern Forfeiture Law: The Symbolic Function of Legal Actions Against Objects' (1999) 11 Yale Journal of Law & the Humanities 1, 2. For a critical perspective, see Jacob Finkelstein, 'The Goring Ox: Some Historical Perspectives on Deodands, Forfeitures, Wrongful Death and the Western Notion of Sovereignty' (1973) 46 Temple Law Quarterly 169, 257.

47 ibid. See also Boister, *An Introduction to Transnational Criminal Law* (n 3) 340, citing Stefan D Cassella, 'Asset Forfeiture in the United States' in Simon NM Young (ed), *Civil Forfeiture of Criminal Property: Legal Measures for Targeting the Proceeds of Crime* (Edward Elgar 2009) 23, 27. Boister observes that the rationale 'has evolved to the more supportable notion that the 'instrumentality' (which can be property as diverse as money or the vehicle in which contraband is smuggled) of crime facilitates the commission of offences.')

48 See Boister, *An Introduction to Transnational Criminal Law* (n 3) 340.

King have argued, the legal safeguards inherent therein are 'frequently seen as providing excessive protection for criminals who, by virtue of operating at a remove, do not risk getting their own hands dirty.'[49] Importantly for the purposes of the present study, this argument can be equally applied to the commission of crimes under the jurisdiction of the ICC.[50]

Like extended confiscation, non-conviction-based confiscation can also be labelled efficient. Its use has therefore been encouraged. According to the Financial Action Task Force (FATF), an intergovernmental body created in 1989 by the Group of Seven (G7) highly industrialised nations,[51] whose membership as of 2019 stood at 38 States and two regional organisations:[52]

> Countries should consider adopting measures that allow such proceeds or instrumentalities to be confiscated without requiring a criminal conviction (non-conviction based confiscation) ... to the extent that such a requirement is consistent with the principles of their domestic law.[53]

But, also as with extended confiscation, scholars have drawn attention to the potential human rights implications of non-conviction-based confiscation.[54] The following section shows that these variants of confiscation also have much in common in terms of their theoretical bases.

2.2.2 *Justifying the Confiscation and Freezing of Assets*

As far as the primary rationale underpinning confiscation is concerned, Peter Alldridge writes as follows: 'Confiscation is said to be justified by a principle, deeply ingrained into the law, that people should not profit from unlawful activity in general and from crime in

---

49 Hendry and King (n 44) 402.

50 ibid fn 13, citing Kai Ambos, 'Command Responsibility and *Organisationsherrschaft*: Ways of Attributing International Crimes to the "Most Responsible"' in André Nollkaemper and Harmen van der Wilt (eds), *System Criminality in International Law* (CUP 2009) 127; Harmen van der Wilt, 'Joint Criminal Enterprise and Functional Perpetration' in André Nollkaemper and Harmen van der Wilt (eds), *System Criminality in International Law* (CUP 2009) 158.

51 Financial Action Task Force (FATF), 'Financial Action Task Force – 30 Years' (FATF 2019) 7.

52 ibid 12 (the European Commission and the Gulf Cooperation Council).

53 FATF, 'International Standards on Combating Money Laundering and the Financing of Terrorism & Proliferation' (FATF 2012) 10.

54 See Johan Boucht, 'Civil Asset Forfeiture and the Presumption of Innocence under Article 6(2) ECHR' (2014) 5 New Journal of European Criminal Law 221; Colin King, 'Civil Forfeiture and Article 6 of the ECHR: Due Process Implications for England & Wales and Ireland' (2014) 34 Legal Studies 371.

particular'.[55] In support of this assertion, Alldridge cites the judgment of Lawton LJ in the English case of *R v Waterfield*:

> The first thing the law should do is to ensure that those who break it ... should not make any money out of their wrongdoing. ... This court is firmly of the opinion that if those who take part in this kind of trade know that on conviction they are likely to be stripped of every penny of profit they make and a good deal more, then the desire to enter it will be diminished.[56]

This is not the only rationale for confiscating assets, whether through criminal or civil means. As Boister observes: 'recovering 'dirty' assets is also justified as a deterrent to offenders, a preventive tool against commission of further crimes, a way of making law enforcement pay for itself and a vehicle for restitution of property to victims.'[57] Other reasons invoked in the academic literature in support of confiscating assets include 'lessen[ing] the economic power of criminal enterprises'[58] and "improv[ing] conditions in crime damaged communities".[59] But these justifications do not operate in isolation; rather, '[f]requently, they are overlapping and mutually reinforcing.'[60] Notwithstanding, the following sections will briefly demarcate these justifications under four headings: (i) punitive; (ii) preventive; (iii) restorative; and (iv) other rationales, with a view to ascertaining which thereof best underpin(s) asset freezing.

2.2.2.1 Punitive

It is not universally believed that confiscation constitutes a punishment. Considering the non-conviction-based variant, Stefan Cassella argues that 'forcing the wrongdoer to disgorge the accouterments of the lavish lifestyle he acquired through his criminal acts' can have as much of a punitive effect on convicted persons as a sentence of imprisonment.[61] On the other hand, David Fried has claimed that even conviction-based confiscation is not particularly punitive, that is, in a denunciatory sense,[62] suggesting instead that this form

---

55 Peter Alldridge, *Money Laundering Law: Forfeiture, Confiscation, Civil Recovery, Criminal Laundering and Taxation of the Proceeds of Crime* (Hart Publishing 2003) 45.

56 ibid, citing *R v Waterfield* (17 February 1975).

57 Boister, *An Introduction to Transnational Criminal Law* (n 3) 333.

58 Stefan D Cassella, 'Civil Asset Recovery: The American Experience' in Jon Petter Rui and Ulrich Sieber (eds), *Non-Conviction-Based Confiscation in Europe: Possibilities and Limitations on Rules Enabling Confiscation without a Criminal Conviction* (Duncker & Humblot 2016) 14, discussing the 'multitude of punitive and remedial purposes' articulated by the US Supreme Court in *Kaley v United States* 134 S Ct 1090 (2014).

59 ibid.

60 ibid.

61 ibid 14-15.

62 Fried (n 26) 333 ('Punishments are penalties, but the reverse is not always true. Unlike penalties, punishments are intended to express moral obloquy through the public infliction of harm. They are addressed not only

of confiscation 'has more in common with civil restitution than with traditional punishments.'[63] In support of this view, Fried asserts that the confiscation of assets during sentencing 'merely restores the status quo ante and, thus lacks the expressive quality of traditional punishments which have the capacity to express the moral opprobrium of the community.'[64]

As mentioned at the outset of this section, asset freezing constitutes a preliminary step in the confiscation process and, consequently, it might be reasonable to argue that the justifications behind the freezing of assets are linked to those underpinning confiscation measures. But can it be said that the rationales behind the freezing 'step' of the process wholly overlap with the aims of the final 'step', that is to say confiscation? In the view of the present author, it is the preventive and restorative functions of confiscation, rather than its disputed punitive purpose, that best justifies the interim measure of freezing assets, an argument that finds further weight in the ICC and UNSC contexts. It is to these purposes that the chapter now turns.

2.2.2.2 Preventive

That freezing and confiscating assets can serve to prevent the commission of (further) crimes is less disputed, if at all. The explanation is straightforward: removing an individual's access to assets that were intended for the commission of crimes 'at least until such time as they are not likely to use it to commit crime',[65] ought to avert such a possibility.

But justifying the confiscation (and therefore freezing as an interim step to this end) of assets as a way to prevent the commission of crimes can only go so far. As Alldridge contends:

> Prevention of crime does not, however, justify the seizure of an item that was lawfully acquired, was used once in the commission of crime, is unlikely to be used in the same way again and has a range of lawful uses.[66]

Taking a pistol and a car as examples, Alldridge draws a distinction between confiscating the objects of crime (for example, 'the gun in the offence of unlawful possession of

---

to the offender but also to the public, announcing to all that certain behavior deserves the stigma of punishment'), citing John H Bogart, 'Punishment and the Subordination of Law to Morality' (1987) 7 Oxford Journal of Legal Studies 421, 426-27.

63 Fried (n 26) 333.

64 ibid.

65 Alldridge (n 55) 61

66 ibid.

firearms'[67]) and the instrumentalities of crime ('the getaway car in a robbery',[68] for instance). This ought not to have much bearing in the ICC context, however, with a draft proposal to empower the Court with the ability to order the forfeiture of instrumentalities as a penalty rejected.[69]

2.2.2.3 Restorative

The confiscation of assets can also be justified for restorative (or restitutive) reasons. In other words, confiscated assets can be used satisfy victims' claims. As Fried has forcefully argued:

> The penalty of forfeiture of criminal profits is closely related to civil restitution on the one hand and enforceable orders of restitution imposed as part of the sentence on the other. All three are intended to effectuate the principle that criminals should not profit by their crimes.[70]

This indicates that restitution may form part of the criminal process, that is to say that a judge may make an order to this end during sentencing, or may be effected by way of a civil claim. The modalities of restitution are dependent on the applicable national law, with certain States offering civil- and/or criminal law-based routes through which victims, if identifiable, of the crimes of which the convicted person has been found guilty might seek restitution.

2.2.2.4 Other

Another reason behind confiscating assets in certain jurisdictions, including the United States and Australia, is so that the proceeds thereof can be diverted to finance the operations of the (generally law enforcement) authorities that 'engineered' the process.[71] Though arguably an incentive for the prospective recipient agencies, using confiscated assets in this way has also been criticised for encouraging dependence on such funds and its potential for abuse.[72]

---

67 ibid 60.

68 ibid.

69 William A Schabas, *The International Criminal Court: A Commentary on the Rome Statute* (2nd edn, OUP 2016) 1163. Schabas observes: 'The potentially enormous scope of such a provision, when war crimes committed by a State or with its complicity are involved, can easily be imagined. Theoretically, an instrumentality could include an aircraft carrier or a military base.'

70 Fried (n 26) 333-334.

71 Boister, *An Introduction to Transnational Criminal Law* (n 3) 350.

72 ibid 350-351, citing Eric Blumenson and Eva Nilsen, 'Policing for Profit: The Drug War's Hidden Economic Agenda' (1998) 65 University of Chicago Law Review 35, 51. According to Boister: 'To counter this potential, in Australia, for example, confiscated funds are placed in the Confiscated Assets Account, a trust separate

There are also procedural rationales behind the freezing and seizure of certain assets in a criminal context that do not apply to their confiscation. For example, assets can be frozen in order to safeguard them for use as evidence to be presented at trial. After the trial ends, such assets are returned to their rightful owners, unless there is an order for confiscation. Otherwise put, freezing and seizing these assets forms part of the criminal procedure for procuring evidence. Having set out a number of rationales that can reasonably be said to support the use of asset freezing processes in criminal law and non-criminal law settings, both with a view to their eventual confiscation and as a (criminal) procedural mechanism for preserving evidence for presentation at trial, the following paragraphs will turn to the justifications for their use in the Rome Statute and UN Charter systems, respectively.

2.3 Situating ICC- and UNSC-Requested Asset Freezing Measures

The ICC considers its asset freezing powers to be part of a wider system of 'asset recovery',[73] which entails the preliminary steps of identification, tracing, freezing and seizure of assets.[74] The primary theoretical underpinnings for the freezing of assets with a view to their eventual forfeiture, that is to say preventive, and restorative purposes, also manifest themselves in the Rome Statute system. Indeed, William Schabas observes that its purpose is 'twofold':[75]

> First, it facilitates enforcement should the accused person be convicted and an order of forfeiture be imposed as part of the sentence. Second, freezing of assets is also important in the process of arrest and surrender, in that it helps to disrupt support networks of suspects.[76]

Forfeiture, as confiscation is termed in the Rome Statute, can (like fines) only be imposed in addition to the penalty of imprisonment.[77] This requirement would appear to reflect the view expressed by Fried that:

> Paradoxically, criminal forfeiture lacks most of the qualities of punishment and more closely resembles a civil penalty. Criminal forfeiture, like civil restitution, only requires the criminal to pay back what he has taken, thus

---

from either the judicial or executive branches, out of which funds are paid to benefit both law enforcement and to fund crime-related social projects.'

73 See ICC, 'Financial investigations and recovery of assets' (ICC 2017) 5.

74 ibid.

75 Schabas (n 69) 1320.

76 ibid.

77 Rome Statute, art 77(2).

> restoring the status quo ante. For this reason it carries no particular moral opprobrium. Nor does criminal forfeiture have any special rehabilitative or deterrent value, contrary to some claims. Thus forfeiture must be combined in most cases with fine or imprisonment to punish adequately.[78]

As far as the idea of using the proceeds of confiscated assets to fund the Court's investigative organ, the Office of the Prosecutor (OTP), is concerned, this is neither likely nor particularly desirable. In the Rome Statute system, the ICC Pre-Trial Chamber can request States to take protective measures for the purpose of forfeiture, which include freezing assets 'in particular for the ultimate benefit of victims'.[79] Indeed, in the event of a conviction, victims' claims to forfeited assets are explicitly prioritised above those of any other prospective claimants, with Rule 221(2) of the ICC RPE stating that, '[i]n all cases, when the Presidency decides on the disposition or allocation of property or assets belonging to the sentenced person, it shall give priority to the enforcement of measures concerning reparations to victims.'[80]

Discussing the imposition of the penalty of forfeiture pursuant to Article 77(2)(c) of the Rome Statute, Kai Ambos expresses the opinion that 'the imposition of economic sanctions adds a reparative and reconciliatory element to sentencing',[81] with the victim(s) being the 'recipient of the ensuing compensation, on the receiving end.'[82] However, as Nader Iskandar Diab has shown,[83] funding reparations to victims has not been easy, with the problem exacerbated by the indigence of a number of convicted persons and/or the obfuscation of their assets.[84] When viewed alongside the size of the (albeit limited number of) reparations awards made by ICTs, the view expressed by Ilaria Bottigliero in respect of courts in the United States rings true for those that form part of the international criminal justice system:

> [There is] a wide gap between the awarding of millions of dollars to victims of serious human rights violations as a matter of formal judgment, and the far

78 Fried (n 26) 358.
79 Rome Statute, art 57(3)(e).
80 ICC RPE, r 221(2).
81 Ambos (n 27) 655.
82 ibid.
83 On which, see Nader Iskandar Diab, 'Challenges in the Implementation of the Reparation Award against Hissein Habré: Can the Spell of Unenforceable Awards across the Globe be Broken?' (2018) 16 Journal of International Criminal Justice 141, 151-52.
84 ibid 152.

> from perfect state of actual execution of the judgment which has left victims mainly without compensation.[85]

For this reason, it is highly unlikely that the proceeds of confiscating assets at the ICC would ever be used to fund the Court, despite pressures on the budget of the latter.[86]

The purposes of asset freezing measures implemented at the behest of the UNSC differ from criminal law-based procedures in one important aspect. According to Jorge Godinho:

> In the field of terrorism, which in principle does not generate profits but rather raises the need for funding, the confiscation of assets works in a purely preventive manner, designed to obstruct the operation of criminal entities by cutting their sources of finance.[87]

A comparable argument can also be made concerning UNSC-requested asset freezes imposed for reasons other than terrorism. For instance, serious violations of international humanitarian law, in response to the (alleged) commission of which the UNSC has mandated UN Member States to impose asset freezing measures against individuals,[88] generally expend considerable resources. But, unlike Godinho's accurate characterisation of terrorism as a mainly non-profit activity, the commission of certain war crimes is able to generate (substantial) income for the perpetrators.[89] Nevertheless, the preventive rationale behind imposing such measures is clear: freezing assets that could be employed in pursuit of activities that, in the determination of the UNSC, undermine international peace and security[90] can be said to constitute, alongside other targeted sanctions, a mechanism '[d]esigned to protect against future acts'.[91]

85 Ilaria Bottigliero, *Redress for Victims of Crimes Under International Law* (Springer 2014) 65. See also Diab (n 83) 150.

86 On the austerities of international criminal justice, see Sara Kendall, 'Commodifying Global Justice: Economies of Accountability at the International Criminal Court' (2015) Journal of International Criminal Justice 113, 129-32.

87 Jorge Godinho, 'When Worlds Collide: Enforcing United Nations Security Council Asset Freezes in the EU Legal Order' (2010) 16 European Law Journal 67, 77.

88 See eg Hilde Roskam, 'Crime-Based Targeted Sanctions: Promoting Respect for International Humanitarian Law by the Security Council' in Terry D Gill and others (eds), *Yearbook of International Humanitarian Law 2016* (TMC Asser Press 2018).

89 See eg Manuel Galvis Martínez, 'Forfeiture of Assets at the International Criminal Court: The Short Arm of International Criminal Justice' (2014) 12 Journal of International Criminal Justice 193, 195-204.

90 That is to say 'any threat to the peace, breach of the peace, or act of aggression', in response to its determining the existence of which the UNSC can mandate UN Member States to impose measures short of the use of armed force. UN Charter, arts 39 and 41.

91 Hadassa Noorda, 'Preventive Deprivations of Liberty: Asset Freezes and Travel Bans' (2015) 9 Criminal Law and Philosophy 521, 526.

As for whether freezes implemented by States at the request of the UNSC can be said to serve only preventive rationales, though some scholars have questioned whether targeted sanctions, including asset freezes, implemented by States at the request of the UNSC are comparable to criminal charges,[92] such measures do not form part of a criminal process in the same way that ICC-requested asset freezes do. It might therefore be difficult to attribute classic criminal law goals, including the punitive and/or restorative justifications behind confiscation measures at issue in the preceding section, to asset freezes imposed under the UN Charter. In other words, the respective 'endgames' of ICC-requested (ie criminal law-based procedures) and UNSC-requested asset freezes differ in that the former is, at least in the first instance, geared towards securing a criminal conviction,[93] with reparations awards following thereafter (the alternative outcome, of course, being an acquittal, after which no reparations award can be made against the acquitted person). On the other hand, asset freezing measures effected pursuant to the UN Charter are aimed toward maintaining or restoring international peace and security. This said, in Resolution 1970, in which it imposed sanctions, including an assets freeze, against the then Libyan leader Muammar Gaddafi and other individuals associated with his regime, the UNSC overtly expressed 'its intention to ensure that assets frozen ... shall at a later stage be made available to and for the benefit of the people of the Libyan Arab Jamahiriya'.[94] The UN organ affirmed this intention shortly thereafter.[95] Although this commitment carries clear restitutive undertones, it also constitutes an exception to the wording typically adopted by the UNSC.[96] As Larissa van den Herik has observed, 'funds frozen pursuant to UN sanctions regimes can generally only be used to fulfil reparatory judgements if the judgements were rendered before the imposition of the sanctions regime.'[97] UNSC-requested asset freezes are accordingly best categorised as underpinned by preventive, rather than restorative (or punitive) rationales.

---

92 Eg Melissa van den Broek, Monique Hazelhorst and Wouter de Zanger, 'Asset Freezing: Smart Sanction or Criminal Charge?' (2011) 27 Utrecht Journal of International and European Law 18.

93 ICC, 'Financial investigations and recovery of assets' (n 73) 5 ('The [Office of the Prosecutor (OTP)] conducts financial investigations and analyses to identify financial flows as part of its investigative activities in accordance with article 54 of the Statute. This is crucial, as such investigations and analyses can contribute to demonstrating: the existence of the crimes themselves; the linkage elements of the crimes; and/or the criminal responsibility and relevant modes of liability of individuals for crimes under the jurisdiction of the Court. Additionally, the OTP conducts financial investigations to identify assets and transmit relevant information to the Chamber to form the basis for possible future forfeiture orders and reparations awards to victims.')

94 UNSC Res 1970 (16 February 2011) UN Doc S/RES/1970, para 18.

95 UNSC Res 1973 (17 March 2011) UN Doc S/RES/1973, para 20.

96 See Larissa van den Herik, 'The Individualization of Enforcement in International Law: Exploring the Interplay between United Nations Targeted Sanctions and International Criminal Proceedings' in Tiyanjana Maluwa, Max du Plessis and Dire Tladi (eds), *The Pursuit of a Brave New World in International Law: Essays in Honour of John Dugard* (Brill Nijhoff 2017) 260.

97 ibid, citing UNSC Res 1970 (n 94) para 19(c).

2.4 Conclusion

This chapter has sought to demonstrate that the freezing of assets serves primarily preventive purposes, whether imposed as part of a criminal law-based confiscation process, (quasi-)civil law proceedings, or under the auspices of the UN Charter. It has also aimed to show that such measures can be justified from a restitutive perspective and, indeed, bear closer resemblance to restitution than punishment, that is when executed during the sentencing phase of domestic or international criminal proceedings. Finally, though the asset freezing procedures available to the ICC and the UNSC differ in terms of their respective 'endgames', with those under the Rome Statute aimed at achieving a conviction (with reparations to victims potentially ensuing thereafter) and those under the UN Charter geared towards the maintenance or restoration of international peace and security, their theoretical bases are remarkably similar. The following chapters will explore the relationship between these procedures in further detail, focusing, in particular, on legal protections.

3 Coexistent but Uncoordinated*

Asset Freezing Measures at the ICC and the UNSC

3.1 Introduction

Both the ICC and UNSC are empowered to request States to freeze individuals' assets. The ICC is authorized to issue such requests to the States Parties to its constituent instrument, the Rome Statute.[1] The power of the UNSC to order States to freeze assets finds its legal basis in Chapter VII of the UN Charter, Article 41 of which permits the organ upon which 'primary responsibility for the maintenance of international peace and security'[2] is conferred to call upon States to implement measures short of the use of armed force to give effect to its decisions.[3] This chapter examines whether the execution of measures requested by UNSC-appointed sanctions committees[4] to freeze individuals' assets could in certain circumstances serve to bolster the Rome Statute framework for the freezing of accused persons' assets.

Part 3.2 further delineates the modalities of the asset freezing powers with which the Court and UNSC are vested, detailing (i) to whom such requests might be addressed, (ii) what sanctions are available to the respective bodies in the event of non-compliance with their respective requests and (iii) under what circumstances and pursuant to which legal bases the two bodies might request States to freeze individuals' assets. Part 3.3 scrutinises the purposes of the respective asset freezing regimes and the broader frameworks of which they form part, namely the Rome Statute system of international criminal justice and the UN Charter system for the maintenance of international peace and security. Part 3.4 discusses the claim made by some scholars that assistance from the UNSC might help the Court in realising its mandate, particularly in encouraging States to cooperate with the ICC. It is also in Part 3.4 that the argument that action requested by the UN organ might

* An earlier version of this chapter was published as Daley J Birkett, 'Coexistent but Uncoordinated: Asset Freezing Measures at the International Criminal Court and the UN Security Council' (2020) 20 International Criminal Law Review 983-1025.

1 Rome Statute, art 93(1)(k). See also Rome Statute, art 57(3)(e).

2 UN Charter, art 24.

3 ibid art 41. The subsequent provision empowers the UNSC to take measures involving the use of armed force, should it 'consider that measures provided for in Article 41 would be inadequate or have proved to be inadequate'. UN Charter, art 42.

4 Pursuant to UNSC Provisional Rules of Procedure, UN Doc S/96/Rev.7, r 28, 'The Security Council may appoint a commission or committee or a rapporteur for a specified question.'

strengthen the Rome Statute's asset freezing regime is deliberated, an issue that is subject to further consideration in the following section. Part 3.5 comprises an analysis of eight cases where the bodies' actions (might) have coincided. This analysis demonstrates that, though the two bodies' respective activities in this area might have overlapped on a number of occasions, they have seldom been coordinated. This, in turn, leads the author to reach the conclusion, in Part 3.6, that to argue in favour of closer, formalised cooperation between the two asset freezing regimes is aspirational but an unlikely outcome.

3.2 MODALITIES

As for the breadth of the two bodies' asset freezing capabilities, the States Parties to the Rome Statute are under an obligation to 'cooperate fully' with the ICC in executing requests for the freezing of assets (as well as their identification, tracing and/or seizure).[5] The ICC is also able to issue requests for cooperation to States not party to the Rome Statute, whether 'on the basis of an ad hoc arrangement, an agreement with such State or any other appropriate basis.'[6] This final category could include situations where the UNSC mandates compliance in accordance with Article 13(b) of the Rome Statute.[7] This provision allows the UN body to refer a situation in which it appears that one or more crimes under the Court's jurisdiction has been committed to the ICC Prosecutor.[8] In such situations,[9] the duty of States not part of the Rome Statute regime to cooperate with the Court would derive from the UN Charter, not the Rome Statute. Where there is an agreement between the ICC and the non-party State to which the request for cooperation is addressed, the requested State would, of course, only be obliged to cooperate with the Court to the extent provided by the provisions of the agreement. Equally, if there were an ad hoc arrangement, the terms thereof would govern the scope of cooperation. As for requests from the UNSC to freeze individuals' assets, all UN Member States are compelled by Article 25 of the UN Charter to 'accept and carry out' its decisions.[10] There are accordingly no constraints upon the UNSC in terms of the States to which it can address its decisions to freeze assets, unlike the regime available to the ICC.

5 Rome Statute, art 86. See also Rome Statute, art 93(1)(k).
6 Rome Statute, art 87(5)(a).
7 Rome Statute, art 13.
8 ibid.
9 See UNSC Res 1593 (31 March 2005) UN Doc S/RES/1593, para 2 (obligating Sudan, a State not party to the Rome Statute to 'cooperate fully with and provide any necessary assistance to the Court and the Prosecutor pursuant to this resolution'); UNSC Res 1970 (16 February 2011) UN Doc S/RES/1970, para 5 (compelling Libya, another State not party to the Rome Statute, to do the same).
10 UN Charter, art 25.

As well as the narrower range of potential recipients of ICC requests for the freezing of assets, the sanctions available to the Court in the event of non-compliance are also more limited than those at the disposal of the UNSC in such cases. In the event that a State Party to the Rome Statute fails to cooperate with the Court when in receipt of an orderly request to do so, the latter is merely empowered to 'make a finding to that effect and refer the matter to the Assembly of States Parties or, where the Security Council referred the matter to the Court, to the Security Council.'[11] The sanctions available to the Court where a State not party to the Rome Statute fails to comply with a request to cooperate in contravention of an agreement or ad hoc arrangement governing such cooperation are equally unlikely to induce compliance.[12] On the other hand, because the UNSC is authorised to take measures in pursuit of the maintenance and restoration of international peace and security,[13] should a State fail to execute a decision to freeze assets taken under Article 41 of the UN Charter, despite bearing an obligation to do so,[14] the UN body could make a determination that the recalcitrant State's conduct itself constitutes a threat to the peace and sanction it under the same provision.[15]

In terms of when the respective institutions might request States to freeze individuals' assets, Article 57(3)(e) of the Rome Statute permits the relevant ICC Pre-Trial Chamber to 'seek the cooperation of states ... to take protective measures for the purpose of forfeiture' on condition that a warrant of arrest or a summons to appear has been issued against the individual targeted by the measures.[16] In order for an arrest warrant or summons to be issued, the ICC Prosecutor is required to demonstrate the existence of 'reasonable grounds to believe' that the person in question has committed one of the crimes within the Court's jurisdiction.[17] This could be one of the four 'most serious crimes of concern to the international community as a whole' listed in Article 5 of the Rome Statute (genocide, crimes against humanity, war crimes or the crime of aggression)[18] or offences against the administration of justice.[19] The Pre-Trial Chamber is also required by Article 57(3)(e) of the Rome Statute to take into account 'the strength of the evidence and the rights of the

11 Rome Statute, 87(7). For an early analysis of some of the weaknesses of the Rome Statute system when faced with States' failure to cooperate with the Court, see Antonio Cassese, 'The Statute of the International Criminal Court: Some Preliminary Reflections' (1999) 10 European Journal of International Law 144, 164-67.

12 Rome Statute, art 87(5).

13 See UN Charter, art 39.

14 ibid art 25.

15 See Antonios Tzanakopoulos, *Disobeying the Security Council: Countermeasures against Wrongful Sanctions* (OUP 2011) 179.

16 Rome Statute, art 57(3)(e).

17 ibid arts 58(1)(a) (for a warrant of arrest) and 58(7) (for a summons to appear).

18 ibid art 5.

19 ibid art 70.

parties concerned'[20] in deciding whether to ask States to freeze individuals' assets. The failure of the Prosecutor to continue to satisfy these important criteria has already led to the suspension of one Pre-Trial Chamber order for the freezing of assets by an ICC Trial Chamber.[21] The few limitations upon the UN body in this regard stem from the UN Charter. First, the UNSC is only able to decide to call upon UN Member States to freeze assets in accordance with Article 41 of the UN Charter after determining the existence of a 'threat to the peace, breach of the peace, or act of aggression'.[22] This condition is found in Article 39 of the UN Charter, which indicates that the power afforded to the UNSC to decide upon measures under Article 41, which have included calling upon States to freeze assets, are for the purpose of maintaining or restoring international peace and security.[23] Article 24(2) of the UN Charter places a second constraint upon the UNSC in exercising its power to request UN Member States to freeze individuals' assets.[24] This provision mandates that the UN organ, in discharging its duties in terms of maintaining international peace and security, 'shall act in accordance with the Purposes and Principles of the United Nations'[25] listed in the first two articles of the constituent instrument of the UN[26] The following section scrutinises the rationales underpinning the respective regimes for asset freezing available to the ICC and the UNSC in further detail.

3.3 Shared Goals?

Scholars and practitioners have attributed a number of purposes to the project of international criminal justice. Minna Schrag, a former prosecutor at the ICTY, compiles the lengthiest list of goals ascribed to the ICTY, the ICC and other ICTs as follows:

- to bring a sense of justice to war-torn places;
- to re-establish the rule of law;
- to provide a sound foundation for lasting peace;
- to enforce international law, and end impunity for violations, especially for senior military and political leaders;
- to bring repose to victims and provide an outlet to end cycles of violence and revenge;
- to demonstrate that culpability is individual, and not the responsibility of entire groups;
- to provide a safe forum for victims to tell their stories;

20 ibid art 57(3)(e). For analysis of 'the rights of the parties concerned', see Chapter 5.
21 *Prosecutor v Kenyatta* (Decision on the implementation of the request to freeze assets) ICC-01/09-02/11-931 (8 July 2014) (*Kenyatta* Implementation Decision) para 29. For discussion, see Chapter 5.
22 UN Charter, art 39.
23 See ibid.
24 See ibid art 24(2).
25 ibid.
26 ibid arts 1-2.

- to demonstrate fairness and the highest standards of due process;
- to provide exemplary procedures to serve as a model for rebuilding a legal system devastated by war crimes and human rights violations;
- to create an accurate historical record, to forestall those who might later try to deny that wide-scale violations of international law occurred;
- public education in general;
- in a didactic mode, to illuminate explanations about what caused the violations, and illustrate particular patterns of violations;
- to develop and expand the application and interpretation of international law and norms;
- to function with maximum transparency and public scrutiny; and
- to provide a forum for considering restitution and reparations.[27]

Nor is this list exhaustive. Other aims attributed to the project of international criminal justice include strengthening 'respect for the law' and newly-elected democratic regimes[28] and goals related to the maintenance and restoration of international peace and security.[29] What is more, it is clear that some of these goals are more or less relevant during different phases of criminal proceedings conducted on the international plane. For example, Denis Abels credibly suggests that the aim of creating an accurate historical record is more relevant during the trial phase of international criminal proceedings than during the enforcement phase thereof.[30]

---

27 Minna Schrag, 'Lessons Learned from ICTY Experience' (2004) 2 Journal of International Criminal Justice 427, 428. For other such lists, see Gary Jonathan Bass, *Stay the Hand of Vengeance: The Politics of War Crimes Tribunals* (Princeton University Press 2000) 284; 'Developments in the Law: International Criminal Law' (2000) 114 Harvard Law Review 1943, 1961-74; UNSC, 'The rule of law and transitional justice in conflict and post-conflict societies: Report of the Secretary-General' (2004) UN Doc S/2004/616 (UN Secretary-General Report), para 38; Jean Galbraith, 'The Pace of International Criminal Justice' (2009) 31 Michigan Journal of International Law 79, 84-97; Jens David Ohlin, 'A Meta-Theory of International Criminal Procedure: Vindicating the Rule of Law' (2009) 14 UCLA Journal of International Law and Foreign Affairs 77, 84-90.

28 See Michael Scharf, 'The Letter of the Law: The Scope of the International Legal Obligation to Prosecute Human Rights Crimes' (1996) 59 Law and Contemporary Problems 41, 42.

29 See UN Secretary-General Report (n 27) para 38; Ohlin (n 27) 88-90; George P Fletcher and Jens David Ohlin, 'The ICC — Two Courts in One?', (2006) 4 Journal of International Criminal Justice 428, 432 (2006); Mirjan Damaška, 'What Is the Point of International Criminal Justice?' (2008) 83 Chicago-Kent Law Review 329, 331.

30 Denis Abels, 'Limiting the Objectives of the Enforcement of International Punishment' in Róisín Mulgrew and Denis Abels (eds), *Research Handbook on the International Penal System* (Edward Elgar 2016) 253.

Asset Freezing at the International Criminal Court and the United Nations Security Council

It is against this background of (unrealistically)[31] high expectations that the ICC, and its asset freezing regime, operates. Turning to the more specific reasons behind empowering the Court with procedures for requesting States to freeze individuals' assets, a number can be identified, all of which require that the person targeted by the measures is not found to be indigent. First, in the event that the person whose assets have been frozen is convicted, cash assets (or, in the case of non-cash assets, such as property, land and investments, the proceeds thereof) can be used to satisfy the payment of fines[32] and legal expenses incurred during the proceedings.[33] A second purpose behind the Court's asset freezing powers is made clear in Article 57(3)(e) of the Rome Statute, which provides that 'protective measures for the purpose of forfeiture [are to be taken] ... in particular for the ultimate benefit of victims.'[34] The Court's case law has further clarified that such measures may be requested not only for the purpose of securing the enforcement of an order for forfeiture but also a future award for reparations to victims of the crime(s) for which a conviction is entered.[35] A third group of objectives can be gleaned when the ICC's asset freezing powers are viewed from a prosecutorial perspective. Indeed, it could be contended that such measures are often sought by the Prosecutor with a view to facilitating the arrest of accused persons.[36]

---

31 See eg Damaška (n 29) 331 ('Unlike Atlas, international criminal courts are not bodies of titanic strength, capable of carrying on their shoulders the burden of so many tasks. Even national systems of criminal justice, with their far greater enforcement powers and institutional support, would stagger under this load'.)

32 See *Prosecutor v Bemba Gombo and others* (Decision on Sentence pursuant to Article 76 of the Statute) ICC-01/05-01/13-2123-Corr (22 March 2017) para 200; *Prosecutor v Bemba Gombo and others* (Decision Re-sentencing Mr Jean-Pierre Bemba Gombo, Mr Aimé Kilolo Musamba and Mr Jean-Jacques Mangenda Kabongo) ICC-01/05-01/13-2312 (17 September 2018) para 109 ('Mr Kilolo may use his frozen bank account to pay his fine, but this account must remain frozen until the fine is paid in full.')

33 See eg *Prosecutor v Bemba Gombo* (Decision on the Defence's Application for Lifting the Seizure of Assets and Request for Cooperation to the Competent Authorities of Portugal) ICC-01/05-01/08-251-Anx (10 October 2008) paras 15, 17.

34 Rome Statute, art 57(3)(e).

35 See *Prosecutor v Lubanga Dyilo* (Decision on the Prosecutor's Application for a warrant of arrest, Article 58) ICC-01/04-01/06-1-Corr-Red (10 February 2006) paras 132-37; *Prosecutor v Lubanga Dyilo* (Decision Establishing the Principles and Procedures to be Applied to Reparations) ICC-01/04-01/06-2904 (7 August 2012) para 277; *Kenyatta* Implementation Decision (n 21) paras 12-15; *Prosecutor v [Redacted]* (Judgment on the appeal of the Prosecutor against the decision of [REDACTED]) ICC-ACRed-01/16 (15 February 2016) paras 49-50. For analysis, see Chapter 5; Carla Ferstman, 'Cooperation and the International Criminal Court: The Freezing, Seizing and Transfer of Assets for the Purpose of Reparations' in Olympia Bekou and Daley J Birkett (eds), *Cooperation and the International Criminal Court: Perspectives from Theory and Practice* (Brill Nijhoff 2016) 233-37.

36 See *Prosecutor v Milošević and others* (Decision on Review of Indictment and Application for Consequential Orders) ICTY-02-54 (24 May 1999) para 27 (in which Judge Hunt notes the ICTY Prosecutor's submission that 'asset freezing may be done for two distinct purposes – for the purpose of granting restitution of property or payment from its proceeds ... , and also for the purpose of preventing an accused who is still at large from using those assets to evade arrest and from taking steps to disguise his assets or putting them beyond the reach of the Tribunal'.) See also Chapter 5; Michael P Scharf, 'The Tools for Enforcing International Criminal Justice in the New Millennium: Lessons from the Yugoslavia Tribunal' (2000) 49 DePaul Law Review 925, 945-46.

Other prosecutorial functions played by measures taken under Article 57(3)(e) of the Rome Statute include disrupting ongoing and preventing future conduct under the ICC's jurisdiction and identifying evidence of financial relationships (through bank records, for example) which could assist the Prosecutor in proving criminal responsibility.[37]

As for asset freezing measures executed at the request of the UNSC, the aims are even more disparate. This is because the framework under Chapter VII of the UN Charter authorises the UNSC to take measures in the event that it has determined the existence of a 'threat to the peace, breach of the peace, or act of aggression',[38] to which a range of responses might be appropriate, depending on the specific circumstances. Article 41 of the UN Charter also recognises the breadth of measures 'not involving the use of armed force'[39] that might be required to give effect to the decisions of the UNSC with a view to maintaining or restoring international peace and security. A non-exhaustive[40] list of options available to the UNSC under Article 41 of the UN Charter 'include complete or partial interruption of economic relations and of rail, sea, air, postal, telegraphic, radio, and other means of communication, and the severance of diplomatic relations.'[41] It is pursuant to this provision that the UNSC 'targeted sanctions' regime has developed. It is to the purposes of this regime, which has evolved to encompass the adoption of asset freezing measures targeting individuals, that the focus of the present chapter now turns.

Biersteker, Tourinho and Eckert have identified multiple political objectives pursued by UNSC decisions to call upon States to apply targeted sanctions against individuals, which the three authors break down into the following categories:

- Armed conflict [which they subcategorise as follows:]
  - Cease hostilities;
  - Peace enforcement;
  - Support peace building; and
  - Negotiation of peace agreement.
- Human rights;
- Democracy support;
- Counter-terrorism;
- Good governance;
- Support judicial process;
- Non-proliferation;

37 See Chapter 5; ICC, 'Financial investigations and recovery of assets' (ICC 2017).
38 UN Charter, art 39.
39 UN Charter, art 41.
40 The list begins with the words 'These may ...'.
41 UN Charter, art 41.

- Support humanitarian effort; and
- Protect population under R2P.[42]

Of these goals, the study's authors gauge that 'more than half (59 per cent) of the UN targeted sanctions episodes have sought to address problems associated with armed conflict.'[43] As for the share of asset freezing measures among the episodes surveyed,[44] Biersteker, Tourinho and Eckert observe that more than half employed this type of individual sanction.[45] Consequently, there might be some overlap between the goals of ICC- and UNSC-requested asset freezing measures in certain cases. But this partial overlap between the purposes of their respective asset freezing regimes has not (yet) translated into the institution by the two bodies of a coordinated, formalised strategy involving the parallel request of such measures.

3.4 Strengthening Cooperation

Few scholars would deny that international criminal justice is but one tool available to respond to the commission of international crimes. Despite the (*de jure* and *de facto*) independence of the Court from the UN system,[46] it has been suggested that the UNSC might assist the ICC in fulfilling its purposes, particularly in respect of the Court's weak cooperation regime.[47] At the same time, it has been claimed that the Court, by pursuing its objectives, can support the UNSC in realising its goals under the UN Charter; in other words, that peace and justice can, and perhaps even ought to, be pursued simultaneously.[48]

42 Thomas J Biersteker, Marcos Tourinho and Sue E Eckert, 'Thinking about United Nations targeted sanctions' in Thomas J Biersteker, Sue E Eckert and Marcos Tourinho (eds) *Targeted Sanctions: The Impacts and Effectiveness of United Nations Actions* (CUP 2016) 23-25.

43 ibid 24.

44 ibid 18 ('[The] quantitative and qualitative databases used to inform the chapters in this volume include the entire universe of UN targeted sanctions imposed since 1991, or twenty-three different country regimes broken down into sixty-three case episodes for comparative analysis.')

45 ibid 24.

46 See ICC-UN Relationship Agreement, preamble ('in accordance with the Rome Statute, the International Criminal Court is established as an independent permanent institution in relationship with the United Nations system').

47 See Morten Bergsmo, 'Occasional Remarks on Certain State Concerns about the Jurisdictional Reach of the International Criminal Court, and Their Possible Implications for the Relationship between the Court and the Security Council' (2000) 69 Nordic Journal of International Law 87, 110.

48 ibid 91-92, 112; Sir Franklin Berman, 'The Relationship Between the International Criminal Court and the Security Council' in Herman von Hebel, Johan G Lammers and Jolien Schukking (eds), *Reflections on the International Criminal Court: Essays in Honour of Adriaan Bos* (TMC Asser Press 1999) 173, 177-78; Matthias Neuner, 'The Security Council and the ICC: Assessing the First Ten Years of Coexistence' (2012) 18 New England Journal of International and Comparative Law 283, 297-98.

For some scholars, there can be 'no peace without justice',[49] while others contend that the removal of international criminals, who may pose obstacles to peace, can serve the interests of both peace and justice.[50] Still others argue that focusing on individual criminal responsibility, rather than collective guilt, is able to prevent future conflict.[51] Despite broad consensus that a relationship exists between the maintenance of international peace and security and international criminal justice,[52] however, tensions between these objectives are also recognised.[53]

It has been contended that this tension flows from the political character of the UNSC and the independent judicial position held by the ICC, which do not neatly converge. In this regard, some scholars propose, on the one hand, that the Court must be allowed to act independently of the will the most powerful States (that is, the P-5),[54] lest it be regarded as a politicised institution, which could entail negative consequences for both its credibility and its legitimacy.[55] At the same time, scholars acknowledge that the ICC must deal with the realities of global politics[56] in its day-to-day operations and that, in order to fulfil its mandate, the ICC may rely upon the exercise of coercive power (military, economic, etc.) by other international actors, not least the five permanent members of the UNSC.[57] Darryl

---

49 M Cherif Bassiouni, 'Justice and Peace: The Importance of Choosing Accountability over Realpolitik' (2003) 35 Case Western Reserve Journal of International Law 191, 204.

50 See Payam Akhavan, 'Beyond Impunity: Can International Criminal Justice Prevent Future Atrocities?' (2001) 95 American Journal of International Law 7, 7; Luigi Condorelli and Annalisa Ciampi, 'Comments on the Security Council Referral of the Situation in Darfur to the ICC' (2005) 3 Journal of International Criminal Justice 590, 592; Payam Akhavan, 'Are International Criminal Tribunals a Disincentive to Peace: Reconciling Judicial Romanticism with Political Realism' (2009) 31 Human Rights Quarterly 624, 629.

51 Antonio Cassese, 'On the Current Trends towards Criminal Prosecution and Punishment of Breaches of International Humanitarian Law' (1998) 9 European Journal of International Law 2, 9.

52 See Ohlin (n 27) 88-90.

53 Janine Natalya Clark, 'Peace, Justice and the International Criminal Court: Limitations and Possibilities' (2011) 9 Journal of International Criminal Justice 521, 542-43; Bruce Broomhall, *International Justice and the International Criminal Court: Between Sovereignty and the Rule of Law* (OUP 2003) 68.

54 Robert Cryer, 'Sudan, Resolution 1593, and International Criminal Justice' (2006) 19 Leiden Journal of International Law 195, 206; William A Schabas, 'The Banality of International Justice' (2013) 11 Journal of International Criminal Justice 545, 550.

55 Lionel Yee, 'The International Criminal Court and The Security Council: Articles 13(b) and 16' in Roy S Lee (ed), *The International Criminal Court: The Making of the Rome Statute: Issues, Negotiations, Results* (Kluwer Law International 1999) 143, 146-47; Lutz Oette, 'Peace and Justice, or Neither? The Repercussions of the Al-Bashir Case for International Criminal Justice in Africa and Beyond' (2010) 8 Journal of International Criminal Justice 345, 356-58.

56 For a prominent proponent of this view, see Kenneth A Rodman, 'Justice as a Dialogue Between Law and Politics: Embedding the International Criminal Court within Conflict Management and Peacebuilding' (2014) 12 Journal of International Criminal Justice 437, 439.

57 ibid 442. See also Kenneth A Rodman, 'Darfur and the Limits of Legal Deterrence' (2008) 30 Human Rights Quarterly 529, 530; Kenneth A Rodman, 'Is Peace in the Interests of Justice? The Case for Broad Prosecutorial Discretion at the International Criminal Court' (2009) 22 Leiden Journal of International Law 99, 108.

Robinson persuasively characterises the foregoing tension as dyadic: 'Legally, the ICC is independent, and indeed its juridical legitimacy hinges on that independence. Yet the ICC is also, factually, utterly dependent'.[58] Consequently, regardless of the path chosen by the Court, it will be open to seemingly opposite criticisms because 'each side of the dyad is based in values that can be credibly regarded as values underlying international criminal justice'.[59]

The utter dependence by the Court upon other actors is most conspicuous in the context of its cooperation procedures, where the ICC is particularly reliant on State action. ICC cooperation procedures are innately weak. According to Antonio Cassese, the framers of the Rome Statute 'left too many loopholes permitting states to delay or even thwart the Court's proceedings.'[60] The weaknesses in the ICC's enforcement mechanisms drew the attention of the international media in June 2015 when the then Sudanese President, Omar Al Bashir, travelled to (and soon thereafter fled from) South Africa, a State Party to the Rome Statute, despite the existence of two outstanding warrants of arrest issued against him by the Court's Prosecutor.[61] The ICC is not only reliant on States Parties to arrest accused persons, but also to recover their assets.[62]

The weaknesses in the Court's cooperation regime can thus have serious implications for its forfeiture powers, pursuant to which fines, forfeiture orders and orders for reparation can be imposed upon persons convicted of crimes under its jurisdiction. Scholars have claimed that, should the TFV[63] be required to operate with insufficient resources, victims of international crimes may be left disappointed and disillusioned with the Court's reparation framework.[64] The significance of this problem is exacerbated by the fact that

58 Darryl Robinson, 'Inescapable Dyads: Why the International Criminal Court Cannot Win' (2015) 28 Leiden Journal of International Law 323, 338 (2015) (footnote omitted).

59 ibid 330.

60 Cassese, 'The Statute of the International Criminal Court' (n 11) 170. See also Göran Sluiter, 'Obtaining Cooperation from Sudan – Where Is the Law?' (2008) 6 Journal of International Criminal Justice 871, 883.

61 See eg Owen Bowcott, 'Sudan president Omar al-Bashir leaves South Africa as court considers arrest' *The Guardian* (15 June 2015) <www.theguardian.com/world/2015/jun/15/south-africa-to-fight-omar-al-bashirs-arrest-warrant-sudan> accessed 31 August 2020.

62 This is not to say that States not party to the Rome Statute cannot assist the ICC; rather, they are not bound to do so under its constituent instrument. See Rome Statute, art 87(5)(a). For the view that this group of States could be obliged to cooperate under customary international law, see Zhu Wenqi, 'On co-operation by states not party to the International Criminal Court' (2006) 88 International Review of the Red Cross 87.

63 See Rome Statute, art 79; Assembly of States Parties, 'Establishment of a fund for the benefit of victims of crimes within the jurisdiction of the Court, and of the families of such victims' (9 September 2002) ICC-ASP/1/Res.6.

64 See Mirjan Damaška, 'The International Criminal Court between Aspiration and Achievement' (2009) 14 UCLA Journal of International Law and Foreign Affairs 19, 31.

some individuals who commit crimes within the Court's jurisdiction may possess substantial personal wealth.[65] Cooperation is therefore paramount to the effective functioning of the ICC reparations system as well as the capacity of the Court to enforce orders for fines and forfeiture of assets.

In response to the weaknesses in the ICC's cooperation regime, some scholars have suggested that a closer relationship between the Court and the UNSC could reinforce the enforcement powers at the Court's disposal.[66] Among the tools available to the UNSC, asset freezes and travel bans have been suggested as valuable tools for strengthening the enforcement capacity of the ICC.[67] Indeed, the Court and the UN have already confirmed the existence of a relationship between their respective responsibilities, particularly in

65 See eg David Wippman, 'Atrocities, Deterrence, and the Limits of International Justice' (1999) 23 Fordham International Law Journal 473, 479 (noting, in discussing the ICTY, that 'most observers believe that indicted leaders such as Milosevic deliberately fostered inter-communal hostility and conflict as a means to secure and maintain political power and personal wealth'); Manuel Galvis Martínez, 'Forfeiture of Assets at the International Criminal Court: The Short Arm of International Criminal Justice' (2014) 12 Journal of International Criminal Justice 193, 195-204. Cf Mahnoush H Arsanjani and W Michael Reisman, 'The Law-in-Action of the International Criminal Court' (2005) 99 American Journal of International Law 385, 401; Christine Van den Wyngaert, 'Victims before International Criminal Courts: Some Views and Concerns of an ICC Trial Judge' (2011) 44 Case Western Reserve Journal of International Law 475, 490. On certain perpetrators of international crimes as 'profiteers', see Alette Smeulers, 'Perpetrators of International Crimes: Towards a Typology' in Alette Smeulers and Roelof Haveman (eds), *Supranational Criminology: Towards a Criminology of International Crimes* (Intersentia 2008) 233, 249-50; Alette Smeulers and Barbora Holá, 'ICTY and the Culpability of Different Types of Perpetrators of International Crimes' in Alette Smeulers (ed), *Collective Violence and International Criminal Justice: An Interdisciplinary Approach* (Intersentia 2010) 186.

66 See eg Dan Sarooshi, 'Aspects of the Relationship between the International Criminal Court and the United Nations' (2001) 32 Netherlands Yearbook of International Law 27, 36-38.

67 See Scharf, 'The Tools for Enforcing International Criminal Justice in the New Millennium: Lessons from the Yugoslavia Tribunal' (n 36) at 944-46; Annie Wartanian, 'The ICC Prosecutor's Battlefield: Combating Atrocities While Fighting for States' Cooperation: Lessons from the U.N. Tribunals Applied to the Case of Uganda' (2005) 36 Georgetown Journal of International Law 1289, 1307; John Litwin, 'Smarter Sanctions: The Use of Targeted Asset Freezes and Travel Bans by the ICC to Effectuate Arrests' (*ICC Forum*, 13 March 2014) <www.iccforum.com/forum/permalink/93/4086> accessed 31 August 2020; Marina Mancini, 'UN Sanctions Targeting Individuals and ICC Proceedings: How to Achieve a Mutually Reinforcing Interaction' in Natalino Ronzitti (ed), *Coercive Diplomacy, Sanctions and International Law* (Brill Nijhoff 2016) 228; Nadia Banteka, 'Mind the Gap: A Systematic Approach to the International Criminal Court's Arrest Warrants Enforcement Problem' (2016) 49 Cornell International Law Journal 521, 541 (2016). See also, on the potential use of UNSC sanctions to bring an end to grave violations of international humanitarian law committed against children, some of which could constitute war crimes under the Rome Statute, David S Koller and Miriam Eckenfels-Garcia, 'Using Targeted Sanctions to End Violations against Children in Armed Conflict' (2015) 33 Boston University International Law Journal 1, 20-21.

respect of peace and security,[68] while the Rome Statute[69] and the ICC-UN Relationship Agreement[70] would appear to contain solid legal bases upon which such closer cooperation might be built. The following section examines eight situations in which the two bodies' actions (could) have interacted, primarily in circumstances related to armed conflict, showing that, despite the UN body having had ample opportunity to play an active role in supporting the ICC in this manner, it has rarely chosen to do so.

3.5 In Search of Coordination

The ICC is not the first ICT whose goals and operations have coincided with those of the UNSC.[71] Certain sanctions regimes established by the latter have interacted with activities at the ICTY,[72] the ICTR,[73] the SCSL[74] and the STL.[75] This is hardly surprising in view of the partially overlapping goals of certain international criminal justice processes and UNSC action examined in Part 3.3. Nor it is startling that the UNSC has called upon States to give effect to targeted sanctions measures under Chapter VII of the UN Charter in multiple

68 See ICC-UN Relationship Agreement, preamble ('Noting the important role assigned to the International Criminal Court in dealing with the most serious crimes of concern to the international community as a whole, as referred to in the Rome Statute, and which threaten the peace, security and well-being of the world'). See also UNGA 'Report of the International Criminal Court on its activities in 2014/15' (28 August 2015) UN Doc A/70/350, para 95 ('United Nations targeted sanctions are an important tool for addressing threats to international peace and security, including atrocity crimes.')

69 Rome Statute, art 87(6) ('The Court may ask any intergovernmental organization to provide information or documents. The Court may also ask for other forms of cooperation and assistance which may be agreed upon with such an organization and which are in accordance with its competence or mandate.) See also Rod Rastan, 'Testing Co-operation: The International Criminal Court and National Authorities' (2008) 21 Leiden Journal of International Law 431, 444.

70 ICC-UN Relationship Agreement, art. 3 ('The United Nations and the Court agree that, with a view to facilitating the effective discharge of their respective responsibilities, they shall cooperate closely, whenever appropriate, with each other and consult each other on matters of mutual interest pursuant to the provisions of the present Agreement and in conformity with the respective provisions of the Charter and the Statute.')

71 See Paul Bentall, 'United Nations targeted sanctions and other policy tools: diplomacy, legal, use of force' in Thomas J Biersteker, Sue E Eckert and Marcos Tourinho (eds), *Targeted Sanctions: The Impacts and Effectiveness of United Nations Action* (CUP 2016) 96-97.

72 UNSC Res 724 (15 December 1991) UN Doc S/RES/724, para 5(b), terminated pursuant to UNSC Res 1074 (1 October 1996) UN Doc S/RES/1074, para 6.

73 UNSC Res 918 (17 May 1994) UN Doc S/RES/918, para 14, terminated pursuant to UNSC Res 1823 (10 July 2008) UN Doc S/RES/1823, para 6.

74 UNSC Res 1521 (22 December 2003) UN Doc S/RES/1521, para 22, terminated pursuant to UNSC Res 2288 (25 May 2016) UN Doc S/RES/2288, para 2; UNSC Res 1532 (12 March 2004) UN Doc S/RES/1532, para 1. UNSC Res 1521 (22 December 2003) UN Doc S/RES/1521 dissolved the committee established under UNSC Res 1343 (7 March 2001) UN Doc S/RES/1343, para 14. In turn, UNSC Res 1343 (7 March 2001) UN Doc S/RES/1343, para 1 dissolved the committee established under UNSC Res 985 (13 April 1995) UN Doc S/RES/1343, para 4.

75 UNSC Res 1636 (31 October 2005) UN Doc S/RES/1636, para 3.

situations in which the ICC Prosecutor has also been engaged in investigative activities. This section analyses eight cases where the two bodies' actions (might) have coincided, with a particular focus on the (non-)parallel execution of asset freezing measures. One aim of this inquiry is to identify situations in which the request of such measures by the UN body has (whether deliberately or incidentally) served to support the actions of the Court. A further objective is to draw attention to cases where UNSC action could have assisted the ICC in achieving its objectives, but the UN body took no such action. A final goal is to ascertain the reasons behind UNSC (in)action in each of the two foregoing scenarios. It is beyond the scope of the chapter to scrutinise cases in which the Court has failed to act in scenarios in which the UNSC has taken coercive action. There have been a number of occasions since the entry into force of the Rome Statute in which the UN body has requested UN Member States to freeze individuals' assets where the ICC has not been engaged.[76] However, in view of the many political objectives for which targeted sanctions measures have been sought by the UNSC compared with the comparatively narrow legal basis on which the ICC can request the execution of such measures,[77] it is the view of the present author that to conduct such an investigation would be of little value.

3.5.1 *Libya: Coexistent and Coordinated?*

The UNSC instituted its (second)[78] sanctions regime for Libya in Resolution 1970.[79] Targeted sanctions were imposed to respond to the actions of the Libyan Government taken against demonstrators protesting against the regime of Muammar Gaddafi (or Qadhafi). As well as imposing measures aimed at preventing the supply, sale or transfer of arms to the Gaddafi regime, a travel ban and asset freezes,[80] the UNSC also referred the situation in Libya to the Prosecutor of the ICC.[81] In addition, Resolution 1970 established a sanctions committee charged with, among other responsibilities, monitoring the execution of the measures imposed, designating individuals for listing and considering exemptions.[82] As for the

76 See eg the sanctions regimes for Iran, established under UNSC Res 1737 (27 December 2006) UN Doc S/RES/1737, terminated pursuant to UNSC Res 2231 (20 July 2015) UN Doc S/RES/2231, and Guinea-Bissau, established under UNSC Res 2048 (18 May 2012) UN Doc S/RES/2048.

77 See Part 3.2.

78 The UNSC had previously imposed targeted sanctions in response to the suspected involvement of Libyan Government officials in the bombing of Pan Am flight 103 and *Union des transports aériens* flight 772. *See* UNSC Res 748 (31 March 1992) UN Doc S/RES/748, paras 4-6; UNSC Res 883 (11 November 1993) UN Doc S/RES/ 883, paras 3-7. The UNSC terminated the sanctions regime in September 2003. See UNSC Res 1506 (12 September 2003) UN Doc S/RES/1506, paras 1-2.

79 UNSC Res 1970 (26 February 2011) UN Doc S/RES/1970, para 24.

80 ibid paras 9-21.

81 ibid paras 4-8.

82 ibid paras 24-25.

targeted individuals, Muammar Gaddafi and five of his children, including his son Saif Al-Islam Gaddafi, became the object of assets freezing measures.[83] While the travel ban also targeted members of the immediate Gaddafi family, senior members of his regime, including Director of Military Intelligence, Abdullah Al-Senussi, were also listed.[84] Mr Al-Senussi was added to the list of individuals subject to an assets freeze in Resolution 1973,[85] in which the UNSC also decided to impose financial sanctions on entities.[86] The sanctions imposed by these two resolutions were partially relaxed after anti-Gaddafi forces captured the Libyan capital, Tripoli.[87] This said, the Libya sanctions regime remains in force, having been renewed with a particular focus on tackling the illicit export of crude oil from Libya.[88] As of 31 August 2020, Muammar Gaddafi,[89] Saif Al-Islam Gaddafi[90] and Abdullah Al-Senussi[91] all remain listed, despite the death of Muammar Gadaffi on 20 October 2011.

After the UNSC referred the situation in Libya to the ICC in Resolution 1970, the Prosecutor successfully applied for the issue of warrants of arrest for three individuals in the first instance. Those were: (i) Muammar Mohammed Abu Minyar Gaddafi;[92] (ii) Saif Al-Islam Gaddafi[93] and (iii) Abdullah Al-Senussi.[94] As for their assets, in the words of the then Prosecutor of the Court, Luis Moreno Ocampo, speaking after the death of Muammar Gaddafi in November 2011:

---

83 UNSC Res 1970 (n 79) Annex II.

84 UNSC Res 1970 (n 79) Annex I.

85 UNSC Res 1973 (17 March 2011) UN Doc S/RES/1973, Annex II.

86 ibid.

87 UNSC Res 2009 (16 September 2011) UN Doc S/RES/2009, paras 13-19.

88 See UNSC Res 2146 (19 March 2014) UN Doc S/RES/2146.

89 Libya Sanctions Committee, 'Muammar Mohammed Abu Minyar Qadhafi' (29 October 2014) <https://www.un.org/securitycouncil/sanctions/1970/materials/summaries/individual/muammar-mohammed-abu-minyar-qadhafi> accessed 31 August 2020 (noting, by way of '[a]dditional information', his '[r]esponsibility for ordering repression of demonstrations' and 'human rights abuses.')

90 Libya Sanctions Committee, 'Saif Al-Islam Qadhafi' (29 October 2014) <https://www.un.org/securitycouncil/sanctions/1970/materials/summaries/individual/saif-al-islam-qadhafi> accessed 31 August 2020 (noting in the '[a]dditional information' category, his '[c]loseness of association with regime' and '[i]nflammatory public statements encouraging violence against demonstrators.')

91 Libya Sanctions Committee, 'Abdullah Al-Senussi' (29 October 2014) <https://www.un.org/securitycouncil/sanctions/1970/materials/summaries/individual/abdullah-al-senussi> accessed 31 August 2020 (noting, under the heading '[a]dditional information', his 'Military Intelligence involvement in suppression of demonstrations', 'suspicion of [his] involvement in [the] Abu Selim prison massacre' and his conviction in absentia for the bombing of *Union des transports aériens* flight 772).

92 *Situation in the Libyan Arab Jamahiriya* (Warrant of Arrest for Muammar Mohammed Abu Minyar Gaddafi) ICC-01/11-01/11-2 (27 June 2011).

93 *Situation in the Libyan Arab Jamahiriya* (Warrant of Arrest for Saif Al-Islam Gaddafi) ICC-01/11-01/11-3 (27 June 2011).

94 *Situation in the Libyan Arab Jamahiriya* (Warrant of Arrest for Abdullah Al-Senussi) ICC-01/11-01/11-4 (27 June 2011).

> The Office will also continue to search out the personal assets of Saif Al-Islam Gaddafi and Abdallah Al-Senussi for the potential benefit of the victims, through reparations awarded by the Court. Since the opening of the situation, the Office has been in contact with the UN Sanctions Committee, which is assisted by a Panel of Experts and with Interpol to coordinate its investigative efforts in relation to the assets of the suspects. The Court has sent at the end of September requests for assistance to Libya, State Parties, and five UN Security Council non-State Parties to identify, trace, seize and freeze all the personal assets belonging to the suspects. The Office strongly encourages the Security Council and States to assist the Court in identifying and isolating these assets.[95]

ICC Pre-Trial Chamber I has since unsealed arrest warrants for two individuals in the situation in Libya: (i) for the alleged former Head of the Libyan Internal Security Agency, Al-Tuhamy Mohamed Khaled, in April 2013[96] and (ii) for an alleged commander in the Al-Saiqa Brigade, one of many armed groups involved in the conflict in post-Gaddafi Libya, Mahmoud Mustafa Busayf Al-Werfalli, in August 2017[97] and again in July 2018.[98]

The coexistent activities of the UNSC and the ICC with regard to Libya might appear to present a suitable occasion on which the two bodies could coordinate their respective asset freezing powers for mutual benefit. Indeed, there is some evidence of coordination in respect of Libya, where the UNSC listed two individuals, Muammar Gaddafi and Saif Al-Islam Gaddafi, later subject to ICC arrest warrants in the same resolution as that which referred the situation in Libya to the Court under Article 13(b) of the ICC Statute, with a third, Abdullah Al-Senussi, following less than one month thereafter. Paul Bentall describes the responses of the UN organ and the ICC to events in Libya, as 'reinforcing', arguing that 'The judicial processes and targeted sanctions pulled logically in the same direction in isolating the Qadhafi regime'.[99] Larissa van den Herik proposes a plausible reason behind the UNSC's reinforcement of the ICC in the situation in Libya, namely is the unanimity of the UN body in deciding to refer the situation to the Court.[100] This can be contrasted

95 ICC Prosecutor, 'Prosecutor's statement to the United Nations Security Council on the situation in Libya, pursuant to UNSCR 1970 (2011)' (New York, 2 November 2011) <https://www.legal-tools.org/doc/bil32o/> accessed 31 August 2020.

96 *Prosecutor v Khaled* (Warrant of Arrest for Al-Tuhamy Mohamed Khaled with under seal and *ex parte* Annex) ICC-01/11-01/13-1 (18 April 2013).

97 *Prosecutor v Al-Werfalli* (Warrant of Arrest) ICC-01/11-01/17-2 (15 August 2017).

98 *Prosecutor v Al-Werfalli* (Second Warrant of Arrest) ICC-01/11-01/17-13 (4 July 2018).

99 Bentall (n 71) 98.

100 Larissa van den Herik, 'The Individualisation of Enforcement in International Law: Exploring the Interplay between United Nations Targeted Sanctions and International Criminal Proceedings' in Tiyanjana Maluwa, Max du Plessis and Dire Tladi (eds), *The Pursuit of a Brave New World in International Law: Essays in Honour of John Dugard* (Brill Nijhoff 2017) 244.

with the situation in Darfur, Sudan, in which she fairly suggests that 'the Council's attitude rather undermined ICC proceedings'.[101]

In 2014, Australia, Finland, Germany, Greece and Sweden sponsored a project studying how to revise and improve the implementation of UNSC sanctions.[102] This project culminated in the publication of the Compendium of the High-level Review of United Nations Sanctions in June 2015.[103] Among the recommendations put forward in the Compendium are several directed at the relationship between targeted sanctions and international(ised) criminal justice institutions.[104] Recommendation 100 resembles the pattern observed with regard to the 2011 situation in Libya:

> With the ICC as an example, sanctions committees should consider enabling the automatic listing of persons sought by the Court once a warrant for their arrest has been issued by a Pre-Trial Chamber for the alleged commission of crimes within the jurisdiction of the Court, particularly where the situation has been referred by the Security Council itself.[105]

Yet, as this chapter will demonstrate in the following sections, practical support for the Court by sanctions committees has very much constituted the exception rather than the rule.

3.5.2 Coexistent but Uncoordinated

3.5.2.1 Democratic Republic of the Congo

The UNSC established a sanctions regime for the DRC in Resolution 1493.[106] The first measures taken in this context were not targeted at individuals, but consisted of an arms embargo against a number of armed groups operating in the North Kivu, South Kivu and Ituri regions.[107] This reflects the objectives pursued by the measures, which primarily

101 ibid 245. See Part 3.5.2.3.
102 'Letter dated 12 June 2015 from the Permanent Representatives of Australia, Finland, Germany, Greece and Sweden to the United Nations addressed to the Secretary-General' (12 June 2015) UN Doc A/69/941–S/2015/432.
103 'Annex to the letter dated 12 June 2015 from the Permanent Representatives of Australia, Finland, Germany, Greece and Sweden to the United Nations addressed to the President of the Security Council' (12 June 2015) UN Doc A/69/941–S/2015/432.
104 ibid 57-59.
105 ibid 59.
106 UNSC Res 1493 (28 July 2004) UN Doc S/RES/1493, para 20.
107 ibid.

related to the armed conflict in the region.[108] It was not until March 2004 that a sanctions committee, with the power *inter alia* to monitor violations of the arms embargo, was established.[109] In a further resolution, adopted in May 2005,[110] the UNSC extended the arms embargo across the DRC.[111] In the same resolution, the UN organ decided that UN Member States should enforce a travel ban and an asset freeze against 'all persons designated by the Committee as acting in violation of' the broadened arms embargo.[112] These measures were extended to target the political and military leadership of foreign armed factions operating in DRC territory and the leaders of Congolese militias in receipt of foreign support.[113] The UNSC decided upon a further extension of the sanctions in July 2006, on this occasion targeting:

- Political and military leaders recruiting or using children in armed conflict in violation of applicable international law; [and]
- Individuals committing serious violations of international law involving the targeting of children in situations of armed conflict, including killing and maiming, sexual violence, abduction and forced displacement[.][114]

The UN body has renewed (and revised) the measures in a series of subsequent resolutions.[115] It was pursuant to the foregoing targeted sanctions that a number of Congolese nationals who later also became the object of ICC-issued arrest warrants were listed by the Resolution 1533 Sanctions Committee.

108 ibid preamble, paras 13-14.
109 UNSC Res 1533 (12 March 2004) UN Doc S/RES/1533, para 8.
110 UNSC Res 1596 (3 May 2005) UN Doc S/RES/1596.
111 ibid para 1.
112 ibid paras 13-16.
113 UNSC Res 1649 (21 December 2005) UN Doc S/RES/1649, para 2.
114 UNSC Res 1698 (31 July 2006) UN Doc S/RES/1698, para 13.
115 UNSC Res 1768 (31 July 2007) UN Doc S/RES/1768; UNSC Res 1771 (10 August 2007) UN Doc S/RES/1771; UNSC Res 1799 (31 March 2008) UN Doc S/RES/1799; UNSC Res 1804 (13 March 2008) UN Doc S/RES/1804; UNSC Res 1857 (22 December 2008) UN Doc S/RES/1857; UNSC Res 1896 (30 November 2009) UN Doc S/RES/1896; UNSC Res 1952 (29 November 2010) UN Doc S/RES/1952; UNSC Res 2021 (29 November 2011) UN Doc S/RES/2021; UNSC Res 2078 (28 November 2012) UN Doc S/RES/2078; UNSC Res 2136 (30 January 2014) UN Doc S/RES/2136; UNSC Res 2198 (29 January 2015) UN Doc S/RES/2198; UNSC Res 2293 (June 23 2016) UN Doc S/RES/2293; UNSC Res 2360 (21 June 2017) UN Doc S/RES/2360; UNSC Res 2424 (29 June 2018) UN Doc S/RES/2424; UNSC Res 2478 (26 June 2019) UN Doc S/RES/2478.

It was the President of the DRC who referred the situation on Congolese territory to the ICC's Prosecutor.[116] The modalities of so-called 'self-referrals'[117] are largely governed by Article 14 of the Rome Statute, according to subsection 1 of which:

> A State Party may refer to the Prosecutor a situation in which one or more crimes within the jurisdiction of the Court appear to have been committed requesting the Prosecutor to investigate the situation for the purpose of determining whether one or more specific persons should be charged with the commission of such crimes.[118]

Having determined that the criteria enabling the initiation of an investigation,[119] including that 'The information available to the Prosecutor provide[d] a reasonable basis to believe that a crime within the jurisdiction of the Court ha[d] been or [was] being committed',[120] were met,[121] the Prosecutor informed the Court's Presidency, which assigned the 'Situation'[122] in the DRC to the Court's Pre-Trial Chamber I.[123] Within this situation, the Prosecutor successfully sought warrants of arrest for multiple individuals, all of whom have also been listed by the Sanctions Committee established by the UNSC pursuant to Resolution 1533.

Thomas Lubanga Dyilo

The DRC Sanctions Committee listed Thomas Lubanga Dyilo, the then leader of a Congolese militia, *Union des Patriotes Congolais* (Union of Congolese Patriots or UPC), on 1 November 2005 for contravening the arms embargo.[124] The narrative summary of reasons[125] for the listing of Mr Lubanga provided by the Committee also notes his

116 ICC Office of the Prosecutor, 'Prosecutor receives referral of the situation in the Democratic Republic of Congo' (24 April 2004) Press Release ICC-OTP-20040419-50.

117 See eg Paola Gaeta, 'Is the Practice of 'Self-Referrals' a Sound Start for the ICC?' (2004) 2 Journal of International Criminal Justice 949.

118 Rome Statute, art 14.

119 ibid art 53(1).

120 ibid art 53(1)(a).

121 *Situation in the Democratic Republic of the Congo* (Decision assigning the situation in the Democratic Republic of Congo to Pre-Trial Chamber I) ICC-01/04-1 (5 July 2005) (DRC Assignment Decision).

122 Rome Statute, art 14. On the legal meaning of the term 'situation' in the Rome Statute system, see Rod Rastan, 'Situation and case: defining the parameters' in Carsten Stahn and Mohamed M El Zeidy (eds), *The International Criminal Court and Complementarity: From Theory to Practice* (CUP 2011) 422-37.

123 DRC Assignment Decision (n 121) 3.

124 DRC Sanctions Committee, 'Thomas Lubanga' (5 December 2016) <https://www.un.org/securitycouncil/sanctions/1533/materials/summaries/individual/thomas-lubanga> accessed 31 August 2020.

125 ibid ('In accordance with paragraph 2 (g) of the Guidelines for the conduct of its work, the Security Council Committee established pursuant to resolution 1533 (2004) concerning the Democratic Republic of the

involvement in the 'recruitment and use of children in Ituri in 2002 to 2003' under the heading '[a]dditional information'.[126] This said, the sole '[r]eason' for his listing is limited to violations of the measures concerning the movement of arms established in Resolution 1493.[127]

As for his ICC arrest warrant, Pre-Trial Chamber I found that there were 'reasonable grounds to believe' that Mr Lubanga was criminally responsible under the Rome Statute for three war crimes, namely enlisting and conscripting children under the age of fifteen and using children under the same age to participate actively in hostilities.[128] It was for this reason, among others, that the Pre-Trial Chamber issued a warrant for Mr Lubanga's arrest. After the issuance of an arrest warrant, in accordance with Article 57(3)(e) of the Rome Statute, the Pre-Trial Chamber ordered the Registry of the Court to transmit requests for cooperation from States with a view to identifying, tracing, freezing and seizing Mr Lubanga's property and assets.[129] In terms of specific assets targeted, Pre-Trial Chamber I's request to the DRC refers to information from the Prosecutor, according to which Mr Lubanga possessed houses in Bunia and Goma as well as a vehicle in the latter.[130] The Prosecutor also indicated that 'funds from a local airline might in fact belong to Mr Lubanga'.[131] Notable for the purposes of the present analysis, in each of the two requests for cooperation issued by the Pre-Trial Chamber (ie one directed at the DRC and the second aimed at other States Parties to the Rome Statute), explicit reference was made to Mr Lubanga's listing by the Sanctions Committee established by the UNSC in Resolution 1533, as follows:

> CONSIDERING that paragraph 15 of United Nations Security Council resolution 1596, states that '... all States shall ... immediately freeze the funds, other financial assets and economic resources which are on their territories from the date of adoption of this resolution, which are owned or controlled,

Congo makes accessible a narrative summary of reasons for the listing for individuals, groups, undertakings and entities included in its sanctions list.')

126 ibid.

127 ibid.

128 *Prosecutor v Lubanga Dyilo* (Warrant of Arrest) ICC-01/04-01/06-2-tEN (10 February 2006).

129 *Prosecutor v Lubanga Dyilo* (Request to the Democratic Republic of the Congo for the purpose of obtaining the identification, tracing, freezing and seizure of property and assets belonging to Mr. Thomas Lubanga Dyilo) ICC-01/04-01/06-22-tEN (9 March 2006) (*Lubanga* DRC Freezing Request); *Prosecutor v Lubanga Dyilo* (Request to States Parties to the Rome Statute for the Identification, Tracing and Freezing or Seizure of the Property and Assets of Mr Thomas Lubanga Dyilo) ICC-01/04-01/06-62-tEN (31 March 2006) (*Lubanga* States Parties Freezing Request). See also *Prosecutor v Lubanga Dyilo* (Decision on the Prosecutor's Application for a warrant of arrest, Article 58) ICC-01/04-01/06-1-Corr-Red (10 February 2006) 64.

130 *Lubanga* DRC Freezing Request (n 129) 3.

131 ibid.

> directly or indirectly, by persons designated by the [Sanctions] Committee pursuant to paragraph 13 above, or that are held by entities owned or controlled, directly or indirectly, by any persons acting on their behalf or at their direction ...';
>
> CONSIDERING that the 'List of individuals and entities subject to the measures imposed by Paragraphs 13 and 15 of Security Council resolution 1596 (2005)', in which the Sanctions Committee identifies Mr Thomas Lubanga Dyilo as one of the persons concerned by the said resolution[.][132]

Prima facie, the respective asset freezing measures adopted by the DRC Sanctions Committee and the Court with respect to Mr Lubanga might appear to indicate concerted action. However, as Annalisa Ciampi contends, 'The ground which justifies the listing [by the DRC Sanctions Committee] ... has little, if anything, to do with the crimes within the jurisdiction of the ICC for which Lubanga [was] charged'.[133] Paul Bentall reaches a similar conclusion, namely that the execution of targeted sanctions against Mr Lubanga under the UN Charter shortly before the ICC issued a warrant for his arrest was 'coincidental',[134] rather than coordinated. Bentall references the fact that the UNSC did not refer the situation in the DRC to the Court in accordance with Article 13(b) of the Rome Statute as further evidence in support of this argument.[135] It is difficult to dispute these conclusions. Mr Lubanga's listing by the DRC Sanctions Committee (despite overtly recognizing his participation in the recruitment and use of children in armed conflict) was for violations of the arms embargo, while the ICC issued a warrant for his arrest for enlisting, conscripting and using child soldiers. Accordingly, though the ICC referred to Mr Lubanga's listing by the DRC Sanctions Committee in requesting the DRC and other States Parties to its constituent instrument to freeze his assets, it is a stretch to describe the respective action of the two bodies here as coordinated. As will be demonstrated in the following paragraphs, similar conclusions can be reached with regard to numerous other DRC-based individuals subject to parallel, if not coordinated, asset freezing requests from the UNSC and the ICC.

Germain Katanga

On the same day that Thomas Lubanga Dyilo was added to the list of targeted individuals, the DRC Sanctions Committee listed Germain Katanga, a commander in the *Force de*

132 ibid. See also *Lubanga* States Parties Freezing Request (n 129) 3.

133 Annalisa Ciampi, 'Security Council Targeted Sanctions and Human Rights' in Bardo Fassbender (ed), *Securing Human Rights? Achievements and Challenges of the UN Security Council* (OUP 2011) 136.

134 Bentall (n 71) 97-98.

135 ibid 97.

résistance patriotique d'Ituri (Front for Patriotic Resistance in Ituri or FRPI), a Congolese armed group, for breaching the arms embargo.[136] Again, similar to the listing of Mr Lubanga, the Sanctions Committee notes Mr Katanga's involvement in recruiting and using children in Ituri between 2002 and 2003 in the '[a]dditional information' category.[137]

Turning to the ICC, Pre-Trial Chamber I issued a warrant of arrest for Mr Katanga on 2 July 2007.[138] The warrant listed multiple allegations of crimes against humanity and war crimes.[139] After the warrant had been issued, Pre-Trial Chamber I requested cooperation from States in the identification, tracing, freezing or seizure of Mr Katanga's property and assets, 'including his moveable and immovable property, bank accounts, [and] shares in a partnership, business or private company'.[140] In a further order on the execution of the arrest warrant, the same Pre-Trial Chamber took note of information supplied by the Prosecutor that, at the time the crimes contained in his application for a warrant were allegedly committed, Mr Katanga 'reportedly had two residences in Aveba [and] that he also can be expected to have retained at least some of the fruits of the crimes in which his combatants frequently engaged'.[141] Pre-Trial Chamber I also decided that the ICC's Registrar ought to transmit a request for cooperation to the DRC with respect to Mr Katanga's assets,[142] having referenced 'resolution 1596 (2005) and the list of persons and entities which are subject to measures imposed by paragraphs 13 and 15 of the resolution'.[143] In this request for cooperation, as with the cooperation requests transmitted to the DRC and other States Parties to the Rome Statute with respect to Thomas Lubanga Dyilo's assets,[144] the Registrar overtly mentioned the inclusion of Mr Katanga on the DRC Sanctions Committee's list of targeted individuals.[145] The wording used is identical to that contained in the request issued to the DRC by Pre-Trial Chamber I in respect of Mr Lubanga's assets,

136 DRC Sanctions Committee, 'Germain Katanga' (5 December 2016) <https://www.un.org/securitycouncil/sanctions/1533/materials/summaries/individual/germain-katanga> accessed 31 August 2020.

137 ibid.

138 *Prosecutor v Katanga* (Warrant of Arrest for Germain Katanga) ICC-01/04-01/07-1-tENG (2 July 2007).

139 ibid 6 (listing the crimes against humanity of murder, other inhumane acts and sexual slavery and the war crimes of wilful killing, inhuman treatment, using children under the age of fifteen years to participate actively in hostilities, sexual slavery, intentionally directing attacks against the civilian population as such or against individual civilians not taking direct part in hostilities and pillaging a town or place, even when taken by assault).

140 *Prosecutor v Katanga* (Request to the Democratic Republic of the Congo for the purpose of obtaining the identification, tracing, freezing and seizure of the property and assets of Germain Katanga) ICC-01/04-01/07-7-tENG (6 July 2007) (*Katanga* DRC Freezing Request) 3.

141 *Prosecutor v Katanga* (Order on the execution of the warrant of arrest against Germain Katanga) ICC-01/04-01/07-54-tENG (5 November 2007) 5.

142 ibid 8.

143 ibid 3.

144 See *Lubanga* DRC Freezing Request (n 129) 3; *Lubanga* States Parties Freezing Request (n 129) 3.

145 *Katanga* DRC Freezing Request (n 140) 2.

but for naming Mr Katanga rather than Mr Lubanga as an individual targeted by the UNSC's targeted sanctions measures.[146]

Bosco Ntaganda

The Sanctions Committee also added Bosco Ntaganda, a UPC military commander, to the list of targeted individuals on 1 November 2005.[147] As with Thomas Lubanga Dyilo and Germain Katanga, Mr Ntaganda was listed for violating the arms embargo,[148] while his involvement in the recruitment and use of children in the armed conflicts in Ituri and North Kivu is mentioned by way of '[a]dditional information'.[149]

ICC Pre-Trial Chamber I issued an arrest warrant for Mr Ntaganda on 7 August 2006.[150] The crimes for which, in the opinion of the Pre-Trial Chamber, there were 'reasonable grounds to believe' that Mr Ntaganda was criminally liable were enlistment and conscription of children under the age of fifteen and use of children under fifteen to participate actively in hostilities,[151] all war crimes under Article 8(2) of the Rome Statute.[152] As for Mr Ntaganda's property and assets, in evaluating the Prosecutor's application for a warrant of arrest,[153] Pre-Trial Chamber I requested that the Court's Registry prepare (and transmit) requests for cooperation from the DRC,[154] Uganda[155] and Rwanda.[156] Pre-Trial Chamber I made this request so that these States might 'identify, trace and freeze or seize the property and assets belonging to Bosco Ntaganda at the earliest opportunity, without prejudice to the rights of third parties',[157] despite the ICC Prosecutor having made 'no application to this effect'.[158]

146 ibid.
147 DRC Sanctions Committee, 'Bosco Taganda' (5 December 2016) <https://www.un.org/securitycouncil/sanctions/1533/materials/summaries/individual/bosco-taganda> accessed 31 August 2020.
148 ibid.
149 ibid ('According to the Office of the [Special Representative of the Secretary-General] on Children and Armed Conflict, he was responsible for recruitment and use of children in Ituri in 2002 and 2003, and 155 cases of direct and/or command responsibility for recruitment and use of children in North Kivu from 2002 to 2009.)
150 *Prosecutor v Ntaganda* (Warrant of Arrest) ICC-01/04-02/06-2-Anx-tEN (22 August 2006).
151 ibid 4.
152 Rome Statute, art 8(2).
153 *Prosecutor v Ntaganda* (Decision on the Prosecution Application for a Warrant of Arrest) ICC-01/04-02/06-1-Red-tENG (6 March 2007).
154 ibid 35. See also para 87.
155 ibid 35. See also para 87.
156 ibid 36. See also para 87.
157 ibid 35, 36.
158 ibid para 88.

It is noticeable that, unlike with Thomas Lubanga Dyilo and Germain Katanga, no mention is made of Mr Ntaganda's preexisting place on the DRC sanctions list, at least not in documents that are publicly available and/or unredacted. This could be seen as an indication that the ICC abandoned its strategy of explicitly referencing an individual's listing by the Resolution 1533 Sanctions Committee when requesting cooperation from States in the freezing of assets. This, in turn, could be viewed as a decline in the already minimal level of coordination between the UNSC and the ICC in this sphere of their respective operations.

Mathieu Ngudjolo Chui

Another individual added to the DRC sanctions list on 1 November 2005 is FRPI commander Mathieu Ngudjolo Chui.[159] Similar to his fellow FRPI leader, Germain Katanga, Mr Ngudjolo was listed for flouting the arms embargo.[160] As with the three foregoing listees, the Sanctions Committee remarked upon Mr Ngudjolo's use of children in armed conflict, this time in Ituri in 2006, under the heading '[a]dditional information'.[161]

The Court's Pre-Trial Chamber I issued a warrant of arrest for Mr Ngudjolo shortly after that of his FRPI colleague, Germain Katanga.[162] The warrants also shared similarities with respect to the crimes contained therein.[163] On 14 November 2007, the Registrar transmitted a request for cooperation from the DRC with a view to identifying, tracing, freezing and/or seizing Mr Ngudjolo's property and assets[164] in accordance with an order by Pre-Trial Chamber I to this effect.[165] The order on the execution of the warrant of arrest for Mr Ngudjolo[166] also resembles that of Germain Katanga. For the purposes of the present

159 DRC Sanctions Committee, 'Mathieu Chui Ngudjolo' (5 December 2016) <https://www.un.org/securitycouncil/sanctions/1533/materials/summaries/individual/mathieu-chui-ngudjolo> accessed 31 August 2020.

160 ibid.

161 ibid.

162 *Prosecutor v Ngudjolo Chui* (Warrant of Arrest for Mathieu Ngudjolo Chui) ICC-01/04-01/07-260-tENG (6 July 2007).

163 ibid 6 (listing the crimes against humanity of murder, other inhumane acts and sexual slavery and the war crimes of wilful killing, inhuman treatment, using children under the age of fifteen years to participate actively in hostilities, sexual slavery, intentionally directing attacks against the civilian population as such or against individual civilians not taking direct part in hostilities and pillaging a town or place, even when taken by assault).

164 *Prosecutor v Ngudjolo Chui* (Demande adressée à la république démocratique du Congo en vue d'obtenir l'identification, la localisation, le gel et la saisie des biens et avoirs de Mathieu Ngudjolo Chui) ICC-01/04-01/07-266 (14 November 2007).

165 ibid 2.

166 *Prosecutor v Ngudjolo Chui* (Version Publique Expurgée de l' « Ordonnance relative à l'exécution du mandat d'arrêt à l'encontre de Mathieu Ngudjolo Chui » rendue le 6 juillet 2007) ICC-01/04-01/07-294 (21 February 2008).

analysis, it is notable that Pre-Trial Chamber I took note of UNSC Resolution 1596 (2005) and the list of persons and entities targeted by measures imposed by paragraphs 13 and 15 thereof.[167] As for specific assets identified as belonging to Mr Ngudjolo, the same Pre-Trial Chamber noted information provided by the Prosecutor that Mr Ngudjolo allegedly had a residence in Ituri at the time of the events covered by the Prosecutor's application for a warrant of arrest, and that he retained part of the proceeds of the crimes in which his troops regularly engaged.[168]

It is important to observe at this stage that the Court's Trial Chamber II acquitted Mr Ngudjolo on 18 December 2012,[169] with the Appeals Chamber upholding this decision on 27 February 2015.[170] Neither of these ICC decisions led to Mr Ngudjolo's de-listing by the DRC Sanctions Committee. On the contrary, he remains a designated individual as of 31 August 2020, that is to say more than seven years after his acquittal at trial. Might the lack of effect on the part of the Court's decision on Mr Ngudjolo's continued presence on the DRC sanctions list indicate an absence of coordination between the two asset freezing processes under examination? Larissa van den Herik offers another possible explanation, namely that 'individuals can be listed and subjected to UN sanctions for different reasons than those underlying ICC prosecutions'.[171] It has been shown that Mr Ngudjolo, like Thomas Lubanga Dyilo, Germain Katanga and Bosco Ntaganda, found himself on the sanctions list for violating the arms embargo. As van den Herik contends: 'most listings are grounded on an individual's contribution to obstructing the peace process and such a reason may maintain or even increase in validity upon return of an acquitted person, thus potentially justifying the continuation of the listing.'[172] To arrive at such a conclusion would appear to be more than reasonable when scrutinizing the cases of the individuals subject to financial sanctions implemented under the auspices of the UNSC and ICC proceedings in the DRC context. It remains to be seen, however, whether an individual designated by a UNSC-established sanctions committee for alleged violations of international humanitarian law and acquitted of those same violations by the ICC would find themselves delisted at the UN level following their acquittal. In view of the state of

167 ibid 2.

168 ibid 5.

169 *Prosecutor v Ngudjolo Chui* (Judgment Pursuant to Article 74 of the Statute) ICC-01/04-02/12-3-tENG (18 December 2012).

170 *Prosecutor v Ngudjolo Chui* (Judgment on the Prosecutor's appeal against the decision of Trial Chamber II entitled "Judgment pursuant to article 74 of the Statute") ICC-01/04-02/12-271-Corr (27 February 2015).

171 van den Herik (n 100) 249.

172 ibid.

sanctions committee practice as far as the delisting of individuals (and entities) is concerned at the time of writing,[173] the present author doubts whether this would be the case.

Callixte Mbarushimana

The Sanctions Committee established by the UNSC in Resolution 1533 listed Callixte Mbarushimana on 3 March 2009.[174] Mr Mbarushimana allegedly had senior roles in the *Forces démocratiques de libération du Rwanda* (Democratic Forces for the Liberation of Rwanda or FDLR), an armed militia active in the eastern DRC.[175] According to the Sanctions Committee, Mr Mbarushimana was targeted by individual sanctions because 'he impeded the disarmament and the voluntary repatriation and resettlement of combatants' in contravention of paragraph 4 of Resolution 1857.[176]

ICC Pre-Trial Chamber I issued a warrant of arrest for Callixte Mbarushimana on 28 September 2010.[177] The arrest warrant contained a list of 11 crimes under the Court's jurisdiction for which Pre-Trial Chamber I was satisfied to the required standard that Mr Mbarushimana was responsible.[178] However, unlike in certain earlier decisions on applications for arrest warrants, the Pre-Trial Chamber made no mention of Mr Mbarushimana's assets.[179] Nor, to the best of the present author's knowledge, was any such mention made in later publicly available filings. Similar to the situation with Mathieu Ngudjolo Chui,[180] despite the Court's Pre-Trial Chamber I declining to confirm the charges[181] against Mr Mbarushimana on 16 December 2011,[182] and with the Appeals Chamber having unanimously dismissed the Prosecutor's appeal against this decision on

173 See Chapter 7, nn 53-54 and accompanying text. On entities, see Dini Sejko and Daley J Birkett, 'When United Nations Sanctions Impact International Financial Governance: Lessons from the Libyan Sovereign Wealth Fund' (2018) 34 American University International Law Review 387, 420-25.

174 DRC Sanctions Committee, 'Callixte Mbarushimana' (5 December 2016) <https://www.un.org/securitycouncil/sanctions/1533/materials/summaries/individual/callixte-mbarushimana> accessed 31 August 2020.

175 ibid.

176 ibid.

177 *Prosecutor v Mbarushimana* (Warrant of Arrest for Callixte Mbarushimana) ICC-01/04-01/10-2-tENG (28 September 2010).

178 ibid para 10 (listing the crimes against humanity of murder, torture, rape, other inhumane acts and persecution and the war crimes of attacks against the civilian population, destruction of property, murder, torture, rape and inhuman treatment).

179 *Prosecutor v Mbarushimana* (Decision on the Prosecutor's Application for a Warrant of Arrest for Callixte Mbarushimana) ICC - 01/04 - 01/10-7 (28 September 2010).

180 van den Herik (n 100) 249.

181 Rome Statute, art 61.

182 *Prosecutor v Mbarushimana* (Decision on the confirmation of charges) ICC-01/04-01/10-465-Red (16 December 2011).

30 May 2012,[183] his name remains on the list of designated individuals. There is therefore limited evidence of coordinated action between the two bodies in this case. A similar conclusion can be reached with regard to Sylvestre Mudacumura.

Sylvestre Mudacumura

The DRC Sanctions Committee listed Sylvestre Mudacumura, the alleged commander of the FDLR-affiliated *Forces Combattantes Abacunguzi*, on 1 November 2005 for trafficking arms in violation of the embargo.[184] The Committee also mentions information from the Office of the Special Representative of the UN Secretary-General on Children and Armed Conflict as regards Mr Mudacumura's responsibility for '27 cases of recruitment and use of children by troops under his command in North Kivu from 2002 to 2007' in the '[a]dditional information' category.[185]

The Court's Pre-Trial Chamber II issued an arrest warrant for Sylvestre Mudacumura on 13 July 2012.[186] The warrant specified multiple war crimes for which the Pre-Trial Chamber was satisfied that there were 'reasonable grounds to believe' that Mr Mudacumura was criminally responsible.[187] In a similar manner to Pre-Trial Chamber I's decision on the arrest warrant for Callixte Mbarushimana, Pre-Trial Chamber II made no mention of Mr Mudacumura's assets, at least not in the unredacted paragraphs of the decision. At the same time, while the Pre-Trial Chamber did not refer to the asset freeze measures imposed against Mr Mudacumura pursuant to his listing by the Sanctions Committee (again, in the unredacted parts of the decision), the Chamber did order the Court's Registrar to take steps to request an exemption from the travel ban imposed by the same listing.[188]

---

183 *Prosecutor v Mbarushimana* (Judgment on the appeal of the Prosecutor against the decision of Pre-Trial Chamber I of 16 December 2011 entitled "Decision on the confirmation of charges") ICC-01/04-01/10-514 (30 May 2012).

184 DRC Sanctions Committee, 'Sylvestre Mudacumura' (5 December 2016) <https://www.un.org/securitycouncil/sanctions/1533/materials/summaries/individual/sylvestre-mudacumura> accessed 31 August 2020.

185 ibid.

186 *Prosecutor v Mudacumura* (Decision on the Prosecutor's Application under Article 58) ICC-01/04-01/12-1-Red (13 July 2012) para 77.

187 ibid 28-29 (listing the war crimes of murder, mutilation, cruel treatment, torture, outrage upon personal dignity, attack against the civilian population, pillaging, rape and destruction of property).

188 ibid 30 ('Orders the Registrar ... to liaise with the Prosecutor in order to invite the DRC and the Kingdom of The Netherlands to request an exemption from the travel ban imposed by the UN Security Council and the Council of the European Union to allow the surrender of Sylvestre Mudacumura to the Court and to enter the territory of the The Netherlands').

3.5.2.2 Côte d'Ivoire

The UNSC first imposed targeted sanctions against individuals and entities in Côte d'Ivoire in November 2004. Acting pursuant to Chapter VII of the UN Charter, and in accordance with Rule 28 of its Provisional Rules of Procedure,[189] the UN organ instituted a sanctions committee in Resolution 1572.[190] The sanctions regime for Côte d'Ivoire aimed to respond to renewed fighting in contravention of a ceasefire agreement brokered following the disputed 2000 Ivorian presidential election, of which Laurent Gbagbo was the victor and from which Alessane Ouattara, among other opposition candidates, was excluded from contesting. As for the sanctions requested, Resolution 1572 includes an arms embargo,[191] a travel ban[192] and asset freezing measures.[193] Thirteen months later, having determined that the situation in Côte d'Ivoire continued 'to pose a threat to international peace and security in the region',[194] the UNSC decided to renew the sanctions imposed by Resolution 1572 for an additional year.[195] Further measures were adopted in the aftermath of the disputed presidential election of 2010, the result of which, a victory for Mr Ouattara, Mr Gbagbo refused to accept. Having implored 'all the Ivorian parties and stakeholders to respect the will of the people and the outcome of the election' in Resolution 1962,[196] in view of Mr Gbagbo's continued refusal to do so,[197] the UNSC adopted further individual sanctions measures targeting Mr Gbagbo, Simone Gbagbo (his wife) and three prominent supporters of his regime.[198] The UNSC renewed and modified the measures on a number of occasions[199] before terminating the sanctions regime for Côte d'Ivoire in Resolution 2283 of 28 April 2016.[200]

The governments led by Mr Gbagbo and Mr Ouattara, respectively, granted jurisdiction over crimes committed in Côte d'Ivoire to the Court. On 18 April 2003, Mr Gbagbo's Minister of Foreign Affairs, Mamadou Bamba, submited a declaration, with validity 'for

189 See n 4.
190 UNSC Res 1572 (15 November 2004) UN Doc S/RES/1572, para 14.
191 ibid para 7.
192 ibid para 9.
193 ibid para 11.
194 UNSC Res 1643 (15 December 2005) UN Doc S/RES/1643, preamble.
195 ibid para 11.
196 UNSC Res 1962 (20 December 2010) UN Doc S/RES/1962, para 1.
197 UNSC Res 1975 (3 March 2011) UN Doc S/RES/1975, para 3.
198 ibid para 12, Annex (listing, in addition to Laurent and Simone Gbagbo, Désiré Tagro, Pascal Affi N'Guessan and Alcide Djédjé).
199 UNSC Res 1980 (28 April 2011) UN Doc S/RES/1980; UNSC Res 2045 (26 April 2012) UN Doc S/RES/2045; UNSC Res 2101 (25 April 2013) UN Doc S/RES/2101; UNSC Res 2153 (29 April 2014) UN Doc S/RES/2153; UNSC Res 2219 (28 April 2015) UN Doc S/RES/2219.
200 UNSC Res 2283 (28 April 2016) UN Doc S/RES/2283, para 1.

an unspecified period of time' from 19 September 2002,[201] under Article 12(3) of the Rome Statute.[202] This provision allows States not party to the ICC's constituent instrument to accept the jurisdiction of the Court on an *ad hoc* basis.[203] Following the 2010 presidential election, Mr Ouattara sent a letter addressed to the ICC's President, Prosecutor and Registrar in which he confirmed the declaration of 18 April 2003.[204] In a further letter to the ICC Prosecutor on 3 May 2011, Mr Ouattara explicitly requested an ICC investigation into crimes committed on Ivorian territory, emphasised Côte d'Ivoire's readiness to cooperate with the Court and confirmed his intention that Côte d'Ivoire become a State party to the Rome Statute 'as soon as practicable'.[205] It was pursuant to the *ad hoc* declaration that the Prosecutor sought authorisation from the Pre-Trial Chamber to commence an investigation into the situation in Côte d'Ivoire,[206] a request granted by ICC Pre-Trial Chamber III on 15 November 2011.[207] Three individuals sanctioned by the Côte d'Ivoire Sanctions Committee thereafter became the object of ICC arrest warrants.

Charles Blé Goudé

Charles Blé Goudé was among three individuals designated by the Resolution 1572 Sanctions Committee in February 2006.[208] In addition to his leadership of the *Congrès Panafricain des Jeunes et des Patriotes* (Pan-African Youth and Patriots Congress or COJEP) a group widely known as the *Jeunes patriotes* (Young Patriots),[209] the Sanctions Committee for Côte d'Ivoire targeted Mr Blé Goudé for the following reasons:

201 *Prosecutor v Gbagbo* (Declaration Accepting the Jurisdiction of the International Criminal Court dated 18 April 2003) ICC-02/11-01/11-129-Anx16-tENG (6 September 2012).

202 Rome Statute, art 12(3).

203 ibid ('... [A] State may, by declaration lodged with the Registrar, accept the exercise of jurisdiction by the Court with respect to the crime in question. The accepting State shall cooperate with the Court without any delay or exception in accordance with Part 9.')

204 *Prosecutor v Gbagbo* (Letter from Alassane Ouattara to the President of the ICC dated 14 December 2010) ICC-02/11-01/11-129-Anx14-tENG (9 October 2012).

205 *Prosecutor v Gbagbo* (Letter from Alassane Ouattara to the Prosecutor of the ICC dated 3 May 2011) ICC-02/11-01/11-129-Anx15-tENG (10 October 2012).

206 *Situation in the Republic of Côte d'Ivoire* (Request for authorisation of an investigation pursuant to article 15) ICC-02/11-3 (23 June 2011).

207 *Situation in the Republic of Côte d'Ivoire* (Corrigendum to "Decision Pursuant to Article 15 of the Rome Statute on the Authorisation of an Investigation into the Situation in the Republic of Côte d'Ivoire") ICC-02/11-14-Corr (15 November 2011).

208 UNSC 'Security Council Committee Concerning Côte d'Ivoire Issues List of Individuals Subject to Measures Imposed by Resolution 1572 (2004)' (7 February 2006) Press Release SC/8631. The other individuals designated by the Sanctions Committee on this date were Eugène Ngoran Kouadio Djué and Martin Kouakou Fofié.

209 ibid.

> repeated public statements advocating violence against United Nations installations and personnel, and against foreigners; direction of and participation in acts of violence by street militias, including beatings, rapes and extrajudicial killings; intimidation of the United Nations, the International Working Group (IWG), the political opposition and independent press; sabotage of international radio stations; obstacle to the action of the IWG, the United Nations Operation in Côte d'Ivoire, (UNOCI), the French Forces [present in Côte d'Ivoire to support UNOCI] and to the peace process as defined by resolution 1633 (2005).[210]

ICC Pre-Trial Chamber III issued a warrant of arrest for Charles Blé Goudé on December 21, 2011, for his alleged responsibility for the crimes against humanity of murder, rape and other forms of sexual violence, other inhumane acts and persecution.[211] To the best of the author's knowledge, no mention of Mr Blé Goudé's designation by the CAR Sanctions Committee is made in publicly available documents. Moreover, as with Mathieu Ngudjolo Chui in the DRC context, the acquittal of Mr Blé Goudé (together with Laurent Gbagbo) by ICC Trial Chamber I on 15 January 2019[212] has not (explicably[213]) resulted in his (nor Mr Gbagbo's) delisting.

Laurent Gbagbo and Simone Gbagbo

It was the UNSC itself that added Laurent Gbagbo and Simone Gbagbo to the list of sanctioned individuals in Resolution 1975.[214] Both were listed for obstructing the peace and reconciliation process in Côte d'Ivoire.[215] Mr Gbagbo was also targeted for rejecting the results of the 2010 presidential election,[216] while Ms Gbagbo, who served as the Chairperson of the Parliamentary Group of the Ivorian Popular Front, the political party co-founded by Mr Gbagbo, was also listed for 'public incitement to hatred and violence.'[217]

---

210 ibid.

211 *Prosecutor v Blé Goudé* (Warrant Of Arrest For Charles Blé Goudé) ICC-02/11-02/11-1 (21 December 2011) 8.

212 *Prosecutor v Gbagbo and Blé Goudé* (Transcript) ICC-02/11-01/15-T-232-FRA (15 January 2019); *Prosecutor v Gbagbo and Blé Goudé* (Reasons for oral decision of 15 January 2019 on the *Requête de la Défense de Laurent Gbagbo afin qu'un jugement d'acquittement portant sur toutes les charges soit prononcé en faveur de Laurent Gbagbo et que sa mise en liberté immédiate soit ordonnée*, and on the Blé Goudé Defence no case to answer motion) ICC-02/11-01/15-1263 (16 July 2019). The Appeals Chamber is seised of an appeal by the Prosecutor against this decision as of 31 August 2020.

213 See nn 171-172 and accompanying text.

214 UNSC Res 1975 (3 March 2011) UN Doc S/RES/1975, Annex I.

215 ibid.

216 ibid.

217 ibid.

ICC Pre-Trial Chamber III issued warrants of arrest for Laurent Gbagbo and Simone Gbagbo on 23 November 2011[218] and 29 February 2012,[219] respectively. Both warrants included the same four crimes against humanity for which, in the judgment of the Pre-Trial Chamber, there were 'reasonable grounds to believe' that Mr Gbagbo and Ms Gbagbo were responsible under the Rome Statute. These were the crimes against humanity of murder, rape and other forms of sexual violence, other inhumane acts and persecution.[220]

Paul Bentall argues that the listing of Laurent Gbagbo by the UNSC a number of months before the Court issued a warrant for his arrest appears 'coincidental'.[221] In support of this conclusion, Paul Bentall again[222] takes note of the mechanism under Article 13 of the ICC Statute pursuant to which the ICC was seised of the situation in Côte d'Ivoire, namely 'self-referral', observing that '[t]he Court's jurisdiction was engaged without Security Council involvement, with targeted sanctions therefore being used coincidentally alongside'[223] ICC activity focused on the same individuals. According to Bentall, further support for this argument can be found in the more than eight months that passed between Mr Gbagbo's listing (3 March 2011) and the issue of a warrant for his arrest (23 November 2011) by the ICC.[224] Such a conclusion is even stronger in the cases of Charles Blé Goudé and Simone Gbagbo, where over five years[225] and a few days short of one year,[226] respectively, passed between their designation at the UN level and the issue of warrants for their arrest by Pre-Trial Chamber III of the Court.

218 *Prosecutor v Gbagbo* (Warrant Of Arrest For Laurent Koudou Gbagbo) ICC-02/11-01/11-1 (23 November 2011) (*Gbagbo* Arrest Warrant).

219 *Prosecutor v Simone Gbagbo* (Warrant of Arrest for Simone Gbagbo) ICC-02/11-01/12-1 (29 February 2012).

220 *Gbagbo* Arrest Warrant (n 218) 7-8.

221 Bentall (n 71) 97-98.

222 See n 135 and accompanying text.

223 Bentall (n 71) 97.

224 ibid 98.

225 The Resolution 1572 Sanctions Committee listed Charles Blé Goudé in February 2006, while ICC Pre-Trial Chamber III issued a warrant for his arrest in December 2011.

226 The UNSC listed Simone Gbagbo on 3 March 2011, while ICC Pre-Trial Chamber III issued a warrant for her arrest on 29 February 2012.

3.5.2.3 Sudan

The genesis of the (second)[227] UNSC sanctions regime for Sudan can be found in Resolution 1556.[228] The first round of sanctions consisted of an arms embargo against 'all non-governmental entities and individuals, including the Janjaweed [militia], operating in the states of North Darfur, South Darfur and West Darfur'.[229] Responding to the protracted armed conflict in the Darfur region, the UNSC established a sanctions committee and an individual sanctions regime, comprising an expanded arms embargo, a travel ban and asset freezing measures, in Resolution 1591 of 29 March 2005.[230] Very shortly thereafter, the UNSC referred 'the situation in Darfur since 1 July 2002' to the Prosecutor of the ICC,[231] thereby enabling the Court to exercise jurisdiction with respect to international crimes allegedly committed in Darfur pursuant to Article 13(b) of the Rome Statute.[232] UNSC Resolution 1672 explicitly named the first four individuals to be added to the list of targeted persons, but none of these individuals was subject to an (unsealed) arrest ICC warrant at the time of their listing (nor, indeed, have they been since that time).[233]

The Court has issued arrest warrants for former Sudanese President, Omar Hassan Ahmad Al Bashir (Omar Al Bashir),[234] the former Minister of the Interior and Special Representative of the President in Darfur, Abdel Raheem Muhammad Hussein,[235] alleged Janjaweed leader, Ali Muhammad Ali Abd-Al-Rahman (Ali Kushayb)[236] and a second former Interior Minister, Ahmad Muhammad Harun (Ahmad Harun).[237]

---

227 UNSC Res 1054 (26 April 1996) UN Doc S/RES/1054, para 3 (instituting a sanctions regime in response to Sudan's failure to extradite three individuals suspected of carrying out an assassination attempt against the then President of Egypt, Hosni Mubarak, in Addis Ababa, Ethiopia). See also UNSC Res 1044 (31 January 1996) UN Doc S/RES/1044, para 4. The UNSC terminated the sanctions regime in UNSC res 1372 (28 September 2001) UN Doc S/RES/1372, para 1.

228 UNSC Res 1556 (30 July 2004) UN Doc S/RES/1556, paras 7-9.

229 ibid para 7.

230 UNSC Res 1591 (29 March 2005) UN Doc S/RES/1591, para 3.

231 UNSC Res 1593 (31 March 2005) UN Doc S/RES/1593, para 1.

232 Rome Statute, art 13(b).

233 UNSC Res 1672 (25 April 2006) UN Doc S/RES/1672, para 1 (adding Major General Gaffar Mohamed Elhassan (Commander of the Western Military Region for the Sudanese Armed Forces), Sheikh Musa Hilal (Paramount Chief of the Jalul Tribe in North Darfur), Adam Yacub Shant (Sudanese Liberation Army Commander) and Gabril Abdul Kareem Badri (National Movement for Reform and Development Field Commander) to the list of sanctioned individuals).

234 *Prosecutor v Al Bashir* (Warrant of Arrest for Omar Hassan Ahmad Al Bashir) ICC-02/05-01/09-1 (4 March 2009); *Prosecutor v Al Bashir* (Second Warrant of Arrest for Omar Hassan Ahmad Al Bashir) ICC-02/05-01/09-95 (12 July 2010).

235 *Prosecutor v Hussein* (Warrant of Arrest for Abdel Raheem Muhammad Hussein) ICC-02/05-01/12-2 (1 March 2012).

236 *Prosecutor v Harun and Kushayb* (Warrant of Arrest for Ali Kushayb) ICC-02/05-01/07-3, (27 April 2007).

237 *Prosecutor v Harun and Kushayb* (Warrant of Arrest for Ahmad Harun) ICC-02/05-01/07-2 (27 April 2007).

The ICC has also issued summonses to appear, an alternative to an arrest warrant issued if the Pre-Trial Chamber is satisfied that serving such a document is sufficient to ensure the person's voluntary appearance before the ICC,[238] for three individuals in the situation in Darfur. These are Bahr Idriss Abu Garda,[239] Saleh Mohammed Jerbo Jamus[240] and Abdallah Banda Abakaer Nourain,[241] all of whom were alleged rebel commanders operating in the Darfur region at the time their summonses to appear before the Court were issued.

Sudan might, at first glance, appear to offer an ideal situation in which the UN organ and the Court could coordinate the asset freezing powers at their disposal. Indeed, the ICC Prosecutor noted the potential support available to the Court through concerted action by the UN body:

> [T]he UNSC can act ... to secure the cooperation for the arrest of Ali Kushayb and Ahmad Harun. The Prosecution understands that the Council can accomplish this under various mechanisms including the existing UNSCR 1591 regime. UNSCR 1591, para 3(c) provides for application of these measures to individuals 'who (...) commit violations of international humanitarian or human rights law or other atrocities.' The UNSCR 1591 regime has already been put into practice through UNSCR 1672, which added four names of individuals to be subject to the measures set out in UNSCR 1591, namely freezing all funds, other financial assets and economic resources owned or controlled by the individuals in question. ... The means to act are entirely within the UNSC's remit. The Prosecution would however urge the UNSC to focus first on individual measures in relation to Kushayb and Harun, in particular the identification and freezing of their assets.[242]

This said, no such support has materialised, with none of the individuals subject to ICC-issued arrest warrants having been added to the Resolution 1591 sanctions list as of August 2020. This is despite the fact that the UNSC referred 'the situation in Darfur' to the Court under Article 13(b) of the ICC Statute, the absence of which has been cited as a reason behind the lack of coordination between the two bodies in the DRC and Côte

---

238 Rome Statute, art 58(7).

239 *Prosecutor v Abu Garda* (Summons to Appear for Bahr Idriss Abu Garda) ICC-02/05-02/09-2 (7 May 2009).

240 *Prosecutor v Banda and Jerbo* (Summons to Appear for Saleh Mohammed Jerbo Jamus) ICC-02/05-03/09-2-RSC (27 August 2009).

241 *Prosecutor v Banda and Jerbo* (Summons to Appear for Abdallah Banda Abakaer Nourain) ICC-02/05-03/09-3 (27 August 2009).

242 ICC Prosecutor, 'Eleventh Report of the Prosecutor of the International Criminal Court to the UN Security Council Pursuant to UNSCR 1593 (2005)' (17 June 2010) <https://legal-tools.org/doc/3krzml> accessed 31 August 2020, paras 63, 66.

d'Ivoire contexts.[243] In order to explain this inconsistency, Paul Bentall plausibly suggests that division between members of the UNSC over referring the situation to the ICC might have spilled over to its consideration of utilising targeted financial sanctions to support Court activity with respect to Sudan, particularly in light of the '[c]ontroversy' that followed the issuance of warrants of arrest for the then Sudanese President Omar Al Bashir.[244] Larissa van den Herik further posits that the heated debate[245] concerning immunities and States' obligations to cooperate with the Court might also have reduced the likelihood of UNSC support for the ICC in relation to its activities in Darfur.[246]

3.5.2.4 Central African Republic

It was through Resolution 2127 that the UNSC established a sanctions regime for the Central African Republic (CAR) by way of response to 'a total breakdown in law and order' across the CAR following the seizure of power by the *Séléka* (Alliance) group of anti-government militias.[247] The UN organ imposed an arms embargo,[248] confirmed its intention to consider imposing measures targeting individuals,[249] and formed a sanctions committee to, among other tasks, monitor the implementation of the arms embargo.[250] With the violence in the CAR not having abated, the UNSC elected to enact targeted measures, ie travel bans[251] and asset freezes,[252] in Resolution 2134 of 28 January 2014. Shortly before the anniversary of Resolution 2134, the UN organ renewed and extended the targeted sanctions measures in Resolution 2196.[253] Further extensions were effected in January 2016,[254] January 2017,[255] and January 2018.[256] Conspicuously, the UNSC explicitly references ICC activity in the CAR in all of these resolutions.[257] In Resolution 2196, the UN body:

---

243 See Bentall (n 71) 97.

244 ibid 98. See also Mancini (n 67) 235.

245 For a contemporaneous discussion of this issue, see Paola Gaeta, 'Does President Al Bashir Enjoy Immunity from Arrest?' (2009) 7 Journal of International Criminal Justice 315; Dapo Akande, 'The Legal Nature of Security Council Referrals to the ICC and its Impact on Al Bashir's Immunities' (2009) 7 Journal of International Criminal Justice 333.

246 van den Herik (n 100) 244.

247 UNSC Res 2127 (5 December 2013) UN Doc S/RES/2127, preamble.

248 ibid 54.

249 ibid 56.

250 ibid 57.

251 UNSC Res 2134 (28 January 2014) UN Doc S/RES/2134, para 30.

252 ibid 32.

253 UNSC Res 2196 (22 January 2015) UN Doc S/RES/2196.

254 UNSC Res 2262 (27 January 2016) UN Doc S/RES/2262.

255 UNSC Res 2339 (27 January 2017) UN Doc S/RES/2339.

256 UNSC Res 2399 (30 January 2018) UN Doc S/RES/2399.

257 UNSC 2127 (n 247) preamble; UNSC Res 2134 (n 251) para 21; UNSC Res 2196 (n 253) preamble; UNSC Res 2262 (n 254) preamble; UNSC Res 2339 (n 255) preamble; UNSC Res 2399 (n 256) preamble.

> Reiterate[d] that all perpetrators of such acts [eg attacks targeting peacekeepers] must be held accountable and that some of those acts may amount to crimes under the Rome Statute ..., to which the CAR is a State party, noting in this regard the opening by the Prosecutor of the [ICC] on 24 September 2014 of an investigation following the request of the national authorities on alleged crimes committed since 2012 and welcoming the ongoing cooperation by the CAR Transitional Authorities in this regard[.][258]

The CAR Government has referred two situations on its territory to the ICC's Prosecutor. The first 'self-referral' came in December 2004,[259] almost a decade *before* the establishment of a UNSC sanctions regime for the CAR. A second referral followed on 30 May 2014,[260] shortly *after* the UN body adopted sanctions measures targeting individuals. But the CAR Sanctions Committee has not (yet) designated any individuals subjected to an ICC arrest warrant in the context of either of these 'situation[s]' within the meaning of Article 14 of the Rome Statute.[261]

Jean-Pierre Bemba Gombo (and others)

It was in the course of investigating the first situation in the CAR that the Court's Prosecutor successfully applied for a warrant of arrest for Mr Jean-Pierre Bemba Gombo.[262] Shortly after the warrant was issued, ICC Pre-Trial Chamber III requested the Court's Registrar to transmit a request for cooperation to the Republic of Portugal.[263] In its decision, the Pre-Trial Chamber requested the Portuguese authorities to identify, locate, freeze or seize the property and assets located in Portugal and owned by Mr Bemba, or in which he had a share, 'in accordance with the procedures provided for by its national legislation'.[264] Mr

258 UNSC Res 2196 (n 253) preamble.

259 *Situation in the Central African Republic* (Decision Assigning Situation in the Central African Republic to PTC III) ICC-01/05-1 (19 January 2005). See also ICC Office of the Prosecutor, 'Prosecutor receives referral concerning Central African Republic' (7 January 2005) Press Release ICC-OTP-20050107-86.

260 *Situation in the Central African Republic II* (Decision Assigning the Situation in the Central African Republic II to PTC II) ICC-01/14-1 (18 June 2014) Annex 1.

261 See Michael Ramsden and Tomas Hamilton, 'Uniting Against Impunity: The UN General Assembly as a Catalyst for Action at the ICC' (2017) 66 International and Comparative Law Quarterly 893, 907.

262 *Prosecutor v Bemba Gombo* (Warrant of Arrest for Jean-Pierre Bemba Gombo) ICC-01/05-01/08-1-tENG (23 May 2008). See also *Prosecutor v Bemba Gombo* (Warrant of arrest for Jean-Pierre Bemba Gombo replacing the warrant of arrest issued on 23 May 2008) ICC-01/05-01/08-15-tENG (10 June 2008).

263 *Prosecutor v Bemba Gombo* (Decision et demande en vue d'obtenir l'identification, la localisation, le gel et la saisie des biens et avoirs adressées a la Republique portugaise) ICC-01/05-01/08-8 (27 May 2008) (*Bemba Gombo* Portugal Freezing Request).

264 ibid 4.

Bemba has also submitted that the ICC issued similar requests to Belgium and the DRC,[265] but notes that these orders remain confidential *ex parte*.[266]

It has been argued that Mr Bemba was never designated on a UNSC sanctions list because there was no UN-level sanctions regime focused on the CAR in place at the time the Court issued his warrant of arrest.[267] This said, the Resolution 2134 Sanctions Committee could have designated Mr Bemba after its establishment in January 2014, especially as he had not yet been acquitted at that time.[268] As to other warrants of arrest issued in the course of the first of two 'situations' in the CAR, these do not concern the commission of the crimes listed in Article 5 of the Rome Statute,[269] but offences against the administration of justice contrary to Article 70 thereof.[270] On 20 November 2013, the Court's Pre-Trial Chamber II ordered the arrest of Mr Bemba, Aimé Kilolo Musamba, Jean-Jacques Mangenda Kabongo, Fidèle Babala Wandu and Narcisse Arido for presenting evidence that the party knows is false or forged and for corruptly influencing witnesses.[271] In the same arrest warrant, the Pre-Trial Chamber also ordered the Registrar to prepare requests for cooperation from the State(s) effecting the arrest of the named individuals and any other relevant State(s) to locate and freeze their assets.[272] It could be contended that offences against the administration of justice, as opposed to the 'most serious crimes of concern to the international community as a whole',[273] are rather less likely to attract UNSC attention under the targeted sanctions framework. This could explain why none of these five individuals has been listed by the CAR Sanctions Committee. From a practical perspective, Marina Mancini also observes that all but one of the individuals had been arrested and transferred to the ICC before Resolution 2134 was adopted.[274]

---

265 *Situation in the Central African Republic* (Public Redacted Version of "Urgent request for partial reconsideration and associated orders") ICC-01/05-01/08-3663-Red (10 December 2018) 34 ('The freezing orders were issued on 23 May 2008 (Belgium), 27 May 2008 (Portugal) and 29 May 2008 (DRC).')

266 ibid (appealing that the requests issued to Belgium and the DRC be reclassified as public, as is the case with the request to Portugal). See *Bemba Gombo* Portugal Freezing Request (n 263).

267 See Mancini (n 67) 234.

268 The Court's Appeals Chamber acquitted Mr Bemba on 8 June 2018. See *Prosecutor v Bemba Gombo* (Judgment on the appeal of Mr Jean-Pierre Bemba Gombo against Trial Chamber III's "Judgment pursuant to Article 74 of the Statute") ICC-01/05-01/08-3636-Red (8 June 2018). Larissa van den Herik describes the failure of the CAR Sanctions Committee to add Mr Bemba to the list of designated individuals as '[r]emarkabl[e]'. See van den Herik (n 100) 246.

269 Rome Statute, art 5 (the crime of genocide, crimes against humanity, war crimes and the crime of aggression).

270 ibid art 70.

271 *Prosecutor v Bemba Gombo and others* (Warrant of arrest for Jean-Pierre Bemba Gombo, Aimé Kilolo Musamba, Jean-Jacques Mangenda Kabongo, Fidèle Babala Wandu and Narcisse Arido) ICC-01/05-01/13-1-tENG (20 November 2013).

272 ibid 15-16.

273 Rome Statute, art 5.

274 Mancini (n 67) 234. Narcisse Arido was transferred to the ICC on 18 March 2014. See *Prosecutor v Bemba Gombo and others* (Decision on "Narcisse Arido's regulation 35 motion to extend time for initial appearance

Asset Freezing at the International Criminal Court and the United Nations Security Council

Alfred Yekatom and Patrice-Edouard Ngaïssona

The CAR Sanctions Committee listed Alfred Yekatom, a former officer in the *Forces Armées Centrafricaines* (CAR armed forces) and alleged leader of a militia in the anti-Balaka alliance of groups engaged in an armed conflict with (ex-)*Séléka*[275] forces, on August 20, 2015.[276] The Sanctions Committee listed Mr Yekatom pursuant to Resolution 2196, namely for:

> engaging in or providing support for acts that undermine the peace, stability or security of the CAR, including acts that threaten or violate transitional agreements, or that threaten or impede the political transition process, including a transition toward free and fair democratic elections, or that fuel violence.[277]

Though the CAR Sanctions Committee has not listed Patrice-Edouard Ngaïssona, his position as 'general coordinator of the anti-Balaka' is mentioned by way of '[a]dditional information' in the listing of Habib Soussou, an alleged anti-Balaka zone commander for the town of Boda and the province of Lobaye.[278] As for the ICC, Pre-Trial Chamber II has issued arrest warrants for both Mr Yekatom[279] and Mr Ngaïssona.[280] Both warrants of arrest followed the listing of Mr Yekatom by the Resolution 2134 Sanctions Committee and, while the Pre-Trial Chamber explicitly states that the protracted armed conflict in the CAR had gained the attention of the UNSC in issuing a warrant for Mr Yekatom's arrest,[281] the latter's designation by the CAR Sanctions Committee is not accorded similar attention.

---

to March 24, 2014 to allow attorney, Abbe Jolles, to travel from Washington DC, USA" dated 18 March 2014) ICC-01/05-01/13-274 (19 March 2014) 3.

275 The then President of the CAR and former leader of the *Séléka*, Michel Djotodia, dissolved the group by way Presidential Decree on 12 September 2013.

276 Security Council Committee established pursuant to resolution 2127 (2013) concerning the Central African Republic (CAR Sanctions Committee), 'Alfred Yekatom' (20 August 2015) <https://www.un.org/securitycouncil/sanctions/2127/materials/summaries/individual/alfred-yekatom> accessed 31 August 2020.

277 ibid.

278 CAR Sanctions Committee, 'Habib Soussou' (20 August 2015) <https://www.un.org/securitycouncil/sanctions/2127/materials/summaries/individual/habib-soussou> accessed 31 August 2020 ('On 28 June 2014, general coordinator of the anti-Balaka Patrice Edouard Ngaïssona appointed Habib Soussou as provincial coordinator for the town of Boda since 11 April 2014 and since 28 June 2014 for the entire province of Lobaye. Targeted killings, clashes and attacks by anti-Balaka in Boda against humanitarian organizations and aid workers have occurred on a weekly basis in areas for which Soussou is the anti-Balaka commander or coordinator.')

279 *Prosecutor v Yekatom* (Public Redacted Version of "Warrant of Arrest for Alfred Yekatom", ICC-01/14-01/18-1-US-Exp, 11 November 2018) ICC-01/14-01/18-1-Red (17 November 2018) (*Yekatom* Arrest Warrant).

280 *Prosecutor v Ngaïssona* (Public Redacted Version of "Warrant of Arrest for Patrice-Edouard Ngaïssona") ICC-01/14-01/18-89-Red (13 December 2018).

281 *Yekatom* Arrest Warrant (n 279) 15.

Joseph Kony

An anomaly in the examination of the overlap between the activities of UNSC-established sanctions committees and the ICC concerns Joseph Kony, the alleged founder and leader of the Lord's Resistance Army (LRA), an armed group with roots in Uganda but which has since been operational across Central Africa, including in the CAR.[282] The CAR Sanctions Committee listed Mr Kony on 7 March 2016, in accordance with Resolution 2262.[283] Among the multiple reasons provided for his listing are his involvement in violations of international human rights law or international humanitarian law, including the use of sexual violence, the targeting of civilians and the recruitment or use of children in armed conflict.[284]

The reason for categorizing Mr Kony's listing by the Sanctions Committee for the CAR as an anomaly stems from the existence of his pre-existing warrant of arrest, issued by the Court in 2005 in the situation in Uganda,[285] rather than in the course of the (first) situation in the CAR. The chapter will return to the (justifiable) lack of UNSC support for the ICC in the Uganda situation, at least in terms of imposing targeted sanctions, in due course.

3.5.2.5 Mali

The UNSC established a sanctions regime, comprising *inter alia* a travel ban, asset freezing measures and the creation of a new sanctions committee, for Mali in Resolution 2374 of 5 September 2017.[286] The UN body decided that coercive action under Chapter VII of the UN Charter was required to respond to violations of various ceasefire agreements, not least by terrorist groups operating on Malian territory. In addition, and of note for the purposes of the present chapter, in the preamble to Resolution 2374, the UNSC:

> Not[ed] with grave concern the involvement of non-state actors, notably terrorist groups, in the destruction of cultural heritage and the trafficking in cultural property and related offences and further [took note] of the fact that on 27 September 2016 the ICC found Mr Al Mahdi guilty of the war crime of

282 CAR Sanctions Committee, 'Joseph Kony' (7 March 2016) <https://www.un.org/securitycouncil/sanctions/2127/materials/summaries/individual/joseph-kony> accessed 31 August 2020.

283 ibid. The Sanctions Committee designated the LRA on the list of sanctioned entities on the same day.

284 ibid.

285 *Situation in Uganda* (Warrant of Arrest for Joseph Kony Issued on 8 July 2005 as Amended on 27 September 2005) ICC-02/04-01/05-53 (27 September 2005) (*Kony* Arrest Warrant).

286 UNSC Res 2374 (5 September 2017) UN Doc S/RES/2374, para 9.

> intentionally directing attacks against religious and historical monuments in Timbuktu.[287]

UNSC action therefore followed ICC activity in the context of the situation in Mali. The sanctions remain in force as of August 2020, having been renewed on three occasions.[288]

Turning to ICC action in Mali, it was the Malian Government that referred the situation on its territory to the Court's Prosecutor in July 2012.[289] It was pursuant to this referral that the ICC Prosecutor successfully applied for a warrant of arrest for Ahmad Al Faqi Al Mahdi,[290] whose conviction in 2016 the UNSC explicitly references in Resolution 2374. Mr Al Mahdi was an alleged member of the *Ansar Dine* group, a movement affiliated with Al-Qaeda in the Islamic Maghreb.[291] The Prosecutor was also successful in her application for an arrest warrant for another alleged member of *Ansar Dine*, and *de facto* chief of the Islamic police in Timbuktu, Al Hassan Ag Abdoul Aziz Ag Mohamed Ag Mahmoud,[292] in March 2018.

Given that the application for a warrant of arrest for Mr Al Mahdi preceded the establishment of the Mali Sanctions Committee, it is perhaps unsurprising that he has not been added to the list of sanctioned individuals. As for Mr Hassan, the situation appears to be less clear-cut. The designation criteria listed in Resolution 2374 include individuals believed 'responsible for or complicit in, or having engaged in … [p]lanning, directing, or committing acts in Mali that violate international human rights law or international humanitarian law'.[293] The latter could include the war crimes for which the Court's Pre-Trial Chamber I found 'reasonable grounds to believe that he is criminally responsible'[294] under the Rome Statute. The same can be said of the former inasmuch as the crimes against humanity for which the same Pre-Trial Chamber was satisfied to the required standard that Mr Hassan was responsible to issue the warrant for his arrest violate international

287 ibid preamble.

288 UNSC Res 2432 (30 August 2018) UN Doc S/RES/2432; UNSC Res 2484 (29 August 2019) UN Doc S/RES/2484; UNSC Res 2541 (31 August 2020) UN Doc S/RES/2541.

289 *Situation in the Republic of Mali* (Decision assigning the situation in the Republic of Mali to Pre-Trial Chamber II) ICC-01/12-1 (19 July 2012) Annex. See also ICC Office of the Prosecutor, 'ICC Prosecutor Fatou Bensouda on the Malian State referral of the situation in Mali since January 2012' (18 July 2012) Press Release ICC-OTP-20120718-PR829.

290 *Prosecutor v Al Mahdi* (Mandat d'arrêt à l'encontre d'Ahmad Al Faqi Al Mahdi) ICC-01/12-01/15-1-Red (18 September 2015).

291 ibid para 5.

292 *Prosecutor v Al Hassan* (Warrant of Arrest for Al Hassan Ag Abdoul Aziz Ag Mohamed Ag Mahmoud) ICC-01/12-01/18-2-tENG (27 March 2018) (*Al Hassan* Arrest Warrant).

293 UNSC Res 2374 (n 286) para 8.

294 *Al Hassan* Arrest Warrant (n 292).

human rights law.[295] Again here, a sanctions committee created under the auspices of the UN Charter was faced with a choice between supporting the Court and not doing so and opted for the latter.

3.5.3 *Neither Coexistent nor Coordinated*

3.5.3.1 Uganda

Uganda was the first State Party to the Rome Statute to refer a situation on its territory to the Prosecutor of the ICC, with the President of Uganda submitting a 'self-referral' in December 2003.[296] It was pursuant to this referral that the Court's Prosecutor succeeded in applying for warrants of arrest for Joseph Kony,[297] Vincent Otti,[298] Raska Lukwiya,[299] Okot Odhiambo[300] and Dominic Ongwen.[301]

The UNSC has not established a sanctions committee for Uganda, although it could be argued that there is some overlap between the work of the Resolution 2127 Sanctions Committee, established for the CAR, and the crimes investigated by the ICC in Uganda. This is because all five individuals for whom the Court has issued warrants of arrest in this situation are members of the LRA, an armed group also designated by the CAR Sanctions Committee. This is not to say, however, that the UN body has ignored the situation. To the contrary, it is clear from various resolutions that members of the UNSC are concerned about events in (northern) Uganda, particularly the activities of the LRA.[302] Instead, it could simply be the case that the UN organ decided to respond to this situation without imposing targeted sanctions under the auspices of a sanctions committee, a reasonable option entirely within its remit. The UNSC adopted a similar approach with regard to Kenya.

---

295 ibid (listing the crimes against humanity of torture, rape and sexual slavery, persecution on religious and gender grounds and other inhumane acts).

296 *Situation in Uganda* (Decision Assigning Situation in Uganda to PTC II) ICC-02/04-1 (5 July 2004) Annex. See also ICC Office of the Prosecutor, 'President of Uganda refers situation concerning the Lord's Resistance Army (LRA) to the ICC' (29 January 2004) Press Release ICC2004012944.

297 *Kony* Arrest Warrant (n 285).

298 *Situation in Uganda* (Warrant of Arrest for Vincent Otti) ICC-02/04-01/05-54 (8 July 2005).

299 *Situation in Uganda* (Warrant of Arrest for Raska Lukwiya) ICC-02/04-01/05-55 (8 July 2005).

300 *Situation in Uganda* (Warrant of Arrest for Okot Odhiambo) ICC-02/04-01/05-56 (8 July 2005).

301 *Situation in Uganda* (Warrant of Arrest for Dominic Ongwen) ICC-02/04-01/05-57 (8 July 2005).

302 See eg UNSC Res 1653 (27 January 2006) UN Doc S/RES/1653, preamble.

3.5.3.2 Kenya

The ICC Prosecutor initiated an investigation into the situation in Kenya under Article 15 of the Rome Statute, which regulates the Prosecutor's *proprio motu* powers.[303] Subparagraph (3) of this provision provides, in relevant part, as follows: 'If the Prosecutor concludes that there is a reasonable basis to proceed with an investigation, he or she shall submit to the Pre-Trial Chamber a request for authorization of an investigation, together with any supporting material collected.'[304] If the Pre-Trial Chamber agrees with the Prosecutor that such a reasonable basis does indeed exist, 'and that the case appears to fall within the jurisdiction of the Court, it shall authorize the commencement of the investigation'.[305] The Prosecutor initiated this process in November 2009 with respect to Kenya, sending a letter to the Court's then President to inform the Presidency of his intention to request the authorization of an investigation pursuant to the Article 15 framework.[306] A formal request followed shortly thereafter.[307]

After Pre-Trial Chamber II authorised the Prosecutor's investigation,[308] he was successful in applications for summonses to appear for William Samoei Ruto, Henry Kiprono Kosgey and Joshua Arap Sang[309] and Francis Kirimi Muthaura, Uhuru Muigai Kenyatta and Mohammed Hussein Ali.[310] The same Pre-Trial Chamber subsequently issued warrants for the arrest of a further three individuals in connection with the alleged commission of crimes under the ICC's jurisdiction in Kenya, namely Walter Osapiri Barasa,[311] Paul Gicheru[312] and Philip Kipkoech Bett,[313] following applications to this end by the second ICC Prosecutor, Fatou Bensouda. As far as the assets of the accused were concerned, less

303 Rome Statute, art 15.

304 ibid art 15(3).

305 ibid art 15(4).

306 *Situation in the Republic of Kenya* (Decision Assigning the Situation in the Republic of Kenya to Pre-Trial Chamber II) ICC-01/09-1 (6 November 2009) Annex.

307 *Situation in the Republic of Kenya* (Request for authorisation of an investigation pursuant to Article 15) ICC-01/09-3 (26 November 2009).

308 *Situation in the Republic of Kenya* (Corrigendum of the Decision Pursuant to Article 15 of the Rome Statute on the Authorization of an Investigation into the Situation in the Republic of Kenya) ICC-01/09-19-Corr (30 March 2011).

309 *Prosecutor v Ruto, Kosgey and Sang* (Decision on the Prosecutor's Application for Summons to Appear for William Samoei Ruto, Henry Kiprono Kosgey and Joshua Arap Sang) ICC-01/09-01/11-1 (8 March 2011) para 59.

310 *Prosecutor v Muthaura, Kenyatta and Ali* (Decision on the Prosecutor's Application for Summonses to Appear for Francis Kirimi Muthaura, Uhuru Muigai Kenyatta and Mohammed Hussein Ali) ICC-01/09-02/11-01 (8 March 2011) para 57.

311 *Prosecutor v Barasa* (Warrant of arrest for Walter Osapiri Barasa) ICC-01/09-01/13-1-Red2 (2 August 2013).

312 *Prosecutor v Gicheru and Bett* (Decision on the "Prosecution's Application under Article 58(1) of the Rome Statute") ICC-01/09-01/15-1-Red (10 March 2015).

313 ibid.

than one month after issuing summonses for the individuals' appearance, Pre-Trial Chamber II instructed the Registrar of the Court 'to prepare and transmit ... in consultation with the Prosecutor, a request for cooperation to the competent authorities of the Republic of Kenya' with the declared aim of identifying, tracing and freezing and/or seizing property and assets owned by Mr Muthaura, Mr Kenyatta and Mr Ali (or under their control) 'without prejudice to the rights of bona fide third parties'.[314]

The UNSC did not establish a sanctions committee by way of response to the post-election violence in Kenya, though the body's President did issue a statement expressing concern at the situation in February 2008.[315] The lack of subsequent action could perhaps be attributed (in part) to the fact that the UN body did not refer the situation to the ICC pursuant to the mechanism under Article 13(b) of the ICC Statute. Indeed, divisions among the membership of the UNSC over ICC action in Kenya are clear from the results of a 2013 vote by the UN body on deferring the investigation by the Court's Prosecutor into crimes allegedly committed by Mr Kenyatta and Mr Ruto in accordance with Article 16 of the Court's constituent instrument.[316]

3.6 Conclusion

The ICC-UN Relationship Agreement foresees the Court and the UNSC functioning in tandem.[317] Indeed, the UN body has requested the execution of asset freezing measures in a number of situations in which the Court has also been actively engaged. Yet, as the chapter has demonstrated, there is negligible evidence of the two bodies acting in concert with a view to facilitating the discharge of their respective responsibilities. It is this absence of 'coordinated' action that leads to the conclusion that to suggest closer, formalised cooperation between the Court and UNSC in this sphere of operations is an unrealistic expectation.

Discussing the ICTY in 2003, the UNSC '[u]rg[ed] Member States to consider imposing measures against individuals and groups or organizations assisting indictees at large to

314 *Prosecutor v Muthaura, Kenyatta and Ali* (Decision Ordering the Registrar to Prepare and Transmit a Request for Cooperation to the Republic of Kenya for the Purpose of Securing the Identification, Tracing and Freezing or Seizure of Property and Assets of Francis Kirimi Muthaura, Uhuru Muigai Kenyatta and Mohammed Hussein Ali) ICC-01/09-02/11-42 (5 April 2011) 5.

315 UNSC Presidential Statement 4 (2008) UN Doc. S/PRST/2008/4.

316 UNSC Verbatim Record (15 November 2013) UN Doc S/PV.7060 (seven members voted in favour of the draft resolution, with eight abstaining).

317 ICC-UN Relationship Agreement, preamble ('a mutually beneficial relationship whereby the discharge of respective responsibilities of the United Nations and the International Criminal Court may be facilitated').

continue to evade justice, including measures designed to restrict the travel and freeze the assets of such individuals, groups, or organizations'.[318] But the foregoing analysis shows that the UN organ has not practiced what it preached in this Resolution with respect to the ICC. Only in response to the situation in Libya can what could be termed 'coordinated' (or 'harmonious'[319]) UNSC support for the Court be observed. Elsewhere such support has been coincidental and, as a result, piecemeal. This is despite the potential benefits of such support, especially for the ICC's operations.

This chapter has not sought to argue that the UNSC ought to appoint a sanctions committee for every situation in which the Court is active. Nor has it explicitly proposed that the UN organ ought to automatically add all individuals subjected to ICC arrest warrants to existing sanctions lists, though the merits of so doing are discussed. Instead, the chapter makes the argument, based on an analysis of eight concrete scenarios in which the two bodies (could) have coordinated the exercise of their enforcement powers, for tempering expectations of the UNSC as far as its support for the Court is concerned. Initial prognoses of the UN body playing an active role in backing the ICC are simply not borne out in practice.

---

318 UNSC Res 1503 (28 August 2003) UN Doc S/RES/1503, preamble.

319 van den Herik (n 100) 244.

4 Recovering Assets at ICTs[*]

Fines, Forfeiture and Orders for Reparations

4.1 Introduction

ICTs have traditionally had two tools at their disposal with which to recover assets, whether ill-gotten or otherwise, belonging to persons convicted of international crimes: fines and orders for forfeiture as penalties additional to imprisonment. However, following the establishment of the permanent ICC, increasingly victim-oriented ICTs have been equipped with a third tool for asset recovery in international crimes cases: orders for reparations. This tool provides a vehicle through which victims of international crimes might be awarded compensation, among other forms of reparation.

This chapter critically analyses the availability and use of these three asset recovery mechanisms at ICTs from Nuremberg until the post-ICC era. It will be shown that, while the majority of ICTs have been empowered to order fines and forfeiture measures, such procedures have been scarcely utilised in practice. An additional aim of the chapter is to show that the Rome Statute system has influenced the approach toward fines, forfeiture (including protective measures) and orders for reparations taken by a number of ICTs established following its adoption in 1998.

4.2 The Post-World War II Military Tribunals

The International Military Tribunal (IMT) was explicitly empowered to order asset forfeiture measures. However, although Article 28 of the IMT Charter afforded the Tribunal 'the right to deprive the convicted person of any stolen property and order its delivery to the Control Council for Germany',[1] this provision was never utilised by the Judges sitting in Nuremberg.[2] The Tribunal found the accused Alfred Rosenberg guilty of war crimes and crimes against humanity based in part upon his 'responsib[ility] for a system of

* An earlier version of this chapter was published as Daley J Birkett, 'Asset Recovery at International(ised) Criminal Tribunals: Fines, Forfeiture and Orders for Reparations' in Nina HB Jørgensen (ed), *The International Criminal Responsibility of War's Funders and Profiteers* (CUP 2020) 455-480.

1 IMT Charter, art 28.

2 For an argument in support of postponing restitution claims, see Stephen Weil, 'The American Legal Response to the Problem of Holocaust Art', (1999) 4 Art, Antiquity and Law 285, 287.

organized plunder of both public and private property throughout the invaded countries of Europe',[3] but it made no orders for restitution against him or other convicted persons under Article 28 of the IMT Charter.[4]

Conversely, the International Military Tribunal for the Far East (IMTFE) had no such explicit power. The IMTFE Charter contains no comparable provision to Article 28 of the IMT Charter, despite the fact that these two ICTs' constituent instruments share several common elements, including with regard to punishment.

As for fines, although neither ICT was explicitly granted the power by its constituent instrument to order fines, it has been suggested that Article 27 of the IMT Charter and Article 16 of the IMTFE Charter did not exclude the possibility of the imposition of financial penalties.[5] These near-verbatim provisions conferred upon the IMT and IMTFE the power to impose upon a convicted person 'death or such other punishment as shall be determined by it to be just.'[6] Although perhaps more likely to refer to 'the most serious forms of punishment, such as imprisonment',[7] Article 27 of the IMT Charter could arguably have allowed for the imposition of fines by the IMT. Further, Article 16 of the IMTFE Charter could have enabled the IMTFE to order fines as well as asset forfeiture measures akin to those provided for in Article 28 of the IMT Charter. In other words, the main focus was on the death penalty or imprisonment, and if fines had ever been in question, the two military tribunals could have asserted the power to impose them even though no such power was explicitly conferred by their constituent instruments. Despite this possibility, no such measures were imposed by either ICT.

Control Council Law No. 10, which was promulgated by the victorious Allied powers after World War II to enable the prosecution of those who were not in the category of major war criminals tried in the main proceedings at Nuremberg, contains more extensive fine and asset forfeiture procedures than those contained in the IMT Charter and IMTFE Charter. Under Article II(3) of Control Council Law No. 10, the tribunals established thereby were able to order the following punishments:

3 *Judgment of the Nuremberg International Military Tribunal 1946* (1947) 41 American Journal of International Law 172, 287.

4 ibid 332. Rosenberg was sentenced to death by hanging.

5 Rebecca Young, 'Fines and Forfeiture in International Criminal Justice' in Róisín Mulgew and Denis Abels (eds), *Research Handbook on the International Penal System* (Edward Elgar 2016) 103.

6 IMT Charter, art 27; IMTFE Charter, art 16.

7 Young (n 5) 104.

(c) Fine .... .

(d) Forfeiture of property. [and]

(e) Restitution of property wrongfully acquired.

(f) ...

Any property declared to be forfeited or the restitution of which is ordered by the Tribunal shall be delivered to the Control Council for Germany, which shall decide on its disposal.[8]

Notably, fine and forfeiture procedures are not listed in Control Council Law No. 10 as available 'in addition to imprisonment'.[9] Rather, these measures are listed as forms of punishment in their own right. Control Council Law No. 10 also provides for the first *pre-conviction* asset forfeiture procedures in the history of international criminal justice. At this time, however, there was no express provision that the forfeited assets were ultimately to be put to use for the benefit of victims. Article III(1) of Control Council Law No. 10 provides as follows:

Each occupying authority, within its Zone of Occupation,

(a) shall have the right to cause persons within such Zone suspected of having committed a crime ... to be arrested and shall take under control the property, real and personal, owned or controlled by the said persons, pending decisions as to its eventual disposition.[10]

Turning to the case law, of the 142 convicted persons in the twelve trials carried out in the American zone of occupation, only the industrialist Alfred Krupp was ordered to forfeit property under Control Council Law No. 10.[11] Moreover, the United States High Commissioner for Germany, John McCloy, later rescinded this forfeiture order,[12] as

8 Control Council Law No 10, art II(3).

9 cf IMT Charter, art 28.

10 Control Council Law No 10, art III.

11 *Judgment of 31 July 1948*, in *Trials of War Criminals Before the Nuremberg Military Tribunals under Control Council Law No. 10*, vol IX (United States Government Printing Office 1950) 1449-50. See also Kevin Jon Heller, *The Nuremberg Military Tribunals and the Origins of International Criminal Law* (OUP 2011) 313.

12 McCloy had the power to do so having created the Advisory Board on Clemency for War Criminals, with the support of then Secretary of State, Dean Acheson. See Heller (n 11) 344, describing Acheson's support as 'reluctant'.

recommended by the Advisory Board on Clemency for War Criminals.[13] McCloy reasoned as follows:

> This is the sole case of confiscation decreed against any defendant by the Nuremberg courts. Even those guilty of personal participation in the most heinous crimes have not suffered confiscation of their property and I am disposed to feel that confiscation in this single case constitutes discrimination against this defendant unjustified by any considerations attaching peculiarly to him. General confiscation of property is not a usual element in our judicial system and is generally repugnant to American concepts of justice[.][14]

The reasons given by McCloy in support of his decision to rescind the forfeiture order against Krupp are unconvincing. As to his first ground, ie the discrimination between Krupp and other convicts, although 'literally correct, ... it conveniently overlooked the difference between confiscating the property of an industrialist and confiscating the property of a soldier or government official.'[15] As to the second ground provided by McCloy, Article II(3) of Control Council Law No. 10 explicitly allowed the tribunals to order the penalty of forfeiture. In addition, American law did not apply to the trials conducted under Control Council Law No. 10. As a result, according to Kevin Heller, McCloy's invocation of American law 'to trump a specific provision of Law No. 10 was ... *ultra vires*.'[16]

The post-World War II military tribunals consequently did not lack the power under their constituent instruments to order fines and forfeiture measures. Nor, as Conor McCarthy has maintained, did those convicted under Control Council Law No. 10 want for wealth;[17] indeed, several affluent industrialists and financiers were convicted of international crimes by the Control Council Law No. 10 tribunals.[18] Instead, these tribunals either focused on sentencing convicted persons with the death penalty and periods of imprisonment or other interests prevailed, as in the case of the decision by John McCloy to revoke the forfeiture order issued against Alfred Krupp. Nonetheless, the inclusion of reasonably broad fine and asset forfeiture measures at this nascent stage of development of the project of international criminal justice is notable.

---

13 See Office of the US High Commissioner for Germany, 'Landsberg: A Documentary Report' (Office of the US High Commissioner for Germany 1951) 10. See also Heller (n 11) 355.

14 ibid.

15 Heller (n 11) 355.

16 ibid.

17 Conor McCarthy, *Reparations and Victim Support in the International Criminal Court* (CUP 2012) 44-45.

18 ibid.

4.3 The *Ad Hoc* International Criminal Tribunals

After the Cold War, the UNSC established the International Criminal Tribunal for the former Yugoslavia (ICTY) and the International Criminal Tribunal for Rwanda (ICTR) in response to the commission of mass atrocities in the former Yugoslavia[19] and Rwanda,[20] respectively. As for asset forfeiture procedures, Article 24(3) of the ICTY Statute permits the Trial Chamber, at the sentencing phase of proceedings, to order forfeiture of assets as follows:

> In addition to imprisonment, the Trial Chambers may order the return of any property and proceeds acquired by criminal conduct, including by means of duress, to their rightful owners.[21]

Article 23(3) of the ICTR Statute is identical to Article 24(3) of the ICTY Statute.[22] The *ad hoc* tribunals were therefore empowered by their constituent instruments to order post-conviction forfeiture measures – but not fines – as a penalty additional to imprisonment, similar to the powers afforded to the IMT.[23] However, Rule 61 of the Rules of Procedure and Evidence of the ICTY and ICTR extends the power of Trial Chambers to order pre-conviction asset freezing measures more akin to those granted to the military tribunals established under Control Council Law No. 10:

> (D) ... Upon request by the Prosecutor or *proprio motu*, after having heard the Prosecutor, the Trial Chamber may order a State or States to adopt provisional measures to freeze the assets of the accused, without prejudice to the rights of third parties.[24]

This Rule was implicated in 1999 in respect of former Serbian President, Slobodan Milošević, and his four co-accused – Milan Milutinović, Nikola Šainovic, Dragoljub Ojdanić and Vlajko Stojiljković.[25] In response to the application for the identification and freezing

19 See UNSC Res 827 (18 May 1993) UN Doc S/RES/827.
20 See UNSC Res 955 (8 November 1994) UN Doc S/RES/955.
21 ICTY Statute, art 24(3).
22 ICTR Statute, art 23(3) ('In addition to imprisonment, the Trial Chambers may order the return of any property and proceeds acquired by criminal conduct, including by means of duress, to their rightful owners.')
23 cf IMT Charter, art 28.
24 ICTY RPE, r 61; ICTR RPE, r 61.
25 *Prosecutor v Milošević and others* (Decision on Review of Indictment and Application for Consequential Orders) ICTY-02-54 (24 May 1999).

of assets by the ICTY Prosecutor,[26] Judge David Hunt ordered 'all States Members of the United Nations [to] make inquiries to discover whether the accused (or any of them) have assets located in their territory and, if so, adopt provisional measures to freeze such assets, without prejudice to the rights of third parties, until the accused are taken into custody.'[27] In discussing the merits of the ICTY Prosecutor's application, Judge Hunt explicitly noted the primary function of pre-trial asset freezing procedures as 'preventing an accused who is still at large from using those assets to evade arrest and from taking steps to disguise his assets or putting them beyond the reach of the Tribunal.'[28] Judge Hunt also accepted the ICTY Prosecutor's submission that a second function of freezing the assets of accused persons at ICTs is to facilitate the 'restitution of property or payment from its proceeds'.[29] Within a month of Judge Hunt's Decision, Switzerland took steps to freeze assets in the possession of Milošević and his co-accused located on its territory.[30]

Ruling on two applications by African NGOs to appear as *amicus curiae*, ICTR trial chambers have confirmed that orders for restitution could only have been made if the accused person(s) had been charged with the unlawful taking of property.[31] No forfeiture order was granted by the ICTR. As for pre-conviction measures, in 1999, the ICTR Prosecutor requested the French Ministry of Justice to freeze bank accounts in the name of Félicien Kabuga,[32] who is accused of genocide and crimes against humanity. The French authorities complied with the request,[33] while the ICTR Prosecutor has also sought the cooperation of Kenya in adopting such measures against Kabuga.[34]

26 Though the ICTY Prosecutor's application was initially based on ICTY RPE, r 54, Judge Hunt ruled that relief under rr 54 and 61(D) may be given 'for the same reasons'. *Milošević and others* Decision (n 25) para 28. ICTY RPE, r 54 provides as follows: 'At the request of either party or *proprio motu*, a Judge or a Trial Chamber may issue such orders, summonses, subpoenas, warrants and transfer orders as may be necessary for the purposes of an investigation or for the preparation or conduct of the trial.'

27 *Milošević and others* Decision (n 25) para 38.

28 ibid para 27. See also McCarthy (n 17) 47; Young (n 5) 104.

29 *Milošević and others* Decision (n 25) para 27.

30 See Swiss Federal Office of Police, 'Décision de l'Office fédéral de la police dans l'affaire *Milosevic Slobodan* et autres' (23 June 1999) <www.admin.ch/opc/fr/federal-gazette/1999/4796.pdf> accessed 31 August 2020. The freezing measures against Milošević's assets were lifted following his death in March 2006. See McCarthy (n 17) 47.

31 See *Prosecutor v Musema* (Decision on an Application by African Concern for Leave to Appear as Amicus Curiae) ICTR-96-13-T (17 March 1999) paras 12-14; *Prosecutor v Bagosora and others* (Decision on Amicus Curiae Request by African Concern) ICTR-98-41-T (23 March 2004) paras 5-11.

32 See *Miscellaneous-Kabuga Family* (Appeal of the Family of Felicien Kabuga against Decisions of the Prosecutor and President of the Tribunal) ICTR-01-A (22 November 2002).

33 ibid.

34 See UNSC 'Speakers in Security Council Call for Rapid Completion of Cases before Tribunals, while Stressing Need for Mechanisms to Tackle Residual Tasks' (4 June 2009) Press Release SC/9670.

The Statute of the International Residual Mechanism for Criminal Tribunals (MICT) largely reverts to the approach of the ICTY and ICTR toward the forfeiture of assets (including protective measures).[35] However, as the MICT was established to conduct some of the remaining tasks of the ICTY and ICTR at the time of their closure,[36] its approach to forfeiture is arguably best regarded as a continuation of that adopted by its predecessors rather than a departure from the post-Rome Statute approach.

The inclusion of asset forfeiture powers, including pre-conviction measures, in the legal frameworks of the two *ad hoc* tribunals created by the UNSC in the mid-1990s represents continuity in the approach adopted in the establishment of the post-World War II military tribunals. These powers were used more extensively by the ICTY and ICTR than their predecessors. At the same time, however, the ICTY and ICTR lacked the power to order fines and neglected to utilise the asset forfeiture measures at their disposal, despite clear indications that certain accused persons possessed property and proceeds susceptible to such measures. This underuse can be imputed, at least in part, to the absence of a holding related to the unlawful taking of property, as indicated in the decisions by ICTR trial chambers in *Musema* and *Bagasora and others*.

4.4 The Rome Statute System

4.4.1 *Fine and Forfeiture Measures*

The Rome Statute provides for the imposition of fines and forfeiture as penalties in addition to imprisonment. Under Article 77(2) of the Rome Statute:

> In addition to imprisonment, the Court may order:
>
> (a) A fine under the criteria provided for in the [RPE];
>
> (b) A forfeiture of proceeds, property and assets derived directly or indirectly from that crime, without prejudice to the rights of bona fide third parties.[37]

---

35 MICT Statute, art 22(4); MICT RPE, r 63(D).

36 UNSC Res 1966 (22 December 2010) UN Doc S/RES/1966, preamble ('*reaffirming* the need to establish an *ad hoc* mechanism to carry out a number of essential functions of the Tribunals … after the closure of the Tribunals') (emphasis in original).

37 Rome Statute, art 77(2).

The Rome Statute definition of proceeds, property and assets prone to forfeiture is noteworthy when compared with that employed at the *ad hoc* ICTs. In contrast to the terminology adopted in the Statutes of the ICTY and ICTR, 'property and proceeds acquired by criminal conduct',[38] the ICC is also able to order forfeiture of proceeds, property and assets derived *indirectly* from the Rome Statute crime(s) of which the convicted person is found guilty.[39] According to Conor McCarthy:

> In sum, Article 77(2)(b) permits the Court to order the forfeiture of property obtained as part of the *actus reus* of the offence; property for the acquisition of which the crime was committed; property purchased with or pursuant to the sale of property directly deriving from the offence in one of the two forgoing ways; and profits from property obtained in any of these ways.[40]

Moreover, the Court's asset freezing powers are much wider than those afforded to earlier international criminal justice mechanisms. Pursuant to Article 93(1)(k) of the Rome Statute, the ICC can request States Parties to identify, trace, freeze and seize assets, proceeds, property and/or instrumentalities of crimes 'in relation to investigations or prosecutions'.[41] The Pre-Trial Chamber can request such measures, under Article 57(3)(e) of the Rome Statute, 'after a warrant of arrest or a summons has been issued'.[42] In other words, the ICC can request an asset freeze at the pre-trial phase of proceedings, before an accused person has been arrested.

The first fines to be ordered by the Court were those against Jean-Pierre Bemba Gombo, a former Vice President of the Democratic Republic of the Congo (DRC), and his co-accused, Aimé Kilolo Musamba. Having been convicted by Trial Chamber VII of offences against the administration of justice, Bemba and Kilolo were fined €300,000 and €30,000, respectively.[43]

---

38 ICTY Statute, art 24; ICTR Statute, art 23.

39 Rome Statute, art 77(2)(b).

40 McCarthy (n 17) 202.

41 Rome Statute, art 93(1)(k).

42 Rome Statute, art 57(3)(e).

43 See *Prosecutor v Bemba Gombo and others* (Decision on Sentence pursuant to Article 76 of the Statute) ICC-01/05-01/13-2123-Corr (22 March 2017) (*Bemba and others* Sentencing Decision) Disposition. The fines were confirmed in *Prosecutor v. Bemba Gombo and others* (Decision Re-sentencing Mr Jean-Pierre Bemba Gombo, Mr Aimé Kilolo Musamba and Mr Jean-Jacques Mangenda Kabongo) ICC-01/05-01/13-2312 (17 September 2018) (*Bemba and others* Re-sentencing Decision) Disposition.

Given the relatively few cases to have reached the sentencing phase at the ICC,[44] it is perhaps unsurprising that the Court had issued only two fines by late 2018 – and, moreover, in the context of proceedings concerning offences against the administration of justice, not international crimes. In the *Bemba and others* Sentencing Decision, Trial Chamber VII took into consideration not only 'Bemba's culpability', but also his 'solvency'[45]. On the other hand, Trial Chamber III, in sentencing Bemba for crimes against humanity and war crimes, offences of which he was acquitted on appeal,[46] did not order fine or forfeiture measures, 'noting that the parties and Legal Representative do not request the imposition of a fine or order of forfeiture'.[47] The lack of enthusiasm for the imposition of fines and asset forfeiture measures for international crimes seen in the practice of the ICTY, ICTR and the post-World War II military tribunals appears to have resurfaced in the sentencing practice of the ICC, despite Bemba's wealth.

In the *Bemba and others* Sentencing Decision, the Trial Chamber observed that the contents of Bemba's bank account had been transferred to the Court in order to meet his Defence expenses.[48] In addition, in the *Bemba and others* Re-sentencing Decision, issued following a partially successful appeal by the Prosecutor against the original decision on sentencing handed down by Trial Chamber VII,[49] the same Trial Chamber held that 'Mr Bemba may use his frozen assets to pay his fine, and once it is paid the asset freezing order issued in this case ceases to have effect with respect to him.'[50] Trial Chamber VII held similarly with respect to Kilolo's frozen bank account.[51]

44 As of 31 August 2020, the cases against Thomas Lubanga Dyilo, Germain Katanga and Ahmad Al Faqi Al Mahdi are at the reparations phase.

45 *Bemba and others* Sentencing Decision (n 43) para 261.

46 The ICC Appeals Chamber acquitted Bemba of war crimes and crimes against humanity on 8 June 2018, thereby vacating his sentence of imprisonment for these crimes. See *Prosecutor v Bemba Gombo* (Judgment on the appeal of Mr Jean-Pierre Bemba Gombo against Trial Chamber III's "Judgment pursuant to Article 74 of the Statute") ICC-01/05-01/08-3636-Red (8 June 2018); *Prosecutor v Bemba Gombo* (Decision on the appeals of the Prosecutor and Mr Jean-Pierre Bemba Gombo against the decision of Trial Chamber III of 21 June 2016 entitled "Decision on Sentence pursuant to Article 76 of the Statute") ICC-01/05-01/08-3637 (8 June 2018) para 8 ('As a result of the Appeal Judgment on Conviction, there is no basis for any sentence to be imposed on Mr Bemba in the present case and the Sentencing Decision therefore ceases to have effect.').

47 *Prosecutor v Bemba Gombo* (Decision on Sentence pursuant to Article 76 of the Statute) ICC-01/05-01/08-3399 (21 June 2016) para 95.

48 *Bemba and others* Sentencing Decision (n 43) para 241.

49 *Prosecutor v Bemba Gombo and others* (Judgment on the appeals of the Prosecutor, Mr Jean-Pierre Bemba Gombo, Mr Fidèle Babala Wandu and Mr Narcisse Arido against the decision of Trial Chamber VII entitled "Decision on Sentence pursuant to Article 76 of the Statute") ICC-01/05-01/13-2276-Red (8 March 2018) paras 359, 361. See also *Bemba and others Re-sentencing Decision* (n 43) para 3.

50 *Bemba and others* Re-sentencing Decision (n 43) para 128.

51 ibid para 109.

Seized assets can thus be used to pay legal fees,[52] but also, if a convicted person is not considered to be indigent, to provide reparations to victims, even if the conviction is for an offence against the administration of justice rather than an international crime. Indeed, one of the principal functions of the fines and forfeiture system in the Rome Statute is to serve as a mechanism facilitating the enforcement of reparation awards. This purpose is confirmed by Article 57(3)(e) of the Rome Statute, which provides that pre-trial protective measures requested by the Court for the purpose of eventual forfeiture are intended 'in particular for the ultimate benefit of victims'.[53]

This is also evidenced by the Court's case law. In its 2012 'Decision establishing the principles and procedures to be applied to reparations',[54] the first decision on reparations issued by a Chamber of the ICC,[55] Trial Chamber I expressed the following view:

> The Statute and [RPE] introduce a system of reparations that reflects a growing recognition in international criminal law that there is a need to go beyond the notion of punitive justice, towards a solution which is more inclusive, encourages participation and recognises the need to provide effective remedies for victims.[56]

Further, in the *Bemba and others* Sentencing Decision, Trial Chamber VII ordered that the proceeds of the fines were to be transferred to the Court's Trust Fund for Victims (TFV),[57] which underscores the reparative nature of the Rome Statute.[58]

52 See *Bemba and others* Sentencing Decision (n 43) para 241. See also, generally, *Prosecutor v Bemba Gombo* (Decision on the Defence's Application for Lifting the Seizure of Assets and Request for Cooperation to the Competent Authorities of Portugal) ICC-01/05-01/08-251-Anx (10 October 2008); *Prosecutor v Bemba Gombo* (Decision on the Second Defence's Application for Lifting the Seizure of Assets and Request for Cooperation to the Competent Authorities of the Republic of Portugal) ICC-01/05-01/08-249 (14 November 2008).

53 Rome Statute, art 57(3)(e).

54 *Prosecutor v Lubanga Dyilo* (Decision Establishing the Principles and Procedures to be Applied to Reparations) ICC-01/04-01/06-2904 (7 August 2012) (*Lubanga* Reparations Decision).

55 ibid para 20.

56 ibid para 177, referring to UNGA 'Basic Principles and Guidelines on the Right to a Remedy and Reparation for Victims of Gross Violations of International Human Rights Law and Serious Violations of International Humanitarian Law' UN Doc A/RES/60/147 (21 March 2006).

57 *Bemba and others* Sentencing Decision (n 43) paras 199, 262. See also *Bemba and others* Re-sentencing Decision (n 43) paras 109, 128.

58 On reparative justice, see Conor McCarthy, 'Reparations under the Rome Statute of the International Criminal Court and Reparative Justice Theory' (2009) 3 International Journal of Transitional Justice 250.

4.4.2 *Orders for Reparations*

If ultimately forfeited after conviction, Article 79 of the Rome Statute provides that assets collected through fines and forfeiture can be transferred to the TFV.[59] Article 75(2) of the Rome Statute further provides as follows:

> The Court may make an order directly against a convicted person specifying appropriate reparations to, or in respect of, victims, including restitution, compensation and rehabilitation. Where appropriate, the Court may order that the award for reparations be made through the Trust Fund provided for in article 79.[60]

Again, as relatively few cases before the ICC have reached the reparations phase of proceedings, the Court has issued orders for reparations[61] directly against convicted persons under Article 75(2) on only three occasions as of August 2020, in the cases against Thomas Lubanga Dyilo, Germain Katanga and Ahmad Al Faqi Al Mahdi. The first order for reparations issued by the ICC was directed against Thomas Lubanga on 3 March 2015,[62] without specifying his individual financial liability, which was later set at $10 million.[63] On 24 March 2017, Trial Chamber II issued an order for reparations against Germain Katanga, finding that, despite his indigence, he was liable for the sum of $1 million.[64] Because of Katanga's inability to pay, the Trial Chamber directed the TFV to consider using the resources at its disposal to implement the order.[65] As for Ahmad Al Faqi Al

59 Rome Statute, art 79(2).
60 ibid art 75.
61 ICC Trial Chamber I established that '[r]eparations fulfil two main purposes that are enshrined in the Statute: they oblige those responsible for serious crimes to repair the harm they caused to the victims and they enable the Chamber to ensure that offenders account for their acts.' *Lubanga* Reparations Decision (n 54) para 179. An 'order for reparations' gives effect to this procedure.
62 *Prosecutor v Lubanga Dyilo* (Order for Reparations) ICC-01/04-01/06-3129-AnxA (3 March 2015).
63 *Prosecutor v Lubanga Dyilo* (Corrected version of the "Decision Setting the Size of the Reparations Award for which Thomas Lubanga Dyilo is Liable") ICC-01/04-01/06-3379-Red-Corr-tENG (21 December 2017).
64 *Prosecutor v Katanga* (Order for Reparations pursuant to Article 75 of the Statute) ICC-01/04-01/07-3728-tENG (24 March 2017) (*Katanga* Reparations Order) para 264. Although Katanga was found to be indigent, Trial Chamber II observed that, because of the potential future identification and freezing of his property and assets and the continued monitoring of his financial situation, 'Katanga's current financial situation cannot be regarded as material to the determination of the size of the reparations award for which he is liable'. ibid para 246. See also *Prosecutor v Lubanga Dyilo* (Judgment on the appeals against the "Decision establishing the principles and procedures to be applied to reparations" of 7 August 2012 with AMENDED order for reparations (Annex A) and public annexes 1 and 2) ICC-01/04-01/06-3129 (3 March 2015) paras 102-105.
65 *Katanga* Reparations Order (n 64) para 342. The TFV is funded from four sources: '(a) Voluntary contributions from governments, international organizations, individuals, corporations and other entities, in accordance with relevant criteria adopted by the Assembly of States Parties; (b) Money and other property

Mahdi, Trial Chamber VIII issued a reparations order against him on 24 March 2017, setting his total individual financial liability at €2.7 million.[66] Although the reparations order was partially amended by the Appeals Chamber in March 2018,[67] the total amount remained undisturbed.

The evident turn toward reparative justice in the Rome Statute has been attributed to a 'growing attention to victims within national criminal justice systems and ... a reaction to criticism of the manner in which victims' concerns were considered by the ICTY and the ICTR'.[68] Further, Shuichi Furuya points to the attention to victims in 'universal and regional human rights systems'.[69] But this turn can also arguably be ascribed to a shift toward more inquisitorial proceedings – which generally provide for more extensive victim reparation (and participation) rights – on the international plane. Several ICTs, discussed in the following section, are based, at least partly, in national jurisdictions with civil law legal traditions. Such a development is likely to lead to a more prominent role for victims in proceedings in view of the more active participation of victims (or their legal representatives) in a number of civil law systems.[70]

---

collected through fines or forfeiture transferred to the Trust Fund if ordered by the Court pursuant to article 79, paragraph 2, of the Rome Statute ... ; (c) Resources collected through awards for reparations if ordered by the Court pursuant to rule 98 of the Rules of Procedure and Evidence; [and] (d) Such resources, other than assessed contributions, as the Assembly of States Parties may decide to allocate to the Trust Fund.' TFV Regulations, reg 21. According to Sara Kendall, compared with the Court's four organs, the 'material resources [of the TFV] are arguably the most tenuous given their voluntary nature, as the Fund relies heavily on annual pledges from interested states'. Sara Kendall, 'Commodifying Global Justice: Economies of Accountability at the International Criminal Court' (2015) 13 Journal of International Criminal Justice 113, 124.

66 *Prosecutor v Al Mahdi* (Reparations Order) ICC-01/12-01/15-236 (17 August 2017) para 134.

67 *Prosecutor v Al Mahdi* (Public redacted Judgment on the appeal of the victims against the "Reparations Order") ICC-01/12-01/15-259-Red2 (8 March 2018).

68 Christine Evans, *The Right to Reparation in International Law for Victims of Armed Conflict* (CUP 2012) 87-88. See also Anne-Marie de Brouwer and Mikaela Heikkilä, 'Victim Issues: Participation, Protection, Reparation, and Assistance' in Göran Sluiter and others (eds), *International Criminal Procedure: Principles and Rules* (OUP 2013) 1300.

69 Furuya Shuichi, 'Victim Participation, Reparations and Reintegration as Historical Building Blocks of International Criminal Law' in Morten Bergsmo and others (eds), *Historical Origins of International Criminal Law: Volume 4* (Torkel Opsahl Academic EPublisher 2015) 839.

70 See eg Charles P Trumbull IV, 'The Victims of Victim Participation in International Criminal Proceedings' (2008) 29 Michigan Journal of International Law 777, 778 ('In these countries, the victim (or often the victim's legal representative) can request investigatory measures, review the evidence against the accused, submit declarations, present evidence, cross-examine witnesses, and make closing arguments'); Salvatore Zappalà, 'Comparative Models and the Enduring Relevance of the Accusatorial – Inquisitorial Dichotomy' in Göran Sluiter and others (eds), *International Criminal Procedure: Principles and Rules* (OUP 2013) 51.

4.5 ICTs Established after the Adoption of the Rome Statute

It is not the aim of this chapter to demonstrate uniformity in the approach of ICTs to the issue of fines and forfeiture; rather, it seeks to demonstrate that while most ICTs have been able to order such measures, they have been barely utilised in practice. This said, after the adoption of the Rome Statute, a more victim-oriented approach to asset forfeiture was followed in the legal instruments of number of ICTs.

4.5.1 *The Special Court for Sierra Leone*

There is no provision for fines in the governing documents of the Special Court for Sierra Leone (SCSL), which was established in 2002. However, Article 19(3) of the SCSL Statute provides for the forfeiture of assets as follows:

> In addition to imprisonment, the Trial Chamber may order the forfeiture of the property, proceeds and any assets acquired unlawfully or by criminal conduct, and their return to their rightful owner or to the State of Sierra Leone.[71]

Rule 104 of the SCSL RPE also allowed the tribunal to order provisional measures as follows:

> (A) After a judgement of conviction ... the Trial Chamber, at the request of the Prosecutor or at its own initiative, may hold a special hearing to determine the matter of property forfeiture, including the proceeds thereof, and may in the meantime order such provisional measures for the preservation and protection of the property or proceeds as it considers appropriate.
>
> (B) The determination may extend to such property or proceeds, even in the hands of third parties not otherwise connected with the crime, for which the convicted person has been found guilty ... .[72]

The limited SCSL case law on this issue, limited to one decision on a request for the freezing of bank accounts,[73] demonstrates an approach akin to that at the ICTY and ICTR, requiring

71 SCSL Statute, art 19.

72 SCSL RPE, r 104.

73 *Prosecutor v Norman and others* (Norman – Decision on *Inter Partes* Motion by Prosecution to Freeze the Account of the Accused Sam Hinga Norman at Union Trust Bank (Sl) Limited or at Any Other Bank in Sierra Leone) SCSL-04-14-PT (19 April 2004).

'clear and convincing evidence that the targeted assets have a nexus with criminal conduct or were otherwise illegally acquired.'[74] The Prosecutor having failed, in the opinion of the Trial Chamber, to adduce sufficient evidence to establish this nexus,[75] the motion to freeze the accounts of Sam Hinga Norman was rejected.[76]

The SCSL did not impose asset forfeiture as a penalty against any convicted person, despite making several findings of guilt in respect of the war crime of pillage,[77] a conspicuously profitable offence,[78] and also hearing evidence that civilians were forced to mine diamonds.[79] But bank accounts belonging to persons accused of crimes under the jurisdiction of the tribunal were frozen at the request of the SCSL. In 2003, Switzerland froze assets amounting to approximately two million Swiss francs in the name of former Liberian President, Charles Taylor, his relatives, members of his regime and his company.[80] However, in 2006, the SCSL Principal Defender determined Taylor to be 'partially indigent'[81] and no order for forfeiture was ultimately made against him.

Similar to the *ad hoc* ICTs, the SCSL does not allow for orders for reparations to be made directly against convicted persons. However, Rule 105 of the SCSL RPE does provide that victims of crimes for which persons were found guilty at the SCSL may attempt to seek compensation in a national court 'or other competent body'.[82] Rather than establishing reparation mechanisms similar to those in the Rome Statute, as will be further discussed below, the drafters of the constituent instruments of several ICTs preferred victims to claim reparations under the relevant provisions of national law. This might be indicative of another trend, namely that reparations procedures at ICTs have developed based on individual experience and that there is no single model.

---

74 ibid para 13.

75 ibid para 16.

76 ibid para 18.

77 See *Prosecutor v Sesay and others* (Judgement) SCSL-04-15-T (2 March 2009) (*Sesay and others* Judgment) paras 679 (in respect of Issa Hassan Sesay), 683 (in respect of Morris Kallon), 686 (in respect of Augustine Gbao).

78 See Manuel Galvis Martínez, 'Forfeiture of Assets at the International Criminal Court: The Short Arm of International Criminal Justice' (2014) 12 Journal of International Criminal Justice 193, 199-201.

79 See eg *Sesay and others* Judgment (n 77) paras 945, 1415, 1433.

80 See Swiss Federal Office of Justice, 'Taylor's accounts blocked as provisional measure: Legal assistance requested by Special Court for Sierra Leone' (Press Release, Bern, Switzerland, 23 June 2013) <https://www.bj.admin.ch/bj/en/home/aktuell/news/2003/2003-06-230.html> accessed 31 August 2020.

81 *Prosecutor v Taylor* (Principal Defender's Determination of Mr. Charles Ghankay Taylor's Indigence) SCSL-03-01-I-85 (3 April 2006). This was a provisional finding.

82 SCSL RPE, r 105.

4.5.2 *The Special Panels for Serious Crimes*

The Special Panels for Serious Crimes (SPSC) in East Timor were empowered by their constituent instrument to impose fines and asset forfeiture measures against persons convicted of international and serious domestic offences falling under their jurisdiction. Section 10.1 of Regulation No. 2000/15 on the Establishment of Panels with Exclusive Jurisdiction over Serious Criminal Offences empowered the SPSC to impose the following penalties:

> (b) A fine up to a maximum of US$ 500,000.
>
> (c) A forfeiture of proceeds, property and assets derived directly or indirectly from the crime, without prejudice to the rights of *bona fide* third parties.[83]

The UN Transitional Administration in East Timor (UNTAET), which promulgated the constituent instrument of the SPSC, also legislated for the possible formation of a Trust Fund. Section 25 of Regulation No. 2000/15 provides as follows:

> 25.1 A Trust Fund may be established ... for the benefit of victims of crimes within the jurisdiction of the panels, and of the families of such victims.
>
> 25.2 The panels may order money and other property collected through fines, forfeiture, foreign donors or other means to be transferred to the Trust Fund.
>
> 25.3 The Trust Fund shall be managed according to criteria to be determined by an UNTAET directive.[84]

This provision reflects Article 79 of the Rome Statute, which establishes the TFV.[85] In practice, such a Trust Fund was never established by UNTAET.

---

83 Regulation No. 2000/15 on the Establishment of Panels with Exclusive Jurisdiction over Serious Criminal Offences (6 June 2008) UN Doc UNTAET/REG/2000/15 (Regulation 2000/15) s 10.

84 ibid s 25.

85 Rome Statute, art 79 ('1. A Trust Fund shall be established by decision of the Assembly of States Parties for the benefit of victims of crimes within the jurisdiction of the Court, and of the families of such victims. 2. The Court may order money and other property collected through fines or forfeiture to be transferred, by order of the Court, to the Trust Fund. 3. The Trust Fund shall be managed according to criteria to be determined by the Assembly of States Parties.')

4.5.3 *The Iraqi High Tribunal*

The influence of the Rome Statute can also be seen in Article 24(f) of the Statute of the Iraqi High Tribunal (IHT), which was established under Iraqi law in 2005 to try Iraqi nationals and residents for international crimes and other violations of Iraqi law. Article 24(f) of the IHT Statute provides as follows with regard to forfeiture:

> The Trial Chambers may order the forfeiture of proceeds, property or assets derived directly or indirectly from that crime, without prejudice to the rights of the bona fide third parties.[86]

The IHT was not empowered by its constituent instrument or Rules of Procedure and Evidence to impose fines as a penalty or to order protective, pre-conviction measures. Additionally, similar to the approach at the ICTY, ICTR and SCSL, the governing documents of the IHT do not allow orders for reparations to be made directly against convicted persons. Of course, each ICT does not, and is not expected to, replicate the institutional design of its predecessors. Where there are discrepancies, these can be attributed to various factors, including but not limited to the tribunal's applicable law.

4.5.4 *The Extraordinary Chambers in the Courts of Cambodia*

The Extraordinary Chambers in the Courts of Cambodia (ECCC), established jointly by the UN and the Government of Cambodia, is also able to order forfeiture of assets as a penalty in addition to imprisonment, but cannot order fines. According to Article 39 of the ECCC Law, one of the tribunal's constituent instruments:[87]

> In addition to imprisonment, the Extraordinary Chamber of the trial court may order the confiscation of personal property, money, and real property acquired unlawfully or by criminal conduct. The confiscated property shall be returned to the State.[88]

This resembles the approach in the constituent instruments of the ICTY, ICTR and SCSL. As of August 2020, the ECCC has yet to order forfeiture as a penalty, although inquiries

86 IHT Statute, art 24(f).

87 The ECCC were established jointly by the ECCC Law and the ECCC Agreement. The tribunal is governed by these documents and the ECCC Internal Rules. See David Scheffer, 'The Extraordinary Chambers in the Courts of Cambodia' in M Cherif Bassiouni (ed) *International Criminal Law Volume III: International Enforcement* (3rd edn, Martinus Nijhoff 2008) 239.

88 ECCC Law, art 39.

were made into the assets of KAING Guek Eav alias Duch,[89] with the Trial Chamber ruling that no assets susceptible to forfeiture were identified.[90]

In addition to allowing for the forfeiture of illicitly gained assets in this manner, the ECCC Internal Rules also provide for an extensive civil party participation – and, of particular note for purposes of the present chapter – reparations regime.[91] According to this schema, civil parties can apply for 'collective and moral reparations', which may not consist of 'monetary payments'.[92] The ECCC, in part as a result of its civil law foundations,[93] perhaps reflects more than any other tribunal the turn towards a more victim-centred internationalised criminal justice after the adoption of the Rome Statute.

4.5.5 *The Special Tribunal for Lebanon*

The Special Tribunal for Lebanon (STL) is also rooted in the civil law tradition. Rule 82 of the STL RPE provides as follows:

> (C) Upon request of the Prosecutor or the Registrar, or *proprio motu* after having heard the Defence, the Pre-Trial Judge or the Trial Chamber may request a State or States to adopt provisional measures to freeze the assets of the accused, without prejudice to the rights of third parties.[94]

Although the STL is not permitted to order fines and forfeiture of assets as penalties additional to imprisonment unlike the majority of ICTs, victims are able to apply to national courts or 'other competent bod[ies]' for compensation pursuant to Article 25 of the STL Statute.[95] This measure is similar to that in the SCSL RPE, according to which victims may, after a decision by the tribunal confirming the guilt of the accused, seek compensation in accordance with the relevant national procedures. The STL and SCSL therefore provide an avenue at the national level, at least in principle, through which victims might seek redress for international crimes.

89 ECCC, *Co-Prosecutors v KAING Guek Eav alias Duch* (Inquiry into income and assets of the Accused) 001/18-07-2007/ECCC/TC (15 October 2009).
90 ECCC, *Co-Prosecutors v KAING Guek Eav alias Duch* (Judgement) 001/18-07-2007/ECCC/TC (26 July 2010).
91 ECCC Internal Rules, r 23.
92 ibid r 23 *quinquies*.
93 The ECCC is housed in the Cambodian court structure and legal system. See Scheffer (n 87) 239.
94 STL RPE, r 82.
95 STL Statute, art 25.

4.5.6 *The Extraordinary African Chambers*

The Extraordinary African Chambers (EAC) were established by the African Union and the Republic of Senegal to try international crimes committed in Chad between 7 June 1982 and 1 December 1990. The EAC are housed within the Senegalese court system, which, like the ECCC and STL, has its basis in the civil law legal tradition.

The EAC is authorised to order fines in accordance with Senegalese law.[96] Under Article 24(2) of the EAC Statute, the EAC is also able to order, as a penalty in addition to imprisonment, forfeiture of proceeds, property and assets derived directly or indirectly from crime(s) for which a person is convicted.[97] Moreover, according to Article 87 *bis* of the Senegalese Code of Criminal Procedure, the EAC may request protective, pre-conviction measures in respect of the assets of an accused person.[98]

As it concerns reparations measures, the EAC is able to order restitution, compensation and rehabilitation under Article 27 of the EAC Statute.[99] In regard to compensation, the EAC can request that such measures be implemented by a trust fund,[100] which is established by Article 28 of the EAC Statute for the benefit of victims of the crimes within the tribunal's jurisdiction as well as their beneficiaries.[101]

Notably, however, the EAC Statute does not include provisions akin to Article 79(2) of the Rome Statute, which permits the ICC to order the transfer of the proceeds of fines and orders for forfeiture to the TFV, [102] or Article 44 of the KSC Law, which allows the KSC to request the sale of forfeited assets to fund reparation awards.[103]

In the case against former President of Chad, Hissène Habré, the EAC did not order the forfeiture of assets or a fine as a penalty. A fine was not requested by the EAC's Prosecutor and the EAC Trial Chamber rejected the Prosecutor's request to impose asset forfeiture,[104] despite assets belonging to Habré having been frozen earlier in the proceedings. The Trial

96 EAC Statute, art 24(1).
97 ibid art 24(2).
98 *Code de Procédure Pénale Sénégalais* (Senegalese Code of Criminal Procedure) art 87 *bis* ('Lorsqu'il est saisi d'un dossier d'information, le juge d'instruction peut d'office ou sur demande de la partie civile ou du ministère public, ordonner des mesures conservatoires sur les biens de l'inculpé.')
99 EAC Statute, art 27(1).
100 ibid art 27(2).
101 ibid art 28(1).
102 See Rome Statute, art 79(2).
103 KSC Law, art 44(6).
104 *Ministère Public c. Hissein Habré* (Jugement) (30 May 2016) para 2329.

Chamber held that the Prosecutor had failed to show that the assets resulted, directly or indirectly, from the commission of Habré's crimes.[105] The failure to charge Habré with the war crime of pillage – a potentially profitable offence – may have caused difficulties for the Prosecutor in meeting this forfeiture threshold, which closely resembles the Rome Statute.[106]

The EAC also ordered significant reparations to Habré's victims. The EAC Appeals Chamber set the total amount of reparations due at more than 82 billion CFA francs, equivalent to over $140 million, and ordered Habré to pay this sum.[107] At the same time, the Appeals Chamber held that, at the time it issued its judgment, Habré's assets were not sufficient to meet the totality of the reparations awarded.[108] Although financing orders for reparations is – and will continue to be – undoubtedly challenging for ICTs in view of their limited resources and reliance on voluntary donations from States,[109] the finding that Habré is individually liable for this amount of compensation, as with Germain Katanga at the ICC, is vital in recognising the harm suffered by the victims of the serious crimes for which these two men were convicted.

4.5.7 *The Kosovo Specialist Chambers*

The most recently established ICT, the Kosovo Specialist Chambers (KSC), adopts an approach to fines, asset forfeiture and orders for reparations similar to that in the Rome Statute. The KSC are permitted to order forfeiture of assets as a penalty and orders for reparations under Article 44(6) of the KSC Law, as follows:

> In addition to imprisonment, the Specialist Chambers may order only the convicted person to make restitution or pay compensation to a Victim or to Victims collectively, or may order the forfeiture of property, proceeds and any assets used for or deriving from the commission of the crime and their return

105 ibid para 2330.
106 Rome Statute, art 77(2)(b). On the failure of the EAC Prosecutor to charge Habré with pillage, see also Daley J Birkett, 'Victims' Justice? Reparations and Asset Forfeiture at the Extraordinary African Chambers' (2019) 63 Journal of African Law 151.
107 *Le Procureur Général c. Hissein Habré* (Arrêt) (27 April 2017) 226. The exact figure was 82 billion and 290 million CFA francs.
108 ibid 226.
109 On which, see Nader Iskandar Diab 'Challenges in the Implementation of the Reparation Award against Hissein Habré: Can the Spell of Unenforceable Awards across the Globe be Broken?' (2018) 16 Journal of International Criminal Justice 141.

> to their rightful owner or sale and share between Victims under Article 22 ('a Reparation Order').[110]

Turning to fines, the KSC Law does not allow for their imposition for international crimes.[111] However, the KSC can order such measures for the failure to comply with witness summonses. Under Article 42 of the KSC Law, failure to appear and refusal to testify as a witness, respectively, are punishable by a fine of up to €250.[112]

As for protective measures, Article 39(11) of the KSC Law provides as follows:

> The Pre-Trial Judge may, where necessary, provide for the protection and privacy of victims and witnesses, the preservation of evidence, the protection of persons and national security information or the preservation of assets which may be subject to a forfeiture under this Law and the Rules of Procedure and Evidence, including temporary freezing orders, temporary confiscation orders or other temporary measures.[113]

This victim-oriented provision provides the Pre-Trial Judge of the KSC with similar powers to those available to Pre-Trial Chambers at the ICC under the Rome Statute. Likewise, Article 53(1)(l) of the KSC Law, which concerns cooperation and judicial assistance, is similar to Article 93(1)(k) of the Rome Statute:

> 1. Subject to the rights of the accused provided for in Article 21, all entities and persons in Kosovo shall co-operate with the Specialist Chambers and Specialist Prosecutor's Office and shall comply without undue delay with any request for assistance or an order or decision issued by Specialist Chambers or Specialist Prosecutor's Office, including, but not limited to, those concerning: …
>
> l. the identification, tracing and freezing or seizure of proceeds, property and assets or instrumentalities of crimes for the purpose of eventual forfeiture, without prejudice to the rights of *bona fide* third parties[.][114]

110 KSC Law, art 44(6).
111 This approach is similar to that adopted at the MICT. See MICT Statute, art 22(1).
112 KSC Law, art 42.
113 ibid art 39(11).
114 ibid art 53(1)(l).

Matthew Cross identifies a subtle difference between the Rome Statute asset freezing regime and that embraced by the drafters of the KSC Law.[115] Cross contends that the wording of the latter, 'proceeds, property and assets *or* instrumentalities of crimes',[116] instead of 'assets *and* instrumentalities of crimes' found in the Rome Statute,[117] 'may broaden the scope of the assets which may be frozen prior to trial'.[118]

In sum, therefore, the KSC have at their disposal a victim-oriented asset freezing and forfeiture regime akin to the Rome Statute system. The KSC are empowered to order both pre- and post-conviction measures to freeze the assets of accused and convicted persons, respectively. Such assets may subsequently be used to provide reparations to victims. That the drafters of the KSC Law included such a regime demonstrates that reparation is viewed as a vital component of the institution's restorative mandate.

4.6 Some Suggested Reasons behind ICTs' Failure to Order Asset Recovery Measures

It has thus far been demonstrated that, although a number of ICTs have been invested with the power to order fines, forfeiture of property, proceeds of crimes and/or assets and, more recently, to orders reparations against convicted persons, these powers have barely been invoked in practice. A key question is therefore why ICTs have appeared to be reluctant to employ the asset recovery tools at their disposal. Three options will be presented in turn.

4.6.1 *Theoretical Basis*

First, the caution on the part of those ICTs empowered to do so to order fines or asset forfeiture measures could arguably be attributable, at least in part, to the grave nature of international crimes. In other words, penalties of a financial corrective nature could seem ill-fitting when imposed for the commission of, in the words of the preamble to the Rome Statute, 'the most serious crimes of concern to the international community as a whole'.[119] This can be contrasted with orders for reparations, which appear to be more readily used by ICTs than fines and forfeiture measures. It is suggested that the former, which find their basis in the law of civil responsibility, do not suffer from this perception. It therefore

115 Matthew E Cross, 'Equipping the Specialist Chambers of Kosovo to Try Transnational Crimes: Remarks on Independence and Cooperation' (2016) 14 Journal of International Criminal Justice 73, 92.
116 KSC Law, art 53(1)(l) (emphasis added).
117 Rome Statute, art 93(1)(k).
118 Cross (n 115) 92.
119 Rome Statute, preamble.

seems reasonable to assume that the ICC, and other ICTs with the capacity to order reparations directly against convicted persons, will employ such powers more readily that fines and forfeiture measures for this reason. Indeed, such a willingness to issue reparations orders is already borne out in the early practice of the ICC, which has found that all three individuals guilty of crimes under its jurisdiction are also liable to make reparations pursuant to Article 75 of the Rome Statute.

4.6.2 *Dearth of Assets*

A second possible reason behind ICTs' reluctance to make use of fines and forfeiture measures is practical: despite certain persons convicted of international crimes having (had) access to substantial assets, ICTs have struggled to have them traced and frozen. For example, although Charles Taylor and Hissène Habré were reported to have held vast sums of money and other assets accumulated during their presidencies of Liberia and Chad, respectively, investigators have not been able to identify, trace, seize and freeze them. This could be because the assets have been located beyond the reach of financial investigators by the suspect (or, depending on the phase of the proceedings, accused person or convicted person) or their ownership disguised.

At the other end of the financial spectrum, it must be acknowledged that many of the persons convicted of international crimes are indigent, meaning that they do not have sufficient assets to fund their defence. When faced with this reality, coupled with the frequently high number of victims potentially eligible for reparations in international crimes cases, the limited use by ICTs of fines and forfeiture measures, with a view to using their proceeds to fund reparation awards, appears rather more justifiable.

4.6.3 *Other Reparations Paradigms*

Although not necessarily a reason behind the lack of enthusiasm shown by a series of ICTs for the imposition of fines and forfeiture measures for the commission of crimes under their jurisdiction, the availability and use of other reparations paradigms ought to be taken into account. For example, it was noted above that only one order for forfeiture of assets, against industrialist Alfred Krupp, was made by the post-World War II military tribunals. It was also observed that the constituent instrument of the IMT, as well as Control Council Law No. 10, failed to provide for the imposition of measures akin to orders for reparations. However, although reparations were not awarded in the course of the *criminal proceedings* before ICTs, this does not mean that victims received no reparations whatsoever for harm suffered. Indeed, post-World War II West Germany developed a reparations programme as a political-administrative tool complementing the criminal process. The measures sought *inter alia* to address the responsibility of the German State to individual victims, as opposed to intra-State reparations, although the latter were also paid.[120] Through a series of federal reparations laws,[121] Germany aimed to indemnify victims of persecution suffered under the Nazi regime.[122]

It is beyond the scope of this chapter to discuss the advantages of different reparations models, within and beyond the criminal process, in respect of the extent to which they meet the need to make restitution to (groups of) victims of war. Nonetheless, it is worth noting that paradigms akin to the foregoing German national reparations scheme, as a political-administrative mechanism designed to complement the criminal process, could function alongside reparations under the ICC system, but only where there is State involvement in the commission of offences, as was the case with Nazi Germany. These mechanisms are therefore limited and operate to meet the responsibility of the State, as opposed to that of individuals, that is to say convicted persons in the ICC system, to make reparations to individual (or groups of) victims. Fines, asset forfeiture, and particularly orders for reparations consequently retain an important role in funding reparations made to the victims of international crimes.

4.7 CONCLUSION

This chapter has sought to demonstrate, first, that most ICTs have been permitted by their constituent instruments to order fines, forfeiture of assets (including protective measures for the purpose of eventual forfeiture) and/or reparations directly against convicted persons. However, despite possessing these powers, and despite evidence that a number of persons found guilty of international crimes had significant wealth, ICTs have seldom invoked such measures in proceedings other than those involving offences against the administration of justice. In addition, the chapter has also aimed to show that the inclusion in the Rome Statute of more victim-centred procedures in respect of fines and forfeiture, targeted at

120 See Ariel Colonomos and Andrea Armstrong, 'German Reparations to Jews after World War II: A Turning Point in the History of Reparations' in Pablo de Greiff (ed), *The Handbook of Reparations* (OUP 2006) 391.

121 *Bundesergänzungsgesetz zur Entschädigung für Opfer der nationalsozialistischen Verfolgung (BEG) vom 18. September 1953* (Federal Supplementary Law for the Compensation of Victims of National Socialist Persecution of 18 September 1953), which was subsequently modified, most pertinently for the purposes of the present chapter, on 29 June 1956 (amending *inter alia* residency and deadline requirements) and 14 September 1965 (amending *inter alia* requirements relating to the burden of proof and eligibility). See Colonomos and Armstrong (n 120) 402-08.

122 See Colonomos and Armstrong (n 120) 402-08.

the provision of reparations, has led to the adoption of similar measures in the law (if not the practice) of certain subsequently-established ICTs.

In order to recover the proceeds of international crimes, and to finance reparations to the victims of such atrocities, ICTs' prosecutors could more readily utilise fines and forfeiture measures. This approach could be especially advantageous in cases where convicted persons (or, in respect of protective, pre-conviction, measures with a view to forfeiture, accused persons) have access to substantial assets. The adoption of an extensive reparations system in the Rome Statute demonstrates a turn toward a more reparative international criminal justice, which is also reflected in the law governing a number of ICTs established after 1998. Most ICTs have at their disposal at least some tools with which they are able to locate and recover assets belonging to those (accused or) convicted of international crimes. Not least to secure the funds required to finance awards for reparations, prosecutors at ICTs could devote greater attention to these tools, for which procedural structures are largely already in place. Of course, however, the more attention paid to these tools, the more the rights of those on the receiving end of such measures are impacted. The following chapter examines the question of how competing rights and interests in the asset freezing process, including those of the individuals against whom such measures are imposed, are secured and balanced in the law and practice of the ICC.

5 Pre-Trial 'Protective Measures for the Purpose of Forfeiture' at the ICC*

Protecting and Balancing Competing Rights and Interests

5.1 Introduction

Under Article 93(1)(k) of the Rome Statute, the ICC is able to request its States Parties to identify, trace, freeze and seize assets 'in relation to investigations or prosecutions'.[1] Such measures can be requested by the Pre-Trial Chamber, under Article 57(3)(e) of the ICC Statute, '[w]here a warrant of arrest or a summons has been issued … having due regard to the strength of the evidence and the rights of the parties concerned'.[2] This chapter explores the rights and interests of the four principal stakeholders in this process: (i) accused persons, (ii) the Prosecutor, (iii) victims and (iv) bona fide third parties, and reflects on how they are safeguarded and balanced.

If forfeited after conviction, frozen and seized assets can be used to fund reparations to the victims of the crimes at issue. This function is confirmed by Article 57(3)(e) of the Rome Statute, which provides that such measures can be requested 'in particular for the ultimate benefit of victims'.[3] However, asset freezing measures at the pre-trial phase of ICC proceedings are not only a vital tool to enable the enforcement of future reparation awards, but may also be an crucial element of prosecutorial strategy. The Prosecutor is therefore a second concerned party within the meaning of the Rome Statute. Third, as accused persons are the direct objects of asset freezing measures requested by pre-trial chambers, their rights are clearly at stake. A fourth category of stakeholders whose rights may be affected is third parties, whether persons or entities, who own the concerned asset(s) and/or who have a right in property in the hands of the accused. This chapter critically examines the practice of the ICC with respect to requesting pre-trial protective measures.

---

* An earlier version of this chapter was published as Daley J Birkett, 'Pre-trial "Protective Measures for the Purpose of Forfeiture" at the International Criminal Court: Safeguarding and Balancing Competing Rights and Interests' (2019) 32 Leiden Journal of International Law 585-602.

1 Rome Statute, art 93(1)(k).

2 ibid art 57(3)(e).

3 ibid.

The previous chapter demonstrated that, although a series of ICTs established before and after the entry into force of the Rome Statute in 2002 have possessed the power to request the imposition of pre-trial protective measures, these bodies have seldom asked States to give effect to such restrictions. The following section will discuss the legal framework at the disposal of the ICC under its constituent instrument and RPE. Reflecting on the law and practice of the Court, the chapter contends that such measures are ultimately essential to enable the Court to meet the interests of victims and to fulfill its restorative mandate. Moreover, even if the ICC were to abandon its restorative aims, such measures are useful prosecutorial tools. After demonstrating that the Rome Statute system introduces a series of checks and balances aimed at guaranteeing the rights and interests of the concerned parties during the pre-trial protective measures process, the chapter concludes that the ICC's approach to date has been progressive and largely consistent.

5.2 Protective measures at the ICC

Article 57(3) of the Rome Statute provides, in relevant part, as follows

> In addition to its other functions under this Statute, the Pre-Trial Chamber may: …
>
> (e) Where a warrant of arrest or a summons has been issued under article 58, and having due regard to the strength of the evidence and the rights of the parties concerned, as provided for in this Statute and the Rules of Procedure and Evidence, seek the cooperation of States pursuant to article 93, paragraph 1 (k), to take protective measures for the purpose of forfeiture, in particular for the ultimate benefit of victims.[4]

According to Article 93(1) of the Rome Statute, ICC States Parties are under an explicit obligation to comply with requests from the Court 'to provide … assistance in relation to investigations or prosecutions'[5] pursuant to their national laws. Subparagraph (k) of the same provision provides that such assistance extends to '[t]he identification, tracing and freezing or seizure of proceeds, property and assets and instrumentalities of crimes for the purpose of eventual forfeiture, without prejudice to the rights of bona fide third parties'.[6]

4 Rome Statute, art 57(3).
5 ibid art 93(1).
6 ibid art 93(1)(k).

As to the 'rights of the parties concerned', the ICC legal framework provides for a series of safeguards, substantive and procedural, enabling it to strike a fair balance between the interests of the four primary stakeholders implicated by the pre-trial protective measures process. These safeguards can be found in both the Rome Statute and the ICC RPE.

5.2.1 *The evidentiary threshold*

One such safeguard can be found in the text of Article 57(3)(e) of the Rome Statute itself. Guariglia and Hochmayr observe that the initial proposed formulations of this provision, which they note was added towards the end of the United Nations Diplomatic Conference of Plenipotentiaries on the Establishment of an International Criminal Court,[7] 'included no clear evidentiary threshold' for the issuance of pre-trial protective measures.[8] Such a state of affairs having 'caused discomfort to many delegations',[9] however, the final text agreed in Rome expressly requires that 'a warrant of arrest or a summons has been issued' under Article 58 of the Rome Statute before the Pre-Trial Chamber can request States to take such measures. The evidentiary threshold required under Article 57(3)(e) of the ICC Statute must therefore be 'reasonable grounds to believe that the person has committed a crime within the jurisdiction of the Court',[10] ie the same as required by Article 58(1)(a) of the ICC Statute.[11] Should the 'strength of the evidence' no longer meet this threshold, the legal basis for any request issued pursuant thereto would cease to exist.

The 'strength of the evidence' has been strictly construed by the Court. In *Kenyatta*, ICC Trial Chamber V(B) took the following factors into account before suspending the Pre-Trial Chamber's order to freeze the assets of Uhuru Muigai Kenyatta and others:[12]

> ... the Prosecution's acknowledgement that it 'now has insufficient evidence to secure a conviction at trial', that any information provided 'may or may not yield evidence relevant to this case', and the directive contained in Article

7 Fabricio Guariglia and Gudrun Hochmayr, 'Article 57' in Otto Triffterer and Kai Ambos (eds), *The Rome Statute of the International Criminal Court: A Commentary* (3rd edn, CH Beck/Hart Publishing/Nomos 2016) 1435.

8 ibid.

9 ibid.

10 Rome Statute, art 58(1)(a).

11 See Guariglia and Hochmayr (n 7) 1435.

12 *Prosecutor v Muthaura, Kenyatta and Ali* (Decision Ordering the Registrar to Prepare and Transmit a Request for Cooperation to the Republic of Kenya for the Purpose of Securing the Identification, Tracing and Freezing or Seizure of Property and Assets of Francis Kirimi Muthaura, Uhuru Muigai Kenyatta and Mohammed Hussein Ali) ICC-01/09-02/11-42 (5 April 2011).

> 57(3)(e) of the Statute that the Chamber pay due regard to the strength of the evidence and the rights of the parties concerned[.][13]

This straightforward application of the 'evidentiary threshold' safeguard found in the text of Article 57(3)(e) of the ICC Statute is evidently paramount to the rights of the accused. When viewed in light of the Prosecutor's failure to bring sufficient evidence to secure a conviction in *Kenyatta*, the reasons behind the discomfort felt by a number of delegations when finalizing the text of the ICC Statute by the lack of a clear evidentiary threshold for the issuance of pre-trial protective measures[14] become even more apparent. Without (the enforcement of) such a threshold, the measures might have remained in force despite the limited prospects of securing a conviction and, thereafter, an order for reparations.

5.2.2 *Prior notification and modification*

Further safeguards can be found in Rule 99 of the ICC RPE. First, Rule 99(2) of the ICC RPE provides that, where such notification could not 'jeopardize the effectiveness of the measures requested ... , the Registrar shall provide notification of the proceedings to the person against whom a request is made and so far as is possible to any interested persons or interested States.'[15] William Schabas argues that the person against whom a request is made may be the accused person, but 'may also be the person or body in possession of the items in question.'[16] Parties other than accused persons, the Prosecutor and victims may therefore benefit from this safeguard against the potential impact of protective measures. As Guariglia and Hochmayr observe, giving prior notification would appear to constitute the exception, rather than the rule.[17] The reason behind this is evident: 'the success of the request depends on its being undisclosed to the person prosecuted by the Court'.[18]

Rule 99(3) of the ICC RPE alludes to a second safeguard, namely the possibility that an order requesting protective measures might be 'revoked or otherwise modified'.[19] Where an order is made without prior notification under Rule 99(2), the person(s) against whom the request is made – as well as other interested persons and States – are invited to make

---

13 *Prosecutor v Kenyatta* (Decision on the implementation of the request to freeze assets) ICC-01/09-02/11-931 (8 July 2014) (*Kenyatta* Implementation Decision) para 29.
14 See Guariglia and Hochmayr (n 7) 1435.
15 ICC RPE, r 99(2).
16 William A Schabas, *The International Criminal Court: A Commentary on the Rome Statute* (2nd edn, OUP 2016) 884.
17 See Guariglia and Hochmayr (n 7) 1436.
18 ibid.
19 ICC RPE, r 99(3).

observations as to the revocation or modification thereof 'as soon as is consistent with the effectiveness of the measures requested'.[20]

5.2.3 *The right to appeal*

A further due process guarantee available under the ICC legal framework is the right to request leave to appeal protective measures decisions pursuant to Article 82(1)(b) of the ICC Statute, which provides as follows: '1. Either party may appeal any of the following decisions in accordance with the Rules of Procedure and Evidence: ... (b) A decision granting or denying release of the person being investigated or prosecuted'.[21] Though at first glance one might question how decisions granting or denying the release of accused persons relate to the identification, tracing and freezing or seizure of assets, this approach was confirmed by ICC Pre-Trial Chamber II in 2014. According to Judge Tarfusser:

> in light of both its provisional nature and the fact that it relates to one of the fundamental rights of an accused, a decision on the seizure of assets can be considered as similar to a decision on the interim release of the accused, which decision can be appealed without the leave of the relevant Chamber pursuant to article 82(1) (b) of the Statute.[22]

Pre-Trial Chamber II also observed that 'a direct right to appeal is also enshrined in article 82(4) and rule 150(1) of the Rules against orders for reparations issued under article 75, which orders may also similarly affect the right to property',[23] which, as noted above, it had explicitly acknowledged as a fundamental right protected by a series of international human rights instruments.

On 28 October 2008, Jean-Pierre Bemba Gombo applied for the release of additional seized funds, an earlier application having already been partially granted on 10 October 2008.[24]

---

20 ibid.

21 Rome Statute art 82(1)(d).

22 *Prosecutor v Bemba Gombo and others* (Decision on Mr Kilolo's "Notice of appeal against the decision of the Single Judge ICC-01/05-01/13-743-Conf-Exp" dated 10 November 2014 and on the urgent request for the partial lifting of the seizure on Mr Kilolo's assets dated 24 November 2014) ICC-01/05-01/13-773 (1 December 2014) (*Kilolo* Notice Decision) 5.

23 ibid.

24 *Prosecutor v Bemba Gombo* (Decision on the Defence's Application for Lifting the Seizure of Assets and Request for Cooperation to the Competent Authorities of Portugal) ICC-01/05-01/08-251-Anx (10 October 2008) (*Bemba* First Lifting Decision).

Pre-Trial Chamber III dismissed Bemba's second application.[25] Among other reasons, the Pre-Trial Chamber observed that the defence team had failed to 'request leave to appeal the Decision of 10 October 2008',[26] thereby giving weight to the appellate safeguarding mechanism enshrined in the Rome Statute and the ICC RPE. The right to appeal decisions concerning protective measures therefore serves two purposes: (i) affording a safeguard against orders against the assets of accused persons that reach beyond the limits imposed by the ICC's legal framework; and (ii) preventing those whose assets have been subjected to freezing or seizure measures from making successive requests for their release without exhausting all legal avenues at their disposal under the Rome Statute and the ICC RPE.

5.2.4 *The 'rights of the parties concerned' and 'the ultimate benefit of victims'*

Article 21(3) of the Rome Statute stipulates that, in applying and interpreting the sources of law at its disposal, including the Statute and RPE,[27] such application and interpretation 'must be consistent with internationally recognized human rights'.[28] Both the ICC Statute and international human rights law guarantee a series of rights on the part of the accused, while Article 57(3)(e) explicitly refers to 'rights of the parties concerned', which has to include the Prosecutor as the second 'party' to the proceedings. The provision also makes reference to the 'ultimate benefit of victims', who hold a unique and significant place in the Rome Statute system of international criminal justice. Finally, Article 93(1)(k) of the ICC Statute safeguards the rights of bona fide third parties in the execution of (pre-trial) enforcement measures with a view to eventual forfeiture.[29] The interests of the principal stakeholders in the protective measures process will consequently be addressed in turn.

5.2.4.1 Accused persons

As the direct objects of the measures, accused persons' rights are clearly implicated by orders for protective measures for the purpose of forfeiture issued at the pre-trial phase. The rights implicated by such measures under Article 57(3)(e) of the ICC Statute include the right to family life. According to Göran Sluiter, the application of human rights norms to the 'unique' circumstances of ICTs inevitably results in reduced protection for accused

25 *Prosecutor v Bemba Gombo* (Decision on the Second Defence's Application for Lifting the Seizure of Assets and Request for Cooperation to the Competent Authorities of the Republic of Portugal) ICC-01/05-01/08-249 (14 November 2008) (*Bemba* Second Lifting Decision) Disposition.

26 ibid para 24. See also para 62.

27 Rome Statute, art 21(1)(a).

28 ibid, art 21(3).

29 ibid, art 93(1)(k).

persons when compared to the interests of the prosecution and/or victims.[30] It is possible that the freezing and seizure of assets in the name of an accused person, where the rights and interests of these three participants, as well as bona fide third parties, must be balanced, could lead to such an outcome, putting assets beyond the reach of the family members etc. of the person(s) against whom the protective measures are sought. Article 21(3) of the Rome Statute ought to provide a safeguard against the interpretation of Article 57(3)(e) in a manner inconsistent with, for example, the right to respect for private and family life.[31] Other rights of the accused that could potentially be implicated by the imposition of pre-trial protective measures for the purpose of forfeiture include the right to the peaceful enjoyment of possessions[32] and the right to a fair trial (ie to be defended by counsel of one's own choosing).[33]

The rights of the accused, as well as those of other interested stakeholders, could also be impacted by the *ex parte* status of requests or decision for protective measures concerning assets that may later be the object of forfeiture measures. Such potential prejudice was acknowledged by Trial Chamber I in *Lubanga*: '*ex parte* procedures are only to be used exceptionally when they are truly necessary and when no other, lesser, procedures are available, and the court must ensure that their use is proportionate given the potential prejudice to the accused'.[34] This proportionality assessment must take into consideration the interests of victims in obtaining reparations in the event of a conviction as well as the interests of the Prosecutor in securing the effective execution of the measures requested. It is therefore difficult to contest the application of *ex parte* proceedings in order to safeguard the rights of the accused in the protective measures process, an argument underscored by the reality that the rights of the accused in terms of participation are fewer during the pre-trial phase of proceedings before the Court compared with the later stages thereof.[35]

30 Göran Sluiter, 'Human Rights Protection in the ICC Pre-Trial Phase' in Carsten Stahn and Göran Sluiter (eds), *The Emerging Practice of the International Criminal Court* (Martinus Nijhoff 2009) 461.

31 As protected in *inter alia* ECHR, art 8.

32 As protected in eg Protocol 1, art 1. Pre-Trial Chamber II explicitly acknowledged the protection of this fundamental right in *Kilolo* Notice Decision (n 22) 5.

33 As protected in *inter alia* Rome Statute, art 67(1)(b) and ECHR, art 6.

34 *Prosecutor v Lubanga Dyilo* (Decision on the procedures to be adopted for ex parte proceedings) ICC-01/04-01/06-1058 (6 December 2007).

35 cf the rights afforded to persons during an investigation under Rome Statute, art 55 and those granted to the accused pursuant to Rome Statute, art 67. On the application of the former, see Christopher Hall and Dov L Jacobs, 'Article 55' in Otto Triffterer and Kai Ambos (eds), *The Rome Statute of the International Criminal Court: A Commentary* (3rd edn, CH Beck/Hart Publishing/Nomos 2016) 1395-96.

5.2.4.1 The Prosecutor

As Judge Hunt noted in his Decision on an application by the ICTY Prosecutor to request States to identify and freeze the assets of Slobodan Milošević, Milan Milutinović, Nikola Šainovic, Dragoljub Ojdanić and Vlajko Stojiljković, the primary function of imposing such measures against accused persons during the pre-trial phase of international criminal proceedings is to facilitate their arrest.[36] Indeed, it is possible to imagine a scenario where an offer to unfreeze (some of) the frozen assets of an accused person who remains at large could be utilised as tool to negotiate their voluntary surrender.

Asset freezing can also disrupt ongoing and prevent future criminal conduct within the jurisdiction of the Court. The commission of international crimes frequently goes hand-in-hand with the purchase of weapons and supplies, payments to troops, as well as other potentially lucrative activities, including the trafficking of persons, arms and narcotics, all of which require the availability of – and access to – (financial) assets.

In addition, financial records may provide evidentiary links between individuals and/or groups, which can assist the Prosecutor in proving, for example, the aiding and abetting of crimes. Such records can be obtained through the identification of assets belonging to accused persons pursuant to the procedures in Article 93(1)(k) of the Rome Statute.

Discussing the role of the Prosecutor with respect to measures under Article 57(3)(e) of the Rome Statute, Pre-Trial Chamber I, having noted that the Prosecutor had not, at the time of its Decision, transmitted requests for co-operation to States Parties with respect to identifying, tracing or seizing Lubanga's assets, expressed the view that, 'as the organ of the Court primarily in charge of the investigation … the effectiveness of the reparation system would greatly benefit from the Prosecution's due consideration of this matter during the investigation stage.'[37]

The interests of the Prosecutor in requesting protective measures during the investigative phase, in the view of Pre-Trial Chamber I, are therefore also linked to future reparations, which may later be found to be payable to victims if the accused is found guilty. It is to the interests of the victims of the crimes at issue that the following section will turn.

---

36 *Prosecutor v Milošević and others* (Decision on Review of Indictment and Application for Consequential Orders) ICTY-02-54 (24 May 1999) para 27. See Chapter 4.

37 *Prosecutor v Lubanga Dyilo* (Decision on the Prosecutor's Application for a warrant of arrest, Article 58) ICC-01/04-01/06-1-Corr-Red (10 February 2006) (*Lubanga* Arrest Warrant Decision) para 141.

5.2.4.3 Victims

Victims play a prominent role in proceedings at the ICC, with broader rights than those afforded by earlier ICTs. The IMT established at Nuremberg, with substantial input from American jurists, focused on punishing individuals for mass crimes within a predominantly adversarial framework.[38] However, after the Cold War, victim-oriented provisions were included in the legal frameworks of a number of ICTs and, most significantly for the purposes of the present chapter, that of the permanent ICC. The *post*-Cold War era also saw significant developments in international human rights law, including recognition that victims of serious violations have a right to reparation.[39] Christine Evans identifies 'growing attention to victims within national criminal justice systems and … a reaction to criticism of the manner in which victims' concerns were considered by the ICTY and the ICTR' as influential factors leading to the adoption of the Court's victim reparations regime.[40] As Liesbeth Zegveld observes:

> With the establishment of the ICC, for the first time in history, individuals can submit claims of a private law nature to an international court. In contrast to the ICTY and ICTR, the ICC may award reparations for the benefit of individual victims. It may do so directly against a convicted person. This reparation may take the form of restitution, compensation and rehabilitation. The ICC can act on an application of a victim or exceptionally on its own motion.[41]

Although not full parties to the proceedings before the ICC in the same way as victims are able to participate before certain national courts or at other ICTs, including the EAC and the ECCC, the interests of victims are evidently paramount to the protective measures procedures found in Article 57(3)(e) of the Rome Statute and Rule 99(1) of the ICC RPE.

5.2.4.4 Bona fide third parties

Article 93(1)(k) of the Rome Statute explicitly provides that States Parties are obliged to assist the Court in identifying, tracing, freezing and seizing assets 'without prejudice to the rights of bona fide third parties'.[42] However, these rights are not further elaborated in

38 See Liesbeth Zegveld, 'Victims' Reparations Claims and International Criminal Courts: Incompatible Values?', (2010) 8 Journal of International Criminal Justice 79, 86-87. The IMTFE reprised this largely retributive model.

39 See eg Christine Evans, *The Right to Reparation in International Law for Victims of Armed Conflict* (CUP 2012)

40 ibid 87-88.

41 Zegveld (n 38) 88.

42 Rome Statute, art 93(1)(k).

the Rome Statute or the ICC RPE.[43] Nevertheless, such third parties constitute an relevant category of stakeholders in the pre-trial protective measures process. For example, their interests, not least their right to the peaceful enjoyment of possessions, could be implicated in two situations. First, the third parties could be in possession of asset(s) belonging to the accused person(s), which could consequently be subjected to pre-trial protective measures. Second, the third parties could have a right in property which, at the time the ICC requests protective measures, is in the hands of the accused. Goldsmith and Linderman claim that such third parties could include owners, creditors, purchasers, business partners and joint tenants, among others.[44] The interests of bona fide third parties must consequently also be safeguarded alongside those of the accused, the Prosecutor and any potential victims. The following section aims to provide an examination of how the ICC has given effect to these rights and interests and, where they are in competition, how it has sought to balance them in its decisions involving persons accused of committing crimes under its jurisdiction.

5.3 The ICC practice

Much of the Court's practice regarding pre-trial 'protective measures for the purpose of forfeiture' remains confidential. However, Pre-Trial Chambers have issued requests for such measures against Thomas Lubanga Dyilo,[45] Germain Katanga,[46] Jean-Pierre Bemba Gombo,[47] Uhuru Muigai Kenyatta and others,[48] and Aimé Kilolo Musamba. It was also

43 See Michael Stiel and Carl-Friedrich Stuckenberg, 'Article 109: Enforcement of fines and forfeiture measures' in Mark Klamberg (ed), *Commentary on the Law of the International Criminal Court* (Torkel Opsahl Academic EPublisher 2017) 705, n 810 ('The only ground for refusal to enforce fines and forfeiture orders mentioned in the Statute is prejudice to the "rights of bona fide third parties", an expression nowhere defined in the Statute or RPE. Hence, it seems that national courts have to determine which rights are relevant and when a party qualifies as bona fide, which not only deviates from inter-State practice but may result in an uneven application'). See also Kai Ambos, *Treatise on International Criminal Law*, vol III (OUP 2016) 655-56.

44 Michael Goldsmith and Mark J Linderman, 'Asset Forfeiture and Third Party Rights: The Need for Further Law Reform' (1989) 5 Duke Law Journal 1254, 1257.

45 See *Prosecutor v Lubanga Dyilo* (Request to the Democratic Republic of the Congo for the purpose of obtaining the identification, tracing, freezing and seizure of property and assets belonging to Mr. Thomas Lubanga Dyilo) ICC-01/04-01/06-22-tEN (9 March 2006); *Prosecutor v Lubanga Dyilo* (Request to States Parties to the Rome Statute for the Identification, Tracing and Freezing or Seizure of the Property and Assets of Mr Thomas Lubanga Dyilo) ICC-01/04-01/06-62-tEN (31 March 2006).

46 See *Prosecutor v Katanga* (Request to the Democratic Republic of the Congo for the purpose of obtaining the identification, tracing, freezing and seizure of the property and assets of Germain Katanga) ICC-01/04-01/07-7-tENG (6 July 2007).

47 *Prosecutor v Bemba Gombo* (Decision et demande en vue d'obtenir l'identification, la localisation, le gel et la saisie des biens et avoirs adressées a la Republique portugaise) ICC-01/05-01/08-8 (27 May 2008) (*Bemba* Seizure Decision).

48 *Prosecutor v Muthaura, Kenyatta and Ali* (Decision Ordering the Registrar to Prepare and Transmit a Request for Cooperation to the Republic of Kenya for the Purpose of Securing the Identification, Tracing

reported in November 2011, by then ICC Prosecutor, Luis Moreno Ocampo, to the UN Security Council, that '[t]he Court ha[d] sent ... requests for assistance to Libya, State Parties, and five UN Security Council non-State Parties to identify, trace, seize and freeze all the personal assets belonging to the suspects',[49] namely Saif Al-Islam Gaddafi and Abdullah Al-Senussi.[50] The following section will examine the practice of the Court with respect to requests for measures under Article 57(3)(3) of the Rome Statute and the relevant RPE, to the extent that its decisions and orders have been classified as public.

5.3.1 *The purpose of protective measures and the range of assets susceptible thereto*

Article 93(1)(k) of the Rome Statute, which governs forms of co-operation that the Court can request from States Parties, does not explicitly provide that the latter should assist the Court in identifying, tracing, freezing and seizing assets for the purpose of *reparations*; rather, such measures can be requested 'for the purpose of eventual forfeiture'.[51] This said, Article 57(3)(e) of the Rome Statute explicitly refers to the 'ultimate benefit of victims' in the context of the Pre-Trial Chamber requesting 'protective measures for the purpose of forfeiture' pursuant to Article 93(1)(k).[52] On a restrictive reading of Articles 93(1)(k) and 57(3)(e) of the Rome Statute, one could conclude that such measures ought to be targeted only at ensuring the enforcement of the penalty of forfeiture in the event of a conviction. Such a narrow reading would have accorded minimal weight to the 'ultimate benefit of victims' in the pre-trial protective measures process, other than those who might have a claim to forfeited 'proceeds, property and assets derived directly or indirectly' from the crime(s) of which the accused was convicted in accordance with the forfeiture procedures contained in the Rome Statute.[53] Such an interpretation was considered, but ultimately rejected, by Pre-Trial Chamber I in *Lubanga*,[54] which instead opined as follows:

---

and Freezing or Seizure of Property and Assets of Francis Kirimi Muthaura, Uhuru Muigai Kenyatta and Mohammed Hussein Ali) ICC-01/09-02/11-42 (5 April 2011) (*Muthaura, Kenyatta and Ali* Seizure Order).

49 ICC Prosecutor, 'Prosecutor's statement to the United Nations Security Council on the situation in Libya, pursuant to UNSCR 1970 (2011)' (New York, 2 November 2011) <https://www.legal-tools.org/doc/bil32o/> accessed 31 August 2020.

50 ibid.

51 Rome Statute, art 93(1)(k).

52 ibid art 57(3)(3).

53 ibid art 77(2) ('In addition to imprisonment, the Court may order: ... (b) A forfeiture of proceeds, property and assets derived directly or indirectly from that crime, without prejudice to the rights of bona fide third parties.')

54 *Lubanga* Arrest Warrant Decision (n 37) para 132 ('The Chamber notes that, although a first reading of article 57 (3) (e) of the Statute might lead to the conclusion that cooperation requests for the taking of protective measures under such a provision can be aimed only at guaranteeing the enforcement of a future

> As the power conferred on the Court to grant reparations to victims is one of the distinctive features of the Court, intended to alleviate, as much as possible, the negative consequences of their victimisation, it will be in the 'ultimate interest of victims' if pursuant to article 57 (3) (e) [of the Rome Statute], the cooperation of States Parties can be sought in order to take protective measures for the purpose of securing the enforcement of a future reparation award.
>
> In the Chamber's view, the reparation scheme provided for in the Statute is not only one of the Statute's unique features. It is also a key feature. In the Chamber's opinion, the success of the Court is, to some extent, linked to the success of its reparation system. In this context, the Chamber considers that early tracing, identification and freezing or seizure of the property and assets of the person against whom a case is launched through the issuance of a warrant of arrest or a summons to appear is a necessary tool to ensure that, if that person is finally convicted, individual or collective reparation awards ordered in favour of victims will be enforced. Should this not happen, the Chamber finds that by the time an accused person is convicted and a reparation award ordered, there will be no property or assets available to enforce the award.
>
> In the Chamber's view, existing technology makes it possible for a person to place most of his assets and moveable property beyond the Court's reach in only a few days. Therefore, if assets and property are not seized or frozen at the time of the execution of a co-operation request for arrest and surrender, or very soon thereafter, it is likely that the subsequent efforts of the Pre-Trial Chamber, the Prosecution or the victims participating in the case will be fruitless.[55]

But this conclusion by Pre-Trial Chamber I was not the end of the matter, with the issue again coming to prominence in the case against Uhuru Muigai Kenyatta and others.

Following disclosure to the public of confidential information, including to the accused, Uhuru Muigai Kenyatta, on 21 October 2014, ICC Trial Chamber V(b) reclassified as

---

penalty of forfeiture under article 77 (2) of the Statute, the literal interpretation of the scope of such provision is not clear, because of the reference to the "ultimate benefit of the victims".')

55 ibid paras 135-37 (footnotes omitted). See also *Prosecutor v Lubanga Dyilo* (Decision Establishing the Principles and Procedures to be Applied to Reparations) ICC-01/04-01/06-2904 (7 August 2012) para 277 ('The identification and freezing of any assets of the convicted person are a fundamental element in securing effective reparations, and pursuant to Article 93(l)(k) of the Statute, State Parties should provide the Court with timely and effective assistance at the earliest possible stage of the proceedings').

public a series of documents concerning pre-trial protective measures in the cases in the *Situation in the Republic of Kenya*.[56] On 5 April 2011, in the case against Francis Kirimi Muthaura, Uhuru Muigai Kenyatta and Mohammed Hussein Ali, Pre-Trial Chamber II ordered the Registrar, in consultation with the Prosecutor, to request co-operation from Kenya 'for purposes of identifying, tracing and freezing or seizing the property and assets belonging to or under the control of Francis Kirimi Muthaura, Uhuru Muigai Kenyatta and Mohammed Hussein Ali, without prejudice to the rights of *bona fide* third parties' and to regularly inform the Chamber of any action taken in the execution of this order.[57]

However, the Government of the Republic of Kenya refused to execute the order. In its submissions, the Kenyan Government expressed the following view:

> ... the Pre-Trial Chamber's Order lacks legal basis and should be revoked. It reiterated its view that Articles 93(1)(k) and 57(3)(e) of the Statute, as well as Rule 99 of the Rules, read together, provide three basic pre-requisites which must be satisfied prior to making a request for cooperation under these provisions: (i) that the criminal offences have been proven, after a full trial; (ii) that the Court found that the person obtained the proceeds, property and assets directly or indirectly from the commission of the crime: and/or (iii) that in committing the crime the accused person employed the property and assets identified.[58]

Trial Chamber V(b), by majority, Judge Henderson dissenting, rejected the submission that, when requesting protective measures, a nexus is required between the assets and the commission of the crime(s). According to the Trial Chamber:

> The Majority observes that Article 93(1)(k) of the Statute is broadly phrased and allows a Chamber to request cooperation from a State in implementing protective measures in respect of proceeds, property and assets, and 'instrumentalities of crimes'. The text makes no distinction concerning whether such property or assets must have been derived directly or indirectly from a crime, as explicitly required under Article 77(2)(b) of the Statute. Read plainly, a request for protective measures in respect of property or assets does not

56 *Prosecutor v Kenyatta* (Order concerning the public disclosure of confidential information) ICC-01/09-02/11-967 (21 October 2014).

57 *Muthaura, Kenyatta and Ali* Seizure Order (n 48) Disposition.

58 *Kenyatta* Implementation Decision (n 13) para 10, citing *Prosecutor v Kenyatta* (Submissions of the Government of the Republic of Kenya pursuant to the 'Order for Submissions on the Implementation of the Request regarding the Freezing of Assets') ICC-01/09-02/11-923-Conf-Corr (28 May 2014) para 12.

> require a nexus between the crimes for which the accused is summoned, charged or convicted, unless it is made solely for the purposes of Article 77(2)(b) of the Statute. In addition, even in those circumstances, any determinative finding as to actual nexus between the proceeds, property or assets in question and crimes could only be made under Article 77(2)(b) of the Statute after conviction.[59]

In *Kenyatta*, Trial Chamber V(b) adopted a broad interpretation of the Rome Statute and RPE in confirming that assets subject to protective measures include those without any nexus to the crimes of which the accused person is suspected, unlike proceeds, property and assets susceptible to the penalty of forfeiture, which, pursuant to Article 77(2)(b) of the Rome Statute, have to be 'derived directly or indirectly from that crime'.[60] However, in his Dissenting Opinion, Judge Henderson expressed the view that Article 57(3)(e) of the Rome Statute and Rule 99(1) of the ICC RPE do not allow the Pre-Trial Chamber to request protective measures for the purpose of an order for reparations,[61] presenting a challenge to the Court's earlier findings in *Lubanga*. According to Judge Henderson:

> I do not read the phrase 'in particular for the ultimate benefit of victims' contained in Article 57(3)(e) of the Statute as expanding the authority of the Pre-Trial Chamber under that Article beyond that which is expressly stated. Rather, I see this phrase as an acknowledgment that in taking the significant step of prospectively freezing or seizing the property or assets of a person who is presumed innocent, the Pre-Trial Chamber shall take into consideration – in addition to the strength of the evidence and the rights of the accused person – whether such measures would in particular be for the ultimate benefit of the victims. ... In my view, this objective can be effectively achieved by the Pre-Trial Chamber requesting protective measures for the purposes of eventual forfeiture, which in appropriate circumstances can be transferred to the Trust Fund and thereafter used for the benefit of the victims in an award for reparations, as provided in the plain text of Article 57(3)(e) of the Statute.[62]

Here, Judge Henderson questions the broad interpretation given to the pre-trial protective measures procedures in the Rome Statute and RPE by the majority of Trial Chamber V(b) in *Kenyatta*, whose view is consistent with that adopted by Pre-Trial Chamber I in the

59 *Kenyatta* Implementation Decision (n 13) para 16.
60 Rome Statute, art 77(2)(b).
61 *Prosecutor v Kenyatta* (Dissenting Opinion of Judge Henderson) ICC-01/09-02/11-931-Anx (8 July 2014).
62 ibid paras 5 and 7.

Lubanga and *Katanga* cases. Judge Henderson's concern is valid. Though the reading of Article 57(3)(e) of the Rome Statute adopted in the Court's earlier case law broadens the range of assets susceptible to protective measures with a view to funding potential future reparations, this has implications for accused persons, who, at the pre-trial stage, must be presumed innocent and remain entitled to the peaceful enjoyment of their possessions.

In *Kilolo*, Judge Schmitt, on behalf of Trial Chamber VII, interpreted Article 57(3)(e) of the Rome Statute in the same manner as Pre-Trial Chamber I in *Lubanga* and the majority of Trial Chamber V(b) in *Kenyatta*, thereby refusing to endorse the narrower interpretation proposed by Judge Henderson in his Dissenting Opinion in the latter case.[63]

The issue was ultimately settled by the Appeals Chamber, which confirmed the approach of the *Kenyatta* majority, in February 2016.[64] Importantly, the Appeals Chamber notes that 'the freezing of assets constitutes a provisional protective measure which must be applied in a manner consistent with article 21 (3) of the Statute'.[65] It might therefore be expected that when such measures are imposed or subject to review, the chamber in question would take the rights and interests of the accused and any bona fide third parties, as well as the ultimate benefit of victims, into consideration. Particularly persuasive in the Judgment of the Appeals Chamber is its discussion of the object and purpose of the Rome Statute as it pertains to reparations to victims.[66] Unlike the ICTY, ICTR and SCSL, all of which had the power to order protective measures but where victims could only claim compensation 'in a national court or other competent body',[67] the ICC is authorised by Article 75 of the Rome Statute to order reparations directly to the victims of crimes under its jurisdiction.[68]

After observing that the Rome Statute also provides for an enforcement mechanism under Article 75(4) and Article 109 of the Rome Statute,[69] the Appeals Chamber concluded:

> an interpretation of the Statute that brings the property and assets of the suspect or accused person that will be potentially subject to reparations orders in the

63 *Prosecutor v Bemba Gombo and others* (Decision on the 'Requête de la défense aux fins de levée du gel des avoirs de Monsieur Aimé Kilolo Musamba') ICC-01/05-01/13-1485-Red (17 November 2015) (*Kilolo* Lifting Decision) paras 17-18.

64 *Prosecutor v [Redacted]* (Judgment on the appeal of the Prosecutor against the decision of [REDACTED]) ICC-ACRed-01/16 (15 February 2016).

65 ibid para 53.

66 ibid.

67 ibid, citing ICTY RPE, r 106 (B); ICTR RPE, r 106 (B); SCSL RPE, r 105 (B).

68 ibid, referring to Rome Statute, art 75 and ICC RPE, r 94.

69 ibid, referring to Rome Statute, arts 75(4) and 109.

> event of conviction within the scope of protective measures under articles 57 (3) (e) and 93 (1) (k) of the Statute consolidates the effectiveness of the reparations system and is thus consistent with the object and purpose of the Statute.[70]

By clarifying the interpretation of these provisions, the Appeals Chamber has given legal certainty to the implicated stakeholders. According to Carla Ferstman, the decision of the majority in *Kenyatta* and, it is argued, its confirmation by Judge Schmitt in *Kilolo* and by the Appeals Chamber, was 'a progressive interpretation of the statutory framework which should encourage legal representatives of victims to actively engage with the OTP and the relevant Chambers on the issue of asset orders, for the ultimate benefit of victims.'[71] In other words, by broadly interpreting the protective measures provisions in the Rome Statute and ICC RPE to take into account orders for reparations, the Court has demonstrated its commitment to the ultimate benefit of victims in Article 57(3)(e) of the ICC Statute. The following section examines how the Court has balanced this consideration with the rights and interests of other stakeholders in the pre-trial protective measures process.

5.3.2 Balancing competing rights and interests in the protective measures process

The ultimate benefit of victims may be in direct competition with the rights and interests accruing to other parties concerned in the Article 57(3)(e) process. Competing rights and interests can be identified most clearly in the Court's case law as between the Prosecutor and victims on the one hand and accused persons and their family members on the other. While the Prosecutor and victims may have a shared interest, albeit perhaps for different reasons, in seeing protective measures ordered (or maintained), accused persons and their dependents may have reasons to request that such measures be denied (or rescinded). In cases where rights and interests are found to be in competition, the Court is able to apply the legal framework at its disposal in order to strike a fair balance between them.

On 24 May 2008, Mr Jean-Pierre Bemba Gombo was arrested near Brussels by Belgian authorities following the issuance of an arrest warrant by the ICC.[72] On 27 May 2008, four

70 ibid.

71 Carla Ferstman, 'Cooperation and the International Criminal Court: The Freezing, Seizing and Transfer of Assets for the Purpose of Reparations' in Olympia Bekou and Daley J Birkett (eds), *Cooperation and the International Criminal Court: Perspectives from Theory and Practice* (Brill Nijhoff 2016) 236.

72 *Prosecutor v Bemba Gombo* (Warrant of Arrest for Jean-Pierre Bemba Gombo) ICC-01/05-01/08-1-tENG (23 May 2008).

days after his arrest warrant was issued, ICC Pre-Trial Chamber III, noting *inter alia* Article 57(3)(e) of the Rome Statute and Rule 99(1) of the RPE, issued a request for co-operation to Portugal to identify, trace, freeze and seize any property and assets belonging to Bemba located on its territory, subject to the rights of bona fide third parties.[73]

Bemba's application for legal assistance having been rejected because he was found not to be indigent,[74] his defence counsel requested a partial lifting of the seizure order.[75] On 10 October 2008, Pre-Trial Chamber III requested the competent Portuguese authorities 'to authorise temporarily the release of the amount of €36,260 on a monthly basis from [Bemba's] account [REDACTED] in Portugal as of 1 October 2008 until a decision on the confirmation of charges has been issued.'[76] These funds were released (1) to enable Bemba to cover fees payable to his defence team and (2) to support his family. Pre-Trial Chamber III reasoned as follows:

> As to the expenses for the Defence of Mr Jean-Pierre Bemba, the Chamber underlines that the disclosure process has just started. The Chamber takes note that the Defence team has to analyse in a short period of time a significant amount of documents. The Chamber considers that at this stage of the proceedings, it is critical that the Defence has adequate time and facilities for the preparation of the confirmation hearing which is scheduled to take place on 4 November 2008.
>
> Furthermore, as to the expenses of Mr Jean-Pierre Bemba to support his family, the Chamber acknowledges that he has financial obligations to his family and must be able to pay for the basic needs of his wife and children.[77]

Pre-Trial Chamber III did not engage in a lengthy discussion of the rights of the accused at issue, that is to say the right to respect for private and family life and the right to a fair trial.[78] Notwithstanding, it can be argued that acknowledging Bemba's familial obligations and the 'needs of his wife and children' implicitly recognizes these rights, guaranteed under

73 *Bemba* Seizure Decision (n 47) para 4, Disposition.
74 *Prosecutor v Bemba Gombo* (Registrar's Decision on the Application for Legal Assistance paid by the Court Filed by Mr Jean-Pierre Bemba Gombo) ICC-01/05-01/08-76-tENG (25 August 2008).
75 *Prosecutor v Bemba Gombo* (Requête en mainlevée de saisie (Application for Lifting the Seizure) ICC-01/05-01/08-81-Conf-tENG (26 August 2008).
76 *Bemba* First Lifting Decision (n 24) Disposition.
77 ibid paras 15-16.
78 cf the extensive discussion of the jurisprudence of the ECtHR by the ICC Presidency in *Prosecutor v Bemba Gombo* (Reasons for the decision on the Applications for judicial review of Mr Jean-Pierre Bemba Gombo of 10 and 11 November 2008) ICC-01/05-01/08-310 (5 December 2008) paras 32-43.

international human rights law and, consequently, Article 21(3) of the Rome Statute. This is not to say that a more extensive discussion of the rights of the accused was necessarily merited in the case at hand. Because Bemba's application for lifting the freezing of assets remains confidential at the time of writing, it cannot be discerned whether he alleged any violation thereof. The manner in which this issue was addressed by the Court thus cannot be found wanting in this respect. Nor can it be claimed that the Decision fails to take the rights afforded to Bemba and his family under international human rights law seriously.

This issue again came to light in Bemba's request for the release of further seized funds. According to Pre-Trial Chamber III's decision disposing of the application:

> Firstly, counsels of Mr Jean-Pierre Bemba requested the lifting of seizure or freezing of € 78,900 on a monthly basis starting on 1 October 2008 to cover both his financial obligations to his family as well as to his counsels. Secondly, the Defence estimated that it would need €100,000 to cover its investigation activities. Thirdly, the Defence requested € 234,000 in order to cover Mr Jean-Pierre Bemba's family expenses and his counsels' fees from the date of his arrest in the Kingdom of Belgium until September 2008.[79]

Pre-Trial Chamber III rejected Bemba's application,[80] emphasizing that he had failed to 'demonstrate any change of circumstances in [his] financial situation … since 10 October 2008 and … support [his] Second Application with any documentation such as official invoices.'[81] It can therefore be reasonably assumed that, had Bemba demonstrated such a change in his circumstances (ie presumably to his detriment), supported by sufficient documentary evidence, the Pre-Trial Chamber might not have dismissed his application. This seems to be a perfectly reasonable application of the legal framework, balancing the interests of the accused (and his family) with those of the Prosecutor and victims.

This balance again came to the fore in the case against Jean-Pierre Bemba Gombo, Aimé Kilolo Musamba, Jean-Jacques Mangenda Kabongo, Fidèle Babala Wandu and Narcisse Arido, specifically as concerns Mr Kilolo, a former member of Bemba's defence team.

On 20 November 2013, Judge Cuno Tarfusser, designated as Single Judge on behalf of ICC Pre-Trial Chamber II, ordered the arrest of Jean-Pierre Bemba Gombo, Aimé Kilolo Musamba, Jean-Jacques Mangenda Kabongo, Fidèle Babala Wandu and Narcisse Arido

---

79 *Bemba* Second Lifting Decision (n 25) para 8.

80 ibid Disposition.

81 ibid para 24.

for their alleged commission of offences against the administration of justice.[82] Pursuant to this order, Belgium seized a bank account under its jurisdiction in Kilolo's name.[83] Kilolo's defence argued that the seizure of his assets was contrary to the Rome Statute. Among other reasons, he submitted that the seizure infringed his right to family life.[84]

Judge Bertram Schmitt, sitting as Single Judge, rejected Kilolo's request in its entirety.[85] As to Kilolo's argument that the seizure of his assets violated his right to family life, Judge Schmitt reasoned as follows:

> As a provisional measure under Article 57(3)(e) of the Statute, the freezing of assets (and its maintenance) must be applied in a manner consistent with Article 21(3) of the Statute. The Single Judge is attentive to Mr Kilolo's argument that the (maintenance of) seizure of said bank account would infringe his right to family life insofar as he purportedly cannot meet his financial obligations towards his family, including his young children. However, … the Single Judge is unconvinced that this provisional measure infringes upon Mr Kilolo's right to family life. The Single Judge recalls that the measure was justified as it was taken in accordance with the law and for a legitimate aim … . The Single Judge also finds that the measure is proportionate vis-à-vis the legitimate aim pursued.[86]

In *Kilolo*, unlike in *Bemba*, Trial Chamber VII explicitly confirmed that, in applying and interpreting Article 57(3)(e) of the Rome Statute and Rule 99(1) of the ICC RPE, both of which are primary sources of law under Article 21(1) of the Rome Statute, the ICC must take steps to ensure their consistency with 'internationally recognized human rights',[87] an important safeguard in the protective measures process. Judge Schmitt, in keeping with the Court's general practice,[88] followed the approach of the ECtHR with regard to limiting

---

82 *Prosecutor v Bemba Gombo and others* (Warrant of arrest for Jean-Pierre Bemba Gombo, Aimé Kilolo Musamba, Jean-Jacques Mangenda Kabongo, Fidèle Babala Wandu and Narcisse Arido) ICC-01/05-01/13-1-tENG (20 November 2013).

83 *Kilolo* Lifting Decision (n 63) para 2.

84 ibid para 15, referring to *Prosecutor v Bemba Gombo and others* (Addendum à la "Requête de la défense aux fins de levée du gel des avoirs de Monsieur Aimé Kilolo Musamba") ICC-01/05-01/13-1014-Conf-Exp (28 July 2015) paras 15, 28.

85 *Kilolo* Lifting Decision (n 63) Disposition.

86 *Kilolo* Lifting Decision (n 63) paras 21-22 (footnotes omitted).

87 *Kilolo* Lifting Decision (n 63) para 21.

88 On which, see Annika Jones, 'Insights Into an Emerging Relationship: Use of Human Rights Jurisprudence at the International Criminal Court' (2016) 16 Human Rights Law Review 701, 724; Nicolas AJ Croquet, 'The International Criminal Court and the Treatment of Defence Rights: A Mirror of the European Court of Human Rights' Jurisprudence?' (2011) 11 Human Rights Law Review 91; and Volker Nerlich, 'Article 21

the exercise of the right, in this instance, to the peaceful enjoyment of (private and) family life. In other words, he assessed whether the protective measure: (i) 'was taken in accordance with the law';[89] (2) 'for a legitimate aim';[90] and (3) whether it was 'proportionate' to that aim.[91] Here, Judge Schmitt uses the approach of the ECtHR to interpret Article 21(3) of the ICC Statute and his reasons for rejecting Kilolo's request are numerous and clear. According to Judge Schmitt:

> Mr Kilolo was released from detention in October 2014 and joined his family in Belgium. He also confirms that he resumed his profession as a lawyer in Brussels. Mr Kilolo is not subjected to any condition which unreasonably impedes the exercise of his profession and, thus, provide for his family. No further specific arguments are provided which demonstrate that Mr Kilolo lacks the means to support his family financially. As a result, the Single Judge finds that Mr Kilolo's right to family life is not unduly interfered with.[92]

As to Kilolo's request for a partial lifting of the seizure order, Judge Schmitt rejected the request as inappropriate. He reasoned:

> As explained above, Mr Kilolo's personal circumstances allow him to provide for his family. Considering the amount seized, a monthly release of [REDACTED] would significantly reduce the sum contained in said bank account, thus rendering the provisional measure meaningless. No other measures appear available which would adequately ensure that the Court's interests underlying the seizure order would still be protected in the event that the seizure were to be partially lifted.[93]

Though the Single Judge rejected the accused's request, it cannot be said that the ultimate benefit of victims was unfairly prioritized above the rights of the accused and his family members in this Decision. Judge Schmitt identifies a number of legitimate aims pursued by the protective measures ordered against Kilolo. These include the need to preserve the assets for the enforcement of a possible penalty of forfeiture in the future,[94] to meet any

(3) of the ICC Statute: Identifying and Applying "Internationally Recognized Human Rights"' in Paolo Lobba and Triestino Mariniello (eds), *Judicial Dialogue on Human Rights: The Practice of International Criminal Tribunals* (Brill Nijhoff 2017) 82.

89 *Kilolo* Lifting Decision (n 63) para 22

90 ibid.

91 ibid.

92 ibid.

93 ibid para 23.

94 ibid para 17.

potential obligations on Kilolo's part vis-à-vis 'other types of forfeiture', ie an order for reparations,[95] to secure the assets 'in order to meet potential fine orders of the Court',[96] and to enable the ICC to recover the costs of Kilolo's legal assistance should he be found to have had the means to cover such expenses.[97] Judge Schmitt then reasons that Kilolo is able to continue his work as a lawyer, the proceeds of which he deems sufficient for the support supporting his family,[98] rendering the protective measures proportionate to these aims. Finally, the Single Judge observes that no measure other than the continued seizure of Kilolo's assets would protect 'the Court's interests underlying the seizure order'.[99] In other words, the interests of the Prosecutor, in enforcing potential future fines and orders for forfeiture, and the ultimate benefit of victims, in seeing that reparations awards are enforced in the event of a conviction, can only be safeguarded through the maintenance of the protective measures. On the other hand, in the view of Judge Schmitt, the interests of Kilolo in meeting his financial obligations towards his family can be met through the continued exercise of his profession, which is not inhibited by the ongoing seizure of his assets. Had Kilolo shown that he 'lack[ed] the means to support his family financially',[100] it would appear reasonable to assume that Judge Schmitt would have decided otherwise.

The ICC's publicly available case law with respect to protective measures has therefore been largely consistent. Assets susceptible to requests for protective measures have not been restricted by the Court to those with a link to the crimes(s) with which an accused person is charged.[101] Further, where conflicting rights and interests have been identified, the Court has applied and interpreted the various safeguards included in the Rome Statute and RPE in a clear and transparent fashion and, moreover, in fulfilment of its duty to do so in a manner that is 'consistent with internationally recognized human rights'.[102]

95 ibid para 18.
96 ibid para 19.
97 ibid para 20, citing ICC RPE, r 21(5) ('Where a person claims to have insufficient means to pay for legal assistance and this is subsequently found not to be so, the Chamber dealing with the case at that time may make an order of contribution to recover the cost of providing counsel.')
98 ibid para 22.
99 ibid para 23.
100 ibid para 22.
101 On which, see Larissa van den Herik, 'The Individualisation of Enforcement in International Law: Exploring the Interplay between United Nations Targeted Sanctions and International Criminal Proceedings' in Tiyanjana Maluwa, Max du Plessis and Dire Tladi (eds), *The Pursuit of a Brave New World in International Law: Essays in Honour of John Dugard* (Brill Nijhoff 2017) 260 ('Article 75(4) of the ICC Statute seems to indicate that protective measures solely for reparation purposes can only be made after conviction. Yet, in practice, Pre-Trial Chambers have effectively ordered the identification, tracing, freezing or seizing of assets already in the pre-trial phase with a view to rendering the reparation system effective. In case of a request for protective measures for reparation purposes, there is no requirement that the assets have a nexus with the crime.')
102 Rome Statute, art 21(3).

5.4 Concluding remarks

Pre-trial 'protective measures for the purpose of forfeiture' are not unique to ICTs. Their availability and use can be seen in the national legal systems of States with both common and civil law legal traditions, including in Senegal, as discussed above.[103] But international criminal proceedings are not national criminal proceedings. Investigations and trials at the international level generally take much longer than domestic criminal cases. According to a study by Alette Smeulers, Barbora Hola and Tom van den Berg, the average length of time between the issuance of the indictment and trial judgment at nine ICTs was 4.9 years, while the average trial length was 2.9 years.[104]

This is not to say that all trials before ICTs take too long. Indeed, it has been argued that ICTs may be generally regarded as more 'efficient' given the complexity of the cases before them.[105] But the time required for international(ised) criminal proceedings to reach completion can lead to problems with respect to assets frozen at the arrest warrant phase, an example of which can be seen in the case of Jean-Pierre Bemba Gombo. At the time of his arrest, unlike most other suspects apprehended by the Court as of August 2020, Bemba had accumulated significant assets including a luxury private jet, as a result of his successful 'business empire'.[106] As of March 2012, it was reported that this aircraft, which had already lost its flightworthiness, had accumulated more than €126,000 in parking fees at Faro Airport, which would likely surpass the value of the aircraft in the near future.[107] On 8 June 2018, Bemba was acquitted of the charges brought against him by the Court's Prosecutor[108] and his defence has subsequently requested that any freezing orders against his assets be lifted.[109] If successful in this application, Bemba's aircraft will presumably be unfrozen and be of negative value as a result of the parking charges accumulated during his time in

---

103 See Senegalese Code of Criminal Procedure, art 87 *bis*.

104 Alette Smeulers, Barbora Hola and Tom van den Berg, 'Sixty-Five Years of International Criminal Justice: The Facts and Figures' (2013) 13 International Criminal Law Review 7, 16-18. The study provides empirical data gathered from the IMT, the IMTFE, the ICTY, the ICTR, the ICC, the SCSL, the ECCC, the STL and the Special Panels for Serious Crimes.

105 Stuart Ford, 'Complexity and Efficiency at International Criminal Courts' (2014) 29 Emory International Law Review 1.

106 At the time of his first appearance before the ICC, Jean-Pierre Bemba Gombo is reported to have owned 'a large business empire'. Marlise Simons, 'Jean-Pierre Bemba, Congolese politician, appears in Hague court' *The New York Times* (4 July 2008) <www.nytimes.com/2008/07/04/world/africa/04iht-05hague.14247286.html> accessed 31 August 2020.

107 See Bruno F Pires, 'Last stop Faro?' *Algarve 123* (15 March 2012) (copy on file with author).

108 *Prosecutor v Bemba Gombo* (Judgment on the appeal of Mr Jean-Pierre Bemba Gombo against Trial Chamber III's "Judgment pursuant to Article 74 of the Statute") ICC-01/05-01/08-3636-Red (8 June 2018).

109 *Situation in the Central African Republic* (Public Redacted Version of "Preliminary application for reclassification of filings, disclosure, accounts and partial unfreezing of Mr. Bemba's assets") ICC-01/05-01/08-3654-Red (30 October 2018). For analysis, see Chapter 8.

detention in The Hague, which, at the time of his acquittal, amounted to over ten years. It is therefore evident that the implications of decisions taken under Article 57(3)(e) of the Rome Statute and Rule 99 of the ICC RPE are potentially far-reaching.

The Rome Statute and ICC RPE include a series of due-process guarantees in respect of protective measures, the application of which can be clearly seen in the ICC's case law. Those most clearly affected are accused persons, the Prosecutor, potential victims and bona fide third parties. The three factors to be considered by the Pre-Trial Chamber under Article 57(3)(e) are: (i) the strength of the evidence; (ii) the rights of the parties concerned in the process; and (iii) the ultimate benefit of victims. Consequently, although not 'parties' to proceedings to the same extent as the Prosecutor and accused persons, victims' interests are given significant weight in the ICC legal framework as concerns protective measures. This is also borne out through an analysis of the Court's case law.

In discussing the most suitable approach to balancing the rights of accused persons with the rights of victims before the ICC, Salvatore Zappalà expressed the following opinion: 'it is often difficult to strike the proper balance between conflicting interests on a case-by-case basis. The case-by-case approach creates problems of consistency in the treatment of different defendants, which in turn threatens the principle of equality before the law.'[110] This chapter has sought to demonstrate that the Court has in its publicly available case law applied the safeguards in its legal framework with an even hand. From this jurisprudence, the parties to, and other participants concerned with, the protective measures process are able to seek largely consistent guidance with respect to ongoing (and future) proceedings pertaining to the protective identification, tracing, freezing and/or seizure of assets. Given the interests at stake, the Court's approach to protective measures is largely praiseworthy. This said, as Chapter 7 shows, there remains scope, on occasion, for clearer reasoning on the part of the ICC as to how the case law of human rights courts is utilised, not least in view of the differences between the institutions' respective mandates. Before turning to this important issue, however, the following chapter assesses the (quasi-)legal protections available to those individuals whose assets are frozen at the request of the UNSC.

110 Salvatore Zappalà, 'The Rights of Victims v. the Rights of the Accused' (2010) 8 Journal of International Criminal Justice 137, 142.

6 UNSC-Requested Asset Freezes and the Legal Protection of Individuals

6.1 Introduction

UNSC sanctions procedures have evolved in manifold ways since their inception in the years following the adoption of the UN Charter. Not only can one witness the employment of more selective measures, including targeted asset freezes, and the propagation of sanctions regimes and committees appointed to monitor their implementation, but also the growth of the number of (quasi-)legal protections granted to those who find themselves listed. This chapter explores those safeguards. In so doing, it finds that the protections afforded to individuals (and entities) varies widely depending on which sanctions committee it is that lists them. It also shows that none of the (quasi-)legal protections, even taken together, can be said to equate to full judicial review. Before turning to the implementation of these protections, the vast majority of which were (first) introduced in the context of the Security Council Committee established pursuant to resolutions 1267 (1999) 1904 (2011) and 2253 (2015) concerning Islamic State in Iraq and the Levant (Da'esh), Al-Qaida and associated individuals, groups, undertakings and entities,[1] however, the evolution of UNSC-requested sanctions will be briefly discussed.

6.2 The Evolution of UNSC Sanctions: From General to Targeted Measures

The UNSC first mandated UN Member States to implement sanctions in 1966 in response to 'the unilateral declaration of independence made by a racist minority in Southern Rhodesia'.[2] In Resolution 232, the UNSC prevented States from *inter alia* importing 'asbestos, iron ore, chrome, pig-iron, sugar, tobacco, copper, meat and meat products and

1 The Resolution 1267 Committee was first instituted to monitor implementation of sanctions against the Taliban before the UNSC split it into two: one for Al-Qaida (later expanded to include ISIL) and one for the Taliban.

2 UNSC Res 216 (12 November 1965) UN Doc S/RES/216, para 1. This resolution did not establish 'mandatory' sanctions. Instead, the UN organ 'call[ed] upon all States not to recognize this illegal racist minority régime in Southern Rhodesia and to refrain from rendering any assistance to this illegal régime'. ibid para 2. For analysis of the sanctions against Southern Rhodesia and subsequent UNSC-ordered sanctions, see Mary Ellen O'Connell, 'Debating the Law of Sanctions' (2002) 13 European Journal of International Law 63.

hides, skins and leather originating in Southern Rhodesia and exported therefrom'.[3] Other restrictions included those on the transfer of funds to Southern Rhodesia for the purpose of promoting such exports and the promotion of the sale or shipment of arms and ammunitions as well as military equipment and vehicles thereto.[4] The UNSC extended these measures in Resolution 253[5] before bringing an end to the sanctions regime in December 1979[6] following 'agreement on the Constitution for a free and independent Zimbabwe providing for genuine majority rule'.[7] In 1977, the UN organ decided to impose a mandatory arms embargo against South Africa on the grounds of, among others, its military activities in neighbouring States and its unrelenting observance of the system of apartheid.[8] These restrictions endured until 1994 when the UNSC 'welcome[d] the first all-race multiparty election and the establishment of a united, democratic, non-racial government of South Africa'[9] and terminated the sanctions regime in response thereto. It was not until the early 1990s, however, that the number of UNSC sanctions regimes proliferated, beginning with the adoption of comprehensive measures, involving a sweeping assets freeze, against Iraq a few days after its invasion and ensuing occupation of Kuwait in August 1990.[10] The appointment of sanctions committees for (and the imposition of comprehensive measures against) Yugoslavia and Haiti followed in 1991-1992[11] and 1993-1994,[12] respectively.

3 UNSC Res 232 (16 December 1966) UN Doc S/RES/231, para 2(a).
4 ibid paras 2(b)-2(f).
5 UNSC Res 253 (29 May 1968) UN Doc S/RES/253.
6 UNSC Res 460 (21 December 1979) para 2.
7 ibid preamble.
8 See UNSC Res 418 (4 November 1977) UN Doc S/RES/418.
9 See UNSC Res 919 (26 May 1994) UN Doc S/RES/919.
10 UNSC Res 661 (6 August 1990) UN Doc S/RES/661.
11 For the establishment of the sanctions committee for Yugoslavia, see UNSC Res 721 (15 December 1991) UN Doc S/RES/721, para 5(b). For the adoption of comprehensive measures, see UNSC Res 757 (30 May 1992) UN Doc S/RES/757, para 4 ff. The UNSC terminated the mandate of the sanctions committee and the comprehensive measures against Yugoslavia in UNSC Res 1074 (1 October 1996) UN Doc S/RES/1074, para 2.
12 For the institution of the sanctions committee for Haiti, see UNSC Res 841 (16 June 1993) UN Doc S/RES/841, para 10. For the imposition of comprehensive measures, see UNSC Res 917 (6 May 1994) UN Doc S/RES/914, para 2 ff. It was in UNSC Res 944 (29 September 1994) UN Doc S/RES/944, paras 4-5, that the UN body brought an end to the comprehensive sanctions and terminated the mandate of the sanctions committee for Haiti.

The measures had negative humanitarian consequences for the civilian populations in Iraq,[13] Yugoslavia,[14] and Haiti,[15] which partially[16] led the UNSC to exclusively adopt 'targeted' or 'smart' sanctions regimes thereafter.[17] According to Biersteker, Tourinho and Eckert:

> Targeted sanctions differ from comprehensive measures in that they are discriminating policy measures. Rather than being applied indiscriminately on an entire country (as comprehensive sanctions are) with resultant harmful humanitarian consequences, targeted sanctions are focused on specific individuals, entities, sectors, and/or regions of a country.[18]

Among other targeted measures, the freezing of individuals' and entities' assets is one of the tools the UNSC has adopted in exercising its responsibilities under the UN Charter.[19] But the use of these measures by the UN body is not unfettered, with several (quasi-)legal protections found in UNSC resolutions appointing sanctions committees and other documents governing the work of these entities. Indeed, even the extensive asset freezing measures imposed against Iraqi assets in the aftermath of its invasion of Kuwait included a humanitarian exception:

13 See eg Richard Garfield, 'Morbidity and Mortality Among Iraqi Children from 1990 Through 1998: Assessing the Impact of the Gulf War and Economic Sanctions' (Campaign Against Sanctions on Iraq (CASI), July 1999) <http://www.casi.org.uk/info/garfield/dr-garfield.html> accessed 31 August 2020; Mohamed M Ali and Iqbal H Shah, 'Sanctions and childhood mortality in Iraq' (2000) 355 The Lancet 1851. See also Geoff Simons, *The Scourging of Iraq: Sanctions, Law and Natural Justice* (Macmillan 1996); Eric Hoskins, 'The Humanitarian Impacts of Economic Sanctions and War in Iraq' in Thomas G Weiss and others (eds), *Political Gain and Civilian Pain: Humanitarian Impacts of Economic Sanctions* (Rowman & Littlefield 1998) 91.

14 See eg Julia Devin and Jaleh Dashti-Gibson, 'Sanctions in the Former Yugoslavia: Convoluted Goals and Complicated Consequences' in Thomas G Weiss and others (eds), *Political Gain and Civilian Pain: Humanitarian Impacts of Economic Sanctions* (Rowman & Littlefield 1998) 149.

15 See eg Elizabeth D Gibbons, *Sanctions in Haiti: Human Rights and Democracy Under Assault* (Praeger 1999); Sarah Zaidi, 'Humanitarian Effects of the Coup and Sanctions in Haiti' in Thomas G Weiss and others (eds), *Political Gain and Civilian Pain: Humanitarian Impacts of Economic Sanctions* (Rowman & Littlefield 1998) 189.

16 The political effectiveness of the measures has also been called into question. See eg Robert A Pape, 'Why Economic Sanctions Do Not Work' (1997) 22 International Security 90; David Cortright and George A Lopez, 'Introduction: Assessing Smart Sanctions: Lessons from the 1990s' in David Cortright and George A Lopez (eds), *Smart Sanctions: Targeting Economic Statecraft* (Rowman & Littlefield 2002) 2 ('these twin impulses – to reduce unintended humanitarian consequences and enhance political effectiveness – have led to the use of targeted and selective sanctions.')

17 Thomas J Biersteker, Marcos Tourinho and Sue E Eckert, 'Thinking about United Nations targeted sanctions' in Thomas J Biersteker, Sue E Eckert and Marcos Tourinho (eds), *Targeted Sanctions: The Impacts and Effectiveness of United Nations Actions* (CUP 2016) 11.

18 ibid 13.

19 For discussion of the legal basis of UNSC sanctions, see Chapter 3.

> Decides that all States shall not make available to the Government of Iraq, or to any commercial, industrial or public utility undertaking in Iraq or Kuwait, any funds or any other financial or economic resources and shall prevent their nationals and any persons within their territories from removing from their territories or otherwise making available to that Government or to any such undertaking any such funds or resources and from remitting any other funds to persons or bodies within Iraq or Kuwait, *except payments exclusively for strictly medical or humanitarian purposes and, in humanitarian circumstances, foodstuffs*[.][20]

The following section identifies and examines the (quasi-)legal protections that form part of some UNSC targeted sanctions regimes.

6.3 Identifying (Quasi-)Legal Protections

6.3.1 *Exemptions*

The UNSC has, beginning with Resolution 1452,[21] authorised exemptions to certain targeted sanctions regimes to allow listed individuals to maintain access the 'necessities of life.'[22] For instance, Resolution 1970, which established a targeted sanctions regime for Libya and which included the adoption of an asset freeze against Muammar Gaddafi and five of his children,[23] provides for three categories exemptions in the following terms:

> [T]he measures imposed … do not apply to funds, other financial assets or economic resources that have been determined by relevant Member States:
>
> To be necessary for basic expenses, including payment for foodstuffs, rent or mortgage, medicines and medical treatment, taxes, insurance premiums, and public utility charges or exclusively for payment of reasonable professional fees

20 UNSC Res 661 (n 10) para 4 (emphasis added).

21 UNSC Res 1452 (20 December 2002) UN Doc S/RES/1452, para 1.

22 Matthew Happold, 'Targeted Sanctions and Human Rights' in Matthew Happold and Paul Eden (eds), *Economic Sanctions and International Law* (Hart Publishing 2016) 93, citing *R (Adam) v Secretary of State for the Home Department* [2005] UKHL 66, [2006] 1 AC 396 [7] (Bingham LJ). Cf UNSC Res 1267 (15 October 1999) UN Doc S/RES/1267, para 4 (deciding that all UN Member States shall '[f]reeze funds and other financial resources, including funds derived or generated from property owned or controlled directly or indirectly by the Taliban, or by any undertaking owned or controlled by the Taliban … except as may be authorized by the Committee on a case-by-case basis on the grounds of humanitarian need'.)

23 UNSC Res 1970 (26 February 2011) UN Doc S/RES/1970, para 17.

> and reimbursement of incurred expenses associated with the provision of legal services in accordance with national laws, or fees or service charges, in accordance with national laws, for routine holding or maintenance of frozen funds, other financial assets and economic resources … ;
>
> To be necessary for extraordinary expenses … ; or
>
> To be the subject of a judicial, administrative or arbitral lien or judgment, in which case the funds, other financial assets and economic resources may be used to satisfy that lien or judgment provided that the lien or judgment was entered into prior to the date of the present resolution, is not for the benefit of a person or entity designated … , and has been notified by the relevant State or Member States to the Committee[.][24]

There are therefore three bases on which certain assets might be deemed exempt from UNSC-requested freezing measures: (i) assets required to meet basic expenses or 'the necessities of life';[25] (ii) assets required to meet 'extraordinary expenses' and (iii) assets required to satisfy certain liens and/or court judgments. The procedures according to which the three categories of exemption might apply to resources frozen at the request of the UNSC also differ *inter se*. For exemptions under the 'basic expenses' category, it is for the relevant State to notify the sanctions committee in the first place.[26] Authorisation will only be confirmed 'in the absence of a negative decision by the Committee within five working days of such notification'.[27] For 'extraordinary expenses', again it is for the relevant State(s) to alert the sanctions committee; the latter must then 'approve' the exemption.[28] As for the third group of exemptions, it is only for the relevant State(s) to inform the sanctions committee; no approval is required.[29] One can observe the use of similar, if not verbatim, wording in resolutions issued in the context of other sanctions committees.[30]

---

24 ibid para 19.

25 Happold, citing Bingham LJ (n 22).

26 UNSC Res 1970 (n 26) para 19(a) ('after notification by the relevant State to the Committee of the intention to authorize, where appropriate, access to such funds, other financial assets or economic resources and in the absence of a negative decision by the Committee within five working days of such notification'.)

27 ibid.

28 ibid para 19(b) ('provided that such determination has been notified by the relevant State or Member States to the Committee and has been approved by the Committee'.)

29 ibid para 19(c).

30 See eg UNSC Res 2134 (28 January 2014) UN Doc S/RES/2134, para 33; UNSC Res 2374 (5 September 2017) UN Doc S/RES/2374, para 5.

6.3.2 *The Focal Point for de-Listing*

It was in Resolution 1730 that the UNSC requested the UN Secretary-General to establish 'a focal point to receive de-listing requests.'[31] In the same resolution, the UNSC referred to 'the statement from its President of 22 June 2006',[32] in which the use of sanctions is discussed in the following terms:

> The Security Council considers sanctions an important tool in the maintenance and restoration of international peace and security. The Council resolves to ensure that sanctions are carefully targeted in support of clear objectives and are implemented in ways that balance effectiveness against possible adverse consequences. The Council is committed to ensuring that fair and clear procedures exist for placing individuals and entities on sanctions lists and for removing them, as well as for granting humanitarian exemptions … .[33]

Staying with the UNSC sanctions committee pursuant to Resolution 1970 (2011) concerning Libya, 'A petitioner seeking to submit a request for de-listing can do so either directly to the Focal Point … or through his/her State of residence or nationality'.[34] In support of a request for de-listing, the petitioner (whether an individual or entity):[35]

> should explain in the de-listing request why the designation does not or no longer meets the criteria described in paragraph 22 of resolution 1970 (2011) or paragraph 23 of resolution 1973 (2011), in particular through countering the reasons for listing as stated in the publicly releasable portion of the statement of case described above. The de-listing request should also include the petitioner's current occupation and/or activities, and any other relevant information.[36]

---

31 UNSC Res 1730 (19 December 2006) UN Doc S/RES/1730, Annex.

32 ibid preamble.

33 UNSC Presidential Statement 28 (2006) UN Doc S/PRST/2006/28.

34 Security Council Committee Established Pursuant to Resolution 1970 (2011) concerning Libya (Libya Sanctions Committee), 'Provisional Guidelines of the Committee for the Conduct of its Work as adopted by the Committee on 25 March 2011 and revised on 25 October 2011' <https://www.un.org/securitycouncil/sanctions/1970/guidelines> accessed 31 August 2020 (Libya Sanctions Committee Guidelines) para 7(c).

35 ibid (para 7(b) refers to 'individual(s), groups, undertakings, and/or entities on the List'.)

36 ibid para 7(e).

Upon receiving a request, among the Focal Point's responsibilities are: to confirm whether it is a new request or a repeated request[37] and to transmit the request to the designating State(s) and the State (or States) of the petitioner's nationality and residence.[38] 'These States are urged to review de-listing petitions in a timely manner and indicate whether they support or oppose the request in order to facilitate the Committee's review.'[39] The Guidelines also 'encourage' these States to consult *inter se* before deciding whether to recommend de-listing.[40] As to the decision-making process within the UNSC-appointed sanctions committee:

> Any member of the Committee may, after consultation with the designating State(s), recommend de-listing by forwarding the request to the Chairman, accompanied by an explanation. (Only one member of the Committee needs to recommend de-listing in order to place the issue on the Committee's agenda.) If after one month, no Committee member recommends de-listing, then it shall be deemed rejected and the Chairman shall inform the Focal Point accordingly[.][41]

Throughout the process, the Focal Point is also tasked with relaying States' communications to the sanctions committee[42] and, at its conclusion, with notifying the petitioner of the success or otherwise of the request.[43]

If the petitioner instead submits their request to their State of nationality or residence, it is for the 'petitioned State' to review the information and to consult with the designating State(s).[44] If the petitioned State so wishes, it may also consult with the State of nationality or residence and the sanctions committee chair.[45] The decision-making process concludes as follows:

> If, after reviewing any additional information, the petitioned State wishes to pursue a de-listing request, it should seek to persuade the designating State(s) to submit jointly or separately a request for de-listing to the Committee. The

37 ibid para 7(g)(ii). Repeated requests containing no new information are to be returned to the petitioner. See ibid para 7(g)(iii).
38 ibid para 7(g)(v).
39 ibid.
40 ibid.
41 ibid.
42 ibid para 7(g)(vii).
43 ibid para 7(g)(viii).
44 ibid para 7(h)(i).
45 ibid para 7(h)(ii).

> petitioned State may, without an accompanying request from the designating State(s), submit a request for de-listing to the Committee, pursuant to the no-objection procedure[.][46]

It is then for the chair of the sanctions committee to notify these States of the outcome of the request.[47] Finally, if the request is successful:

> The Secretariat shall, within one week after a name is removed from the List, notify the Permanent Mission of the country or countries where the individual or entity is believed to be located and, in the case of individuals, the country of which the person is a national (to the extent this information is known). The letter shall remind States receiving such notification that they are required to take measures, in accordance with their domestic laws and practices, to notify or inform the concerned individual or entity of the de-listing in a timely manner.[48]

Turning to the use of this procedure, as of 31 August 2020,[49] 101 requests had been submitted to the Focal Point by 80 individuals and 39 entities.[50] When compared with the total number of individuals and entities listed by one of the many UNSC-appointed sanctions committees, a modest number of those designated have applied for their de-listing, while the proportion of those successful in these applications is even smaller.

6.3.3 *Other (Quasi-)Legal Protections*

The UNSC has introduced a number of additional (quasi-)legal protections for those targeted by asset freezing measures and other targeted sanctions with respect to the ISIL (Da'esh) and Al-Qaida Sanctions Committee, many of which have since been embraced by other sanctions committees. For instance, in Resolution 1735, the UNSC directed States to employ a generic cover sheet when putting names forward for inclusion on the sanctions list 'in order to ensure clarity and consistency in requests for listing'.[51] The cover sheet is divided into two sections: one for 'identifier information' (including name(s), address(es), date(s) and place(s) of birth, passport details, location, etc.) and the other for the 'basis for

46 ibid para 7(h)(iii).
47 ibid para 7(h)(iv).
48 ibid para 7(i).
49 UNSC, 'De-listing requests' <https://www.un.org/securitycouncil/sanctions/delisting/de-listing-request-stats> accessed 31 August 2020.
50 ibid. These figures are calculated from twelve UNSC-appointed sanctions committees.
51 UNSC Res 1735 (22 December 2006) UN Doc S/RES/1735, para 7.

listing' (which explicitly refers to paragraphs of Resolution 1617).[52] The cover sheet also invites States to attach a 'Statement of the Case' to elaborate on the basis for listing.[53] According to Feinäugle, this sheet, replaced by the 'standard form for listing' in Resolution 1904,[54] helps to guarantee 'that sanctions are *carefully targeted* in the sense of paragraph 29 of the [Declaration of the High-level Meeting of the General Assembly on the Rule of Law at the National and International Levels]',[55] the relevant paragraph of which provides as follows:

> Recognizing the role under the Charter of the United Nations of effective collective measures in maintaining and restoring international peace and security, we encourage the Security Council to continue to ensure that sanctions are carefully targeted, in support of clear objectives and designed carefully so as to minimize possible adverse consequences, and that fair and clear procedures are maintained and further developed.[56]

The UNSC has also introduced an obligation upon the ISIL (Da'esh) and Al-Qaida Sanctions Committee to provide 'a narrative summary of reasons for listing',[57] a measure subsequently implemented by other UNSC-appointed sanctions committees. For example, the committee established under Resolution 1533 concerning the DRC includes the following in the guidelines it adopted for the conduct of its work:

> Following a new listing, the Committee, with the assistance of the Group of Experts on the DRC, and in coordination with the relevant designating State(s),

52 ibid Annex I, citing UNSC Res 1617 (29 July 2005) UN Doc S/RES/1617, paras 2-3 (detailing 'acts or activities indicating that an individual, group, undertaking, or entity is "associated with" Al-Qaida, Usama bin Laden or the Taliban').

53 ibid ('including: (1) specific information supporting the association or activities alleged; (2) the nature of the information (e.g., intelligence, law enforcement, judicial, media, admissions by subject, etc.) and (3) supporting information or documents that can be provided. Include details of any connection with a currently listed individual or entity.')

54 UNSC Res 1904 (17 December 2009) UN Doc S/RES/1904, para 13.

55 Clemens A Feinäugle, 'UN Smart Sanctions and the UN Declaration on the Rule of Law' in Matthew Happold and Paul Eden (eds), *Economic Sanctions and International Law* (Hart Publishing 2016) 126 (emphasis in original).

56 UNGA Res 67/1 (30 November 2012) UN Doc A/RES/67/1, para 29. Cf UNSC Presidential Statement 28 (n 33).

57 UNSC Res 1822 (30 June 2008) UN Doc S/RES/1822, para 13 ('Directs the Committee, with the assistance of the Monitoring Team and in coordination with the relevant designating States, after a name is added to the Consolidated List, to make accessible on the Committee's website a narrative summary of reasons for listing for the corresponding entry or entries on the Consolidated List, and further directs the Committee, with the assistance of the Monitoring Team and in coordination with the relevant designating States, to make accessible on the Committee's website narrative summaries of reasons for listing for entries that were added to the Consolidated List before the date of adoption of this resolution'.)

> shall make accessible on the Committee's website a narrative summary of reasons for listing for the corresponding entry or entries on the List.[58]

Together with the annual review of listed individuals and entities, another measure embraced by the ISIL (Da'esh) and Al-Qaida Sanctions Committee at the request of the UNSC,[59] it has been argued that providing such a summary of reasons serves due process purposes.[60]

It was again concerning the ISIL (Da'esh) and Al-Qaida Sanctions Committee that the UNSC established a further quasi-legal protection mechanism for listed individuals and entities: the Office of the Ombudsperson.[61] The Ombudsperson's mandate can be broken down into three phases: (i) a four-month 'information gathering' phase, which can be extended only once for up to a further two months;[62] followed by (ii) a two-month 'dialogue' phase; which, like the first phase, can be prolonged once for up to an additional two months,[63] and, finally (iii) the 'discussion' phase, at the close of which the sanctions committee takes a decision on the de-listing request.[64] In Resolution 1904, the same resolution in which the UNSC established the Office of the Ombudsperson, the body also decided that individuals and entities listed by the ISIL (Da'esh) and Al-Qaida Sanctions

58 Security Council Committee Established Pursuant to Resolution 1533 (2004) concerning the Democratic Republic of the Congo (DRC Sanctions Committee), 'Guidelines of the Committee for the Conduct of its Work as adopted by the Committee on 6 August 2010' <https://www.un.org/securitycouncil/sanctions/1533/guidelines> accessed 31 August 2020 (DRC Sanctions Committee Guidelines) para 5(g).

59 UNSC Res 1822 (n 36) para 26 ('Further directs the Committee ... to conduct an annual review of all names on the Consolidated List that have not been reviewed in three or more years, in which the relevant names are circulated to the designating states and states of residence and/or citizenship, where known, pursuant to the procedures set forth in the Committee guidelines, in order to ensure the Consolidated List is as updated and accurate as possible and to confirm that listing remains appropriate').

60 Feinäugle (n 55) 126.

61 UNSC Res 1904 (17 December 2009) UN Doc S/RES/1904, para 20. The UNSC extended the Ombudsperson's mandate in UNSC Res 1989 (17 June 2011) UN Doc S/RES/1989, para 21; UNSC Res 2083 (17 December 2012) UN Doc S/RES/2083, para 19; UNSC Res 2161 (17 June 2014) UN Doc S/RES/2161, para 41; UNSC Res 2253 (17 December 2015) UN Doc S/RES/2253, para 54; UNSC Res 2368 (20 July 2017) UN Doc S/RES/2368, para 60.

62 UNSC Res 2368 (n 61) Annex II, paras 1-5. For a first-hand perspective on the modalities of the mandate of the Ombudsperson, see Kimberly Prost, 'A Reflection on Innovations in the Security Council: The International Tribunals, Counterterrorism, and the Office of the Ombudsperson' (2014) 46 *Case Western Reserve Journal of International Law* 465, 472-476; Kimberly Prost, 'The Office of the Ombudsperson: A case for fair process' in Jeremy Farrall and Hilary Charlesworth (eds), *Strengthening the Rule of Law through the UN Security Council* (Routledge 2016) 181. Judge Prost served as the first Ombudsperson, having been appointed to the office by the UN Secretary-General in June 2010. See UNSC 'Letter dated 3 June 2010 from the Secretary-General addressed to the President of the Security Council' (4 June 2010) UN Doc S/2010/282.

63 ibid paras 6-8.

64 ibid paras 9-19.

Committee should no longer submit their requests for de-listing to the Focal Point, but to the Ombudsperson.[65] However, the UNSC also added that 'the Focal Point shall continue to receive requests from individuals and entities seeking to be removed from other sanctions lists'.[66] Therefore, to the extent that the Ombudsperson offers greater (quasi-)legal protection to those on the ISIL (Da'esh) and Al-Qaida sanctions list, the benefits of such protection do not extend to individuals and entities designated by any of the other active UNSC-appointed sanctions committees. As far as the broader protections offered to those with access to the Office of the Ombudsperson are concerned, since Resolution 1989, which equipped the Office with greater powers,[67] the Ombudsperson has been authorised to provide the committee with a 'recommendation to retain the listing or a recommendation that the Committee consider delisting'.[68] This process operates such that the obligation on States to give effect to the sanctions measures in their domestic legal orders ceases to apply 60 days after the Ombudsperson recommends de-listing:

> unless the Committee decides by consensus before the end of that 60 day period that the requirement shall remain in place with respect to that individual, group, undertaking or entity; provided that, in cases where consensus does not exist, the Chair shall, on the request of a Committee Member, submit the question of whether to delist that individual, group, undertaking or entity to the Security Council for a decision within a period of 60 days[.][69]

In other words, 'the support of a single member of the Committee would entail the enforcement of the Ombudsperson's recommendation subject to possible referral to the UN Security Council for its decision'.[70] This represents a more robust de-listing procedure than the Focal Point for De-listing process, which the first Ombudsperson to be appointed to the role, Judge Kimberly Prost, describes in the following terms: 'I don't like to refer to [the Focal Point] as a mailbox, but she's responsible simply to take communications and pass them to the committee.'[71] This description stands in stark contrast to way in which she describes the role of the Office of the Ombudsperson as performing 'an independent

65 UNSC Res 1904 (n 61) para 21.

66 ibid.

67 UN Doc S/RES/1989 (n 61). For a thorough analysis of the development of the mandate of the Ombudsperson from the perspective of human rights, see Paul Eden, 'United Nations Targeted Sanctions, Human Rights and the Office of the Ombudsperson' in Matthew Happold and Paul Eden (eds), *Economic Sanctions and International Law* (Hart Publishing 2016) 135.

68 ibid para 21.

69 ibid para 23. The same approach applies where the designating State submits a delisting request. See para 27.

70 Eden (n 67) 153.

71 Prost, 'A Reflection on Innovations in the Security Council' (n 62) 471.

de novo assessment of the information.'[72] The Office of the Ombudsperson does, however, remain subject to criticism, not least with respect to its lack of independence within the UN apparatus.[73] Before leaving the Office, Judge Prost raised similar concerns.[74] A further concern, of course, is one already mentioned: namely that those listed by sanctions committees other than that established in response to ISIL (Da'esh) and Al-Qaida do not have recourse to the more robust Office of the Ombudsperson procedure, but must instead channel any requests for de-listing through the Focal Point for De-listing or through their State of nationality or residence. Consequently, the Office of the Ombudsperson does not represent a (quasi-)legal protection available to all individuals and entities subjected to UNSC-requested asset freezing measures, but only a fraction (albeit sizeable) thereof. As for why the Ombudsperson's remit extends only to those listed by the ISIL (Da'esh) and Al-Qaida Sanctions Committee, the following extract from a press conference held shortly after the appointment of Judge Prost to the role, at which Thomas Mayr-Harting, then Chair of the Resolution 1267 Committee, was also in attendance, is illuminating:

> Asked why the office of Ombudsperson had been created only for the 1267 Committee and not other sanctions bodies, Mr. Mayr-Harting said the 1267 Committee was 'the mother regime of all sanctions regimes', in which the lack of due process was most criticized in court. If the Office proved effective in strengthening due process and the rule of law, it should serve as a model for others in the Organization.[75]

However, at the time of writing, ten years have elapsed since the Office was established and the UNSC has yet to extend its brief to cover those listed by other UNSC-appointed sanctions committees, thereby leaving a significant number of individuals and entities unable to benefit from the additional (quasi-)legal protections at the disposal of this mechanism.[76]

---

72 ibid 474.

73 See eg UNSC 'Improving fair and clear procedures for a more effective United Nations sanctions system: Input paper by the Group of Like-Minded States on Targeted Sanctions (Austria, Belgium, Costa Rica, Denmark, Finland, Germany, Liechtenstein, the Netherlands, Norway, Sweden and Switzerland)' (21 April 2014) UN Doc S/2014/286 ('The Office of the Ombudsperson should be made permanent and the contractual arrangements for the position of the Ombudsperson should be modified and improved. The status and privileges of the position should fully reflect the independence required to perform the tasks of the Ombudsperson effectively.')

74 See UNSC 'Report of the Office of the Ombudsperson pursuant to Security Council resolution 2161 (2014)' (14 July 2015) UN Doc S/2015/533, paras 55-69.

75 UNSC 'Press Conference to Present Ombudsperson of Security Council's 1267 Committee' (15 July 2010) <https://www.un.org/press/en/2010/100715_1267.doc.htm> accessed 31 August 2020.

76 The Group of Like-Minded States on Targeted Sanctions made the argument in 2014 in support of extending the Ombudsperson's mandate to cover other sanctions regimes. See UNSC, 'Improving fair and

Feinäugle categorises UNSC-instituted sanctions regimes into three groups according to 'the degree to which rule of law requirements … are achieved'.[77] The three groups he identifies are: (i) advanced; (ii) medium-developed; and (iii) less-developed sanctions regimes.[78] Only the ISIL (Da'esh) and Al-Qaida sanctions regime falls into the first category.[79] Feinäugle lists multiple reasons in support of this classification, including the introduction of:

- exemptions for basic expenses;[80]
- the Focal Point for De-listing;[81]
- the cover sheet for listings,[82] later the 'standard form for listing';[83]
- the requirement to provide a narrative summary of reasons for listing;[84]
- the regular review of listed individuals and entities;[85] and
- the Office of the Ombudsperson.[86]

In comparison, according to Feinäugle, other sanctions regimes would appear to fall short of 'advanced' status for want of one or more of the foregoing legal protections.[87] Yet, even the many (quasi-)legal protections available to individuals and entities listed in accordance with the 'advanced' Resolution 1267 sanctions regime do not represent 'proper judicial review'.[88] Another concern expressed in the literature is that 'different sanctions regimes

clear procedures for a more effective United Nations sanctions system' (n 73) ('Currently, only individuals and entities listed on the Al-Qaida Sanctions List have access to the Ombudsperson process. Yet, similar due process concerns exist in other Security Council sanctions regimes. … The Security Council should therefore consider the possibility of extending the mandate of the Ombudsperson to other (appropriate) regimes on the occasion of their next mandate renewals. The possibility of adapting the mandate of the Ombudsperson to the various sanctions regimes should also be explored.')

77 Feinäugle (n 55) 125.

78 ibid.

79 ibid 125-128.

80 ibid 125.

81 ibid 126.

82 ibid.

83 ibid 127.

84 ibid 126.

85 ibid.

86 ibid 127.

87 ibid 128-131. Feinäugle scrutinises *inter alia* the UNSC-appointed sanctions committees for Somalia/Eritrea, Liberia, Guinea-Bissau, South Sudan (classified as medium-developed sanctions regimes), Iraq and Kuwait and Lebanon (classified as less-developed sanctions regimes).

88 ibid 128. See also Happold (n 22) 103 ('the Focal Point procedure … is avowedly not a form of judicial review. Listed persons continue to be unable to know the full reasons for their listing, and consequently to respond to them when drafting their applications. During the process, petitioners cannot respond to new points raised by designating (or other) States, as they are not party to the proceedings. And there is no obligation on sanctions committees to give reasoned decisions; so that the bases for their conclusions remain opaque'). For human rights concerns about the Office of the Ombudsperson, see Happold (n 22) 105 ('petitioners remain unable to see all the evidence against them, and decisions of the Ombudsperson are not formally binding. … To this, one might add a certain precarity concerning the Ombudsperson's position.

have different procedures and each sanctions committee is, largely, a law unto itself',[89] a concern borne out in Feinäugle's categorisation of multiple sanctions committees in terms of their adherence to rule of law requirements.

6.4 Conclusion

This chapter has demonstrated that several (quasi-)legal mechanisms exist within the UNSC sanctions apparatus to protect individuals (and entities) listed by UNSC-appointed sanctions committees. It has also shown that there are a number of shortcomings within the system of available protections, leading to *inter alia* those designated by certain sanctions committees being better protected than those listed by others. This discrepancy is most evident when one compares the protections granted to those listed by the ISIL (Da'esh) and Al-Qaida Sanctions Committee with committees established by other UNSC resolutions. And yet it has also been suggested that even these legal protections do not constitute review akin to that offered by an independent and impartial tribunal. This is not to say, however, that individuals (and entities) listed by UNSC sanctions committees do not have recourse to such review; rather, this has to take place, if at all, at the (supra)national level and before regional human rights courts. How such protections are given effect in two fora extraneous to the UN system, ie the ECtHR and IACtHR, will be examined in the following chapter.

Not only is the Ombudsperson's mandate subject to regular renewals but, it has been argued, the administrative structures relied on to support the mandate lack autonomy and independence.')

89 Happold (n 22) 102.

7 Asset Freezing at the European and Inter-American Courts of Human Rights*

Lessons for the ICC, the UNSC and States

7.1 Introduction

Both the ICC and the UNSC are authorised to request States to freeze individuals' assets. Although there are differences in the modalities of the procedures available thereto,[1] both bodies are also constrained by human rights in the exercise of their respective powers. As for the ICC, whose asset freezing powers are tied to the question of the potential criminal responsibility of the accused and therefore subject to the checks and balances applicable to criminal procedures, including fair trial considerations, Article 21(3) of the Rome Statute stipulates that the application and interpretation of its applicable law must be 'consistent with internationally recognized human rights'.[2] Göran Sluiter has therefore argued that Article 21(3) should occupy a 'prominent place as a systematic and obligatory human rights review standard for each and every activity of the Court and activity that is of benefit to the proceedings before the Court'.[3] In a similar manner, Article 24(2) of the UN Charter requires that the UNSC 'act in accordance with the Purposes and Principles of the United Nations' in discharging its duties.[4] Article 1(3) of the UN Charter, which lists three of the four purposes of the organisation, includes 'promoting and encouraging respect for human rights'.[5] UNSC-requested asset freezing measures, which are ordered at the behest of the UNSC, albeit subject to the legal constraints on UNSC action detailed in Article 24(2) of the UN Charter and by peremptory norms of international law,[6] must consequently also

* An earlier version of this chapter was published as Daley J Birkett, 'Asset Freezing at the European and Inter-American Courts of Human Rights: Lessons for the International Criminal Court, the United Nations Security Council and States' (2020) 20 Human Rights Law Review 502-525.

1 See Part 3.2.

2 Rome Statute, art 21(3). The full provision reads: 'The application and interpretation of law pursuant to this article must be consistent with internationally recognized human rights, and be without any adverse distinction founded on grounds such as gender as defined in article 7, paragraph 3, age, race, colour, language, religion or belief, political or other opinion, national, ethnic or social origin, wealth, birth or other status.'

3 Göran Sluiter, 'Human Rights Protection in the ICC Pre-Trial Phase' in Carsten Stahn and Göran Sluiter (eds), *The Emerging Practice of the International Criminal Court* (Martinus Nijhoff 2009) 475.

4 UN Charter, art 24(2).

5 UN Charter, art 1(3).

6 UN Charter, art 24(2) ('In discharging these duties the Security Council shall act in accordance with the Purposes and Principles of the United Nations. The specific powers granted to the Security Council for the

be constrained by human rights. This chapter examines the principal human rights implicated by both processes through the lens of a series of cases decided by the ECtHR and the IACtHR under the European Convention on Human Rights (ECHR) and the American Convention on Human Rights (ACHR), respectively. This is not to say that the rights at issue in the present chapter are not protected in other international and/or regional human rights instruments. Rather, the focus rests on these two courts because they have produced the case law deemed most germane to answering the research question.

Further to the relationship between the application of ICC-requested and UNSC-ordered asset freezing measures and human rights, the ECtHR also provides an especially apt lens through which to conduct the present enquiry because the ICC regularly refers to the legal findings of the Strasbourg court in its own case law.[7] At the same time, although certain ICTs established before the entry into force of the Rome Statute were authorised by their constituent instruments to order provisional and/or post-conviction asset freezing measures,[8] such measures were barely used in practice.[9] As a result, there is limited discussion of the relationship between the application of these measures and their consequent impact on fundamental human rights in the jurisprudence of the ICTs that predate the ICC. In addition, because the Court has seen relatively few cases proceed to

---

discharge of these duties are laid down in Chapters VI, VII, VIII, and XII.') See also Erika de Wet, *The Chapter VII Powers of the United Nations Security Council* (OUP 2004) 187-91 (on *jus cogens* as a substantive limit to UNSC discretion), 191-95 (on the purposes and principles of the UN as substantive limits to the powers of the UNSC) and 219-26 (on human rights limitations to economic sanctions); Erika de Wet, 'Human Rights Limitations to Economic Enforcement Measures Under Article 41 of the UN Charter and the Iraqi Sanctions Regime' (2001) 14 Leiden Journal of International Law 284, 286–89; David Schweigman, *The Authority of the Security Council under Chapter VII of the UN Charter: Legal Limits and the Role of the International Court of Justice* (Kluwer Law International 2001) 172, 202; Antonios Tzanakopoulos, *Disobeying the Security Council: Countermeasures against Wrongful Sanctions* (2011) 31-32; Alexander Orakhelashvili, 'The Impact of Peremptory Norms on the Interpretation and Application of United Nations Security Council Resolutions' (2005) 16 European Journal of International Law 59, 63-67 (for fundamental human rights as constraints, see 64-66); Devon Whittle, 'The Limits of Legality and the United Nations Security Council: Applying the Extra-Legal Measures Model to Chapter VII Action' (2015) 26 European Journal of International Law 671. One scholar even goes so far as to suggest that UN Charter, art 55 imposes similar '[h]umanitarian [c]onstraints' on the UNSC when imposing financial sanctions. See Evan J Criddle, 'Humanitarian Financial Intervention' (2013) 24 European Journal of International Law 583, 605.

7 On this practice, see Nicolas AJ Croquet, 'The International Criminal Court and the Treatment of Defence Rights: A Mirror of the European Court of Human Rights' Jurisprudence?' (2011) 11 Human Rights Law Review 91; Annika Jones, 'Insights Into an Emerging Relationship: Use of Human Rights Jurisprudence at the International Criminal Court' (2016) 16 Human Rights Law Review 701; Paolo Lobba and Triestino Mariniello (eds), *Judicial Dialogue on Human Rights: The Practice of International Criminal Tribunals* (2017).

8 The IMT was explicitly empowered to order post-conviction forfeiture, the IMTFE was arguably authorised to do so, the tribunals established under Control Council Law No 10 were permitted to order fines as well as provisional and post-conviction forfeiture measures, while the ICTY and the ICTR had similar powers, without the capacity to order fines as a penalty. See Chapter 4.

9 ibid.

the sentencing phase, while other accused and/or convicted persons have been found to be indigent and many filings remain confidential, the ICC has developed only a relatively limited jurisprudence on the execution of asset freezing measures.[10]

This is not to say that this issue is not of significant import for the Court's activities in the future. As will be demonstrated in this chapter, the application of such measures has been contested before the ICC's pre-trial, trial and appeals chambers, with the impact of these measures on the human rights guaranteed under the Rome Statute regularly under discussion. Why, then, might the case law of the ECtHR and IACtHR be relevant for the UNSC? As will be discussed in this chapter, the execution of UNSC-ordered asset freezing measures has been determined to have violated the ECHR in certain cases. The efficacy of these measures, at least in the territories of the High Contracting Parties to the ECHR, therefore depends upon their compatibility with the rights protected therein. As to the IACtHR, its case law sheds light on a subject of immediate relevance to the operations of the ICC), namely the impact upon human rights caused by the mismanagement of assets frozen at the Court's request. As for the cases under examination, each is selected because of its immediate relevance to the research question at the heart of this book.

The chapter demonstrates that the case law of the ICC has, by and large, complied with the human rights principles identified but could benefit from clearer reasoning as to why the ICC elected to rely upon the jurisprudence of a particular regional human rights court. As for UNSC-ordered asset freezes, the chapter shows that the UN organ vested with 'primary responsibility for the maintenance of international peace and security'[11] is given a wide margin of appreciation in framing such measures. At the same time, however, there is a risk that UN Member States, in executing UNSC-requested measures, could be found to have violated the human rights protected in regional instruments to which they are parties.

7.2 ASSET FREEZING IN THE LAW AND PRACTICE OF THE STRASBOURG AND SAN JOSÉ COURTS

At the outset, it is important to note the difference between provisional measures with a view to possible forfeiture and post-conviction forfeiture measures, both of which require

10 On which, see Chapter 5; Carla Ferstman, 'Cooperation and the International Criminal Court: The Freezing, Seizing and Transfer of Assets for the Purpose of Reparations' in Olympia Bekou and Daley J Birkett (eds), *Cooperation and the International Criminal Court: Perspectives from Theory and Practice* (Brill Nijhoff 2016) 233-37.

11 UN Charter, art 24(1).

assets to be frozen by States. The former are protective measures, explicitly designed to safeguard any assets that might later be subject to an order for forfeiture (or, in the Rome Statute system, an order for reparations to victims),[12] while the latter constitute a penalty imposed by a criminal court following a guilty verdict. Both types of measures have been brought to the attention of the ECtHR, from which a series of principles useful to the work of the ICC, chiefly as concerns the application and interpretation of its applicable law consistent with internationally recognised human rights, can be gleaned. Similarly, the execution of UNSC sanctions, including asset freezing procedures, has been challenged in Strasbourg. In addition, the IACtHR has also examined the human rights implications of the mismanagement of assets frozen at the request of responsible domestic authorities.

The principles developed by the two human rights courts in this context will also be examined with a view to identifying their potential for promoting and encouraging respect for human rights by the UNSC and, more specifically, by UN Member States in their national implementation of the administrative asset freezing measures requested at the international level. This is because UNSC resolutions ordering UN Member States to freeze the assets of individuals (and entities) included on sanctions lists are not self-executing.[13] Nor are ICC-issued cooperation requests for the freezing of assets capable of self-execution.[14] Rather, such requests, whether they originate from the UNSC or the Court, require (legislative) action by the receiving States to give effect to the measures in their national legal orders.

Another important difference that ought to be acknowledged is that between the purpose of asset freezing measures executed by States based on a request from the Court and the aims of asset freezing under the auspices of UNSC sanctions regimes. At the Court, one can identify several such purposes, including the prevention of ongoing or future criminal conduct under ICC jurisdiction, the preservation of assets for the payment of future fines, orders for forfeiture or orders to make reparations to victims and the payment of defence fees. While the UNSC has also requested States to give effect to asset freezing measures

12 Rome Statute, art 75(2) ('The Court may make an order directly against a convicted person specifying appropriate reparations to, or in respect of, victims, including restitution, compensation and rehabilitation.') On the development of the ICC's case law concerning the request of provisional asset freezing measures to safeguard assets for the enforcement of possible future reparations orders, see Chapter 5; Ferstman (n 10) 233-36.

13 See Vera Gowlland-Debbas, 'Implementing Sanctions Resolutions in Domestic Law' in Vera Gowlland-Debbas (ed), *National Implementation of United Nations Sanctions: A Comparative Study* (Martinus Nijhoff 2004) 35.

14 See Rome Statute, art 88 ('States Parties shall ensure that there are procedures available under their national law for all of the forms of cooperation which are specified under this Part.') For discussion of this important provision, see Olympia Bekou, 'A Case for Review of Article 88, ICC Statute: Strengthening a Forgotten Provision' (2009) 12 New Criminal Law Review 468.

against individuals under the guise of so-called targeted sanctions, some of which could be said to premised on similar purposes to those of the Court in seeking to put an end to impunity for the perpetrators of mass atrocities,[15] the freezing of assets pursuant to UNSC resolutions can also serve other varied purposes. These have included, among others, deterring the proliferation and alleged testing of nuclear weapons,[16] denouncing a military coup,[17] and condemning repeated violations of ceasefire arrangements by armed groups.[18] This distinction might be relevant in determining whether the measures comply with the human rights principles applicable to asset freezing, particularly in the appraisal of whether the implementation of such measures satisfies the 'general interest' or 'legitimate aim' criterion.[19]

It is also important to note the differences between the freezing of assets on the one hand and the identification, tracing, seizure and (forms of) forfeiture and confiscation thereof on the other.[20] Distinguishing these types of measures ought to clarify the terminology employed in the ensuing analysis of the case law of the ECtHR and IACtHR as regards asset freezing and its implications for the ICC, the UNSC and the States party to the Rome Statute and UN Charter. According to guidance approved by the UNSC Al-Qaida Sanctions Committee:[21]

> *Freeze* of funds and other financial assets and economic resources includes preventing their use, alteration, movement, transfer or access … . *Freeze* of economic resources also includes preventing their use to obtain funds, goods, or services in any way, including, but not limited to, by selling, hiring or

15 The measures, which have included asset freezes, have been labelled 'crime-based targeted sanctions'. See Hilde Roskam, 'Crime-Based Targeted Sanctions: Promoting Respect for International Humanitarian Law by the Security Council' in Terry D Gill and others (eds), *Yearbook of International Humanitarian Law 2016* (TMC Asser Press 2018). The UNSC has ordered such measures in a number of situations, including in Côte d'Ivoire, the DRC, the CAR and Libya. This said, it ought to be noted that the UNSC measures, although arguably 'crime-based', remain administrative.

16 Security Council Committee established pursuant to resolution 1718 (2006) (concerning the Democratic People's Republic of Korea).

17 Security Council Committee established pursuant to resolution 2048 (2012) concerning Guinea-Bissau.

18 Security Council Committee established pursuant to resolution 2374 (2017) concerning Mali.

19 See infra.

20 cf Rome Statute, art 93(1)(k).

21 Security Council Committee pursuant to resolutions 1267 (1999) 1989 (2011) and 2253 (2015) concerning Islamic State in Iraq and the Levant (Da'esh), Al-Qaida and associated individuals, groups, undertakings and entities (Al-Qaida Sanctions Committee).

> mortgaging them. The term '*freeze*' does not mean confiscation or transfer of ownership.[22]

The identification and/or tracing of assets are steps that may need to be taken preliminary to their freezing. After freezing, assets may, but need not necessarily, be seized, forfeited and/or confiscated. As the foregoing Al-Qaida Sanctions Committee guidance stipulates, UNSC-requested asset freezes do not require the confiscation or transfer of ownership of the assets by UN Member States.[23] In the Rome Statute system, the ICC can only request the forfeiture of assets in the event of a conviction[24] and the 'identification, tracing and freezing or seizure of proceeds, property and assets and instrumentalities of crimes'[25] can be requested 'for the purpose of eventual forfeiture'.[26] In other words, where an acquittal is entered, there is no legal basis for an order for forfeiture of assets by the Court.

Much of the ECtHR's case law concerning asset freezing has developed in the context of challenges brought in the context of forfeiture proceedings, which take a number of forms at the domestic level.[27] But this does not mean that the ECtHR has necessarily developed a thorough approach thereto. In the words of Judge Pinto de Albuquerque:

> Under the *nomen juris* of confiscation, the States have introduced *ante delictum* criminal prevention measures, criminal sanctions (accessory or even principal criminal penalties), security measures in the broad sense, administrative measures adopted within or outside criminal proceedings, and civil measures *in rem*. Confronted with this enormous range of responses available to the State, the Court has not yet developed any consistent case-law based on principled reasoning.[28]

---

22 Al-Qaida Sanctions Committee, 'Assets Freeze: Explanation of Terms' (24 February 2015) <https://www.un.org/securitycouncil/sites/www.un.org.securitycouncil/files/eot_assets_freeze_-_english.pdf> accessed 31 August 2020, paras 9-11 (emphases in original).

23 ibid para 11.

24 cf Rome Statute, art 75(2) ('In addition to imprisonment, the Court may order … (b) A forfeiture of proceeds, property and assets derived directly or indirectly from that crime, without prejudice to the rights of bona fide third parties.')

25 ibid art 93(1)(k).

26 ibid.

27 See Chapter 2.

28 *Varvara v Italy* App no 17475/09 (ECtHR, 29 October 2013) para 14 (Partly Concurring and Partly Dissenting Opinion of Judge Pinto De Albuquerque). See also Michele Simonato, 'Confiscation and fundamental rights across criminal and non-criminal domains' (2017) 18 ERA Forum 365, 366 ('Human rights law … has not yet provided a firm answer to all questions arising about the compatibility of new forms of confiscation with fundamental rights.')

The following section analyses this case law in respect of two rights protected under the ECHR and ACHR frameworks with which the imposition of asset freezing measures necessarily interferes, namely the right to the peaceful enjoyment of one's possessions and the right to respect for one's private and family life, home and correspondence. A second justification for focusing on these rights is that both have been subject to judicial scrutiny in cases brought before the ECtHR and IACtHR by applicants challenging the implementation of asset freezing measures by State authorities. This is not to say that these are the only relevant rights in this context. Indeed, the right to a fair trial, particularly as it concerns the presumption of innocence, is also implicated and will be considered alongside the analysis of the two principal rights under examination where relevant. A further reason behind focusing on these rights is that both have been discussed by the ICC in its case law on the execution of asset freezing measures. The analysis therefore also aims to distil principles from the Strasbourg and San José courts' case law relevant to the execution of asset freezing measures by States at the request of the ICC and UNSC, respectively.

7.2.1 *Protection of property*

One human right that is evidently implicated by the imposition of asset freezing measures can be found in the (first) Protocol to the Convention for the Protection of Human Rights and Fundamental Freedoms (Protocol 1):

> Every natural or legal person is entitled to the peaceful enjoyment of his possessions. No one shall be deprived of his possessions except in the public interest and subject to the conditions provided for by law and by the general principles of international law.
>
> The preceding provisions shall not, however, in any way impair the right of a State to enforce such laws as it deems necessary to control the use of property in accordance with the general interest or to secure the payment of taxes or other contributions or penalties.[29]

29 Protocol 1, art 1.

This right is also enshrined in Article 21 of the ACHR in the following terms:

> 1. Everyone has the right to the use and enjoyment of his property. The law may subordinate such use and enjoyment to the interest of society.
>
> 2. No one shall be deprived of his property except upon payment of just compensation, for reasons of public utility or social interest, and in the cases and according to the forms established by law.[30]

7.2.1.1 Džinić v Croatia

The impact of protective (that is, pre-conviction) asset freezing measures on the right to the peaceful enjoyment of one's possessions came to the attention of the ECtHR in *Džinić v Croatia*,[31] a case involving the provisional seizure of the applicant's property with a view to securing the enforcement of a potential future order for forfeiture.[32] The applicant had been charged with the misappropriation of shares and the misuse of company assets and facilities, which allegedly led to a pecuniary gain of approximately €1 million.[33] This gain was later found to be roughly €240,000,[34] but the domestic court refused to lift the seizure order,[35] despite the total value of the property seized from the applicant being closer to €10 million.[36] The applicant brought his complaint to the ECtHR, with the matter for determination by thc Strasbourg court being whether the disproportionate asset seizure infringed his Protocol 1 right to the peaceful enjoyment of his possessions.[37]

It is notable that the parties did not dispute whether the seizure of the applicant's property constituted an interference with his possessions.[38] On the contrary, both parties were of the view, confirmed by the ECtHR,[39] that Article 1 of Protocol 1 was necessarily implicated by the seizure of property in his possession – that is, assets of which he was the lawful owner – 'by prohibiting its alienation or encumbrance'.[40] In the words of the ECtHR: 'the seizure of property for legal proceedings normally relates to the control of the use of

30 ACHR, art 21.
31 *Džinić v Croatia* App no 38359/13 (ECtHR, 17 May 2016).
32 ibid para 14.
33 ibid para 9.
34 ibid para 31.
35 ibid para 32
36 ibid para 27. The total value of the property seized from the applicant (ten plots of land, two houses and a commercial building) was estimated at €9,887,084. ibid para 12.
37 ibid para 42.
38 ibid para 59.
39 ibid.
40 ibid.

property, which falls within the ambit of the second paragraph of Article 1 of Protocol No. 1 to the Convention'.[41] In addition, the ECtHR expressed the following view in relation to protective, pre-conviction asset seizure measures:

> [T]he seizure of the applicant's property did not purport to deprive him of his possessions but placed a temporary restriction on its use ... which, in circumstances where the disposition of the property was associated with the applicant's lawful business, also inevitably affected the capacities of his business activity ... . [It is also] important to note that the seizure of the applicant's property was applied as a provisional measure aimed at securing enforcement of a possible confiscation order imposed at the outcome of the criminal proceedings in relation to the obtained proceeds of crime[.][42]

The freezing of individuals' assets by States at the request of the ICC and UNSC therefore infringes upon the ECHR-protected right to the peaceful enjoyment of one's possessions and, as a result, must be justified. It is important to reiterate here that UNSC decisions that States must freeze assets need not be taken with a view to their eventual forfeiture during criminal proceedings.[43] Nevertheless, it is argued that the principles that can be deduced from the case law of the ECtHR might also have consequences for the implementation of freezing measures executed under the auspices of UNSC targeted sanctions and therefore ought to be analysed alongside their application to the Rome Statute system. For example, the ECtHR could find a High Contracting Party to the ECHR, all of whom are also UN Member States, to have violated the ECHR in attempting to give domestic effect to UNSC-requested asset freezing measures, if the State's national implementing legislation fails to adhere to the principles detailed in the ECtHR's jurisprudence.[44] It is to these principles, grouped under four headings, namely (i) time limits; (ii) legality; (iii) legitimate aim; and (iv) proportionality, that the focus of analysis now shifts.

41 ibid para 60.
42 ibid para 61 (emphases added).
43 See nn 15-18 and accompanying text.
44 As Erika de Wet notes, 'the *Nada* decision of the ECtHR has indicated that even where the language of a UNSC resolution leaves no apparent scope for interpretation, States remain under an obligation to find a way to give some effect to international human rights standards.' Erika de Wet, 'From *Kadi* to *Nada*: Judicial Techniques Favouring Human Rights over United Nations Security Council Sanctions' (2013) 12 Chinese Journal of International Law 787, 806.

Time limits

In *Džinić v Croatia*, the ECtHR stressed that protective, pre-conviction measures carried out with a view to the prospective forfeiture of the assets in question are of an impermanent nature. Both ICC- and UNSC-requested asset freezing measures are customarily time-limited and are thus comparable with the seizure under discussion. As for the UNSC, although the body has broad discretion in deciding on which measures are to be employed to give effect to its decisions under Chapter VII and, more specifically, Article 41 of the UN Charter,[45] the UNSC has rarely imposed targeted financial sanctions without specifying an end date or, at least, 'a commitment to review' the measures.[46] Kristen Boon compares UNSC sanctions to counter-terrorism legislation adopted in states of emergency because they are aimed at addressing security-related situations.[47] In her view, as 'derogations from the norm of co-existence and State sovereignty, there is a powerful argument that coercive measures must be inherently time bound and departures from this premise must be supported by [the UNSC] in the form of renewals.'[48] Should the UNSC be of the opinion that the situation to which it had responded by imposing asset freezing measures no longer merits their application, the body can, of course, terminate the measures under Chapter VII.

As for the ICC, protective asset freezing measures are given effect by States following a request for cooperation issued thereto by the Court, which has discussed their termination in the following terms:

> an acquittal or other cessation of proceedings does not render the original cooperation requests nor the coercive measures invalid, null or void. The cooperation requests issued in this case remain, but cease to have effect in the sense that States are no longer required to comply with them, for instance by keeping any assets frozen. This, however, does not mean that assets are

45 See Alexander Orakhelashvili, *Collective Security* (OUP 2011) 189-91; *Prosecutor v Tadić* (Decision on the Defence Motion for Interlocutory Appeal on Jurisdiction) ICTY-94-1 (2 October 1995) para 31 ('Once the Security Council determines that a particular situation poses a threat to the peace or that there exists a breach of the peace or an act of aggression, it enjoys a wide margin of discretion in choosing the course of action').

46 Kristen Boon, 'Timing Matters: Termination Policies for UN Sanctions' in Larissa van den Herik (ed), *Research Handbook on UN Sanctions and International Law* (Edward Elgar 2017) 239-42 (discussing three termination methods for UNSC sanctions: (i) resolutions with sunset clauses, (ii) resolutions with no expiry date; and (iii) resolutions with a commitment to review). Boon observes that the third option is the most frequently used option by the UNSC in the 41 resolutions forming the subject of her analysis, with the second option the least frequently employed. ibid 240.

47 ibid 247.

48 ibid.

> automatically released in the requested State. It is rather for the State to determine what action to take under domestic law as a result of the conclusion of its obligation to assist the Court through the freezing of assets.[49]

Asset freezing measures, whether implemented by States at the request of the ICC or the UNSC, consequently ought to be provisional restrictions.

This is not to say that the temporary asset freezes imposed at the respective request of the ICC and UNSC cannot endure for many years. For example, at the ICC, assets belonging to Jean-Pierre Bemba Gombo were frozen in the weeks after his arrest on 24 May 2008.[50] Following his acquittal on 8 June 2018, counsel for Mr Bemba submitted that '[t]here is no legal basis to continue to freeze [his] assets'.[51] According to a filing lodged at the ICC by counsel for Mr Bemba, all of these assets remained frozen as of December 2018, more than ten years after his arrest and almost five months following his acquittal.[52] The application of long-term asset freezing measures can also been seen at the UNSC, where, by way of example, the asset freeze by States at the behest of the UNSC against a number of the children of former Libyan leader Muammar Gadhafi, as a result of their association with their father's regime, has endured since 26 February 2011.[53] These measures remain

49 *Situation in the Central African Republic* (Public redacted version of "Decision on Mr Bemba's preliminary application for reclassification of filings, disclosure, accounts, and partial unfreezing of Mr Bemba's assets and the Registry's Request for guidance", 18 October 2018) ICC-01/05-01/08-3660-Red2 (20 November 2018) para 13.

50 *Situation in the Central African Republic* (Public Redacted Version of "Preliminary application for reclassification of filings, disclosure, accounts and partial unfreezing of Mr. Bemba's assets") ICC-01/05-01/08-3654-Red (30 October 2018) paras 7-9.

51 ibid para 25.

52 See *Situation in the Central African Republic* (Public Redacted Version of "Urgent request for partial reconsideration and associated orders") ICC-01/05-01/08-3663-Red (10 December 2018) para 1 ('In the 22 days since Trial Chamber III's [20 November 2018] "Decision on Mr Bemba's preliminary application for reclassification of filings, disclosure, accounts, and partial unfreezing of Mr Bemba's assets and the Registry's Request for guidance", not one of the assets (whether in the name of Mr Bemba or somebody else) in Portugal, Belgium, or the Democratic Republic of Congo ("the States") has been returned to its owner. Mr. Bemba has received no direct communication from the States, nor indeed are any of them apparently prepared to entertain such communication.') (footnote omitted).

53 For example, the asset freezes (and travel bans) imposed at the request of the Security Council Committee Established Pursuant to Resolution 1970 (2011) concerning Libya (Libya Sanctions Committee) with respect to Muammar Gadhafi's daughter, Aisha, and two of his sons, Mohammed Muammar and Hannibal, remain in force as of August 2020. See UNSC, 'United Nations Security Council Consolidated List' <scsanctions.un.org/consolidated/> accessed 31 August 2020. The Libya Sanctions Committee listed all three because of their proximity to their father's regime, rather than any alleged involvement in the perpetuation of the civil war. See UNSC, 'Narrative Summaries of Reasons for Listing' <www.un.org/securitycouncil/sanctions/narrative-summaries> accessed 31 August 2020. Compare the reasons for the listing two of Gaddafi's other sons, Khamis and Saadi, who, in addition to their closeness to the regime, were listed because of their 'Command of military units involved in repression of demonstrations.' ibid.

in force as of 31 August 2020,[54] despite their father's death, and the overthrow of his regime, on 20 October 2011.

The protracted application of asset freezing measures could potentially call into question their classification as temporary or provisional restrictions. Such a concern was expressed by the EU General Court in *Yassin Abdullah Kadi v. European Commission*,[55] which, in turn, cited a report by the UN High Commissioner for Human Rights for the UN General Assembly.[56] According to the General Court, it might be asked whether:

> [G]iven that now nearly 10 years have passed since the applicant's funds were originally frozen – it is not now time to call into question the finding ... according to which the freezing of funds is a temporary precautionary measure which, unlike confiscation, does not affect the very substance of the right of the persons concerned to property in their financial assets but only the use thereof. ... In the scale of a human life, 10 years in fact represent a substantial period of time and the question of the classification of the measures in question as preventative or punitive, protective or confiscatory, civil or criminal seems now to be an open one[.][57]

This human rights concern could have implications for the length of ICC proceedings, to which the duration of protective measures is tied, as well as UNSC-ordered asset freezes, which may be (and, indeed, have been) subjected to challenges on the domestic, regional and international planes, should they be renewed consecutively over many years.[58]

54 ibid.

55 Case T-85/09 *Yassin Abdullah Kadi v. European Commission* [2010] ECR II-5177.

56 UNHCHR, 'Report of the United Nations High Commissioner for Human Rights on the protection of human rights and fundamental freedoms while countering terrorism' (2 September 2009) UN Doc A/HRC/12/22, para 42 ('Because individual listings are currently open-ended in duration, they may result in a temporary freeze of assets becoming permanent which, in turn, may amount to criminal punishment due to the severity of the sanction. This threatens to go well beyond the purpose of the United Nations to combat the terrorist threat posed by an individual case.') See also para 41: 'The freezing of assets has an impact on several human rights including the right to property. It impacts directly on the right to work and the right to freedom of movement associated with it.'

57 *Kadi* (n 55) para 150. See also de Wet, 'From *Kadi* to *Nada*' (n 44) fn 42.

58 On the judicial review of UNSC sanctions and its human rights implications, which is beyond the scope of the present chapter, see Erika de Wet, 'Human Rights Considerations and the Enforcement of Targeted Sanctions in Europe: The Emergence of Core Standards of Judicial Protection' in Bardo Fassbender (ed), *Securing Human Rights? Achievements and Challenges of the UN Security Council* (OUP 2011); Lisa Ginsborg and Martin Scheinin, 'You Can't Always Get What You Want: The Kadi II Conundrum and the Security Council 1267 Terrorist Sanctions Regime' (2011) 8 Essex Human Rights Review 7.

Having found that the asset seizure implicated Article 1 of Protocol 1, the ECtHR turned to consider the questions whether the measure was lawful,[59] whether it was executed 'in accordance with the general interest'[60] or, in other words, pursuant to a legitimate aim,[61] and whether it was proportionate – that is, 'whether there existed a reasonable relationship of proportionality between the means employed and the aim sought to be realised'.[62] In turn, the Strasbourg court found that the measure was conducted in accordance with domestic law permitting their use[63] and that 'the application of provisional measures in the context of judicial proceedings, aimed at anticipating a possible confiscation of property, was in the "general interest" of the community'.[64]

Legality

As regards the legality of asset freezing measures requested by the ICC and UNSC, both require the requested States to give domestic effect thereto. Any ECHR-based challenge stemming from the application of ICC- or UNSC-requested measures at the national level will therefore require an assessment of whether the national asset freezing measures were adopted in accordance with the domestic legislation enacted to give effect to the measures requested by the Court or decided upon by the UNSC on the international plane. In *Nada v Switzerland*, the ECtHR observed that 'the impugned measures were taken pursuant to the Taliban Ordinance [i.e. Swiss legislation], adopted to implement the relevant Security Council resolutions ... [and] therefore had a sufficient legal basis.'[65] In a similar vein, measures adopted by States at the domestic level to give effect to ICC requests for cooperation in the freezing of assets pursuant to Article 93(1)(k) of the Rome Statute ought to satisfy this principle.[66]

Legitimate aim

As for what might constitute the 'general interest', in the Rome Statute system there are several stakeholders with rights and interests invested in the pre-trial protective measures process. These include the accused, the Prosecutor, and *bona fide* third parties.[67] Further,

59 *Džinić v Croatia* (n 31) paras 63-64.
60 Protocol 1, art 1.
61 *Džinić v Croatia* (n 31) paras 65-66.
62 ibid paras 67-82.
63 ibid paras 63-64.
64 ibid paras 65-66.
65 *Nada v Switzerland* App no 10593/0856 (ECtHR, 12 September 2012) para 173.
66 For discussion of whether the ICC has taken the legality of measures into account when examining their continued application, see n 123; Chapter 5.
67 On which, see Chapter 5.

Article 57(3)(e) of the Rome Statute provides that protective measures for the purpose of forfeiture are to be taken 'in particular for the ultimate benefit of victims.'[68] ICC pre-trial chambers must therefore take into account the interests of all four groups of stakeholders, which frequently fail to neatly align, when ordering or renewing such measures.

Turning to UNSC-requested asset freezing measures, what might constitute the 'general interest' or 'legitimate aim' will necessarily relate to the purpose of the UNSC resolutions implemented by the domestic legislation in question. For example, in *Nada v Switzerland*, the ECtHR found that 'as the relevant Security Council resolutions had been adopted to combat international terrorism under Chapter VII of the United Nations Charter ("Action with respect to threats to the peace, breaches of the peace, and acts of aggression"), they were also capable of contributing to Switzerland's national security and public safety.'[69]

The responsibility of the UNSC to maintain or restore international peace and security under Article 24(1), Article 39 and Article 41 of the UN Charter will always provide the legal basis for the adoption of sanctions measures, whatever their specific aim might be.[70] The Strasbourg court also held that seeking to prevent crime constituted a legitimate aim of the UNSC sanctions under examination.[71] This finding could also have consequences for ICC-requested asset freezes, given that their aims include the cessation and deterrence of the commission of ongoing or prospective crimes under its jurisdiction.

Proportionality

Turning to its proportionality assessment, which represented the majority of the analysis by the ECtHR in *Džinić v Croatia*, the Strasbourg court noted the margin of appreciation granted to States under paragraph 2 of Article 1 of Protocol 1.[72] The ECtHR then stressed that the execution of such measures, because of their potentially significant impact on the ability of the applicant to manage his assets, should be constrained by 'certain procedural safeguards'.[73] Additionally, 'while any seizure or confiscation entails damage, the actual

68 Rome Statute, art 57(3)(e). See also Chapter 5.

69 *Nada v Switzerland* (n 65) para 174.

70 See UN Charter, art 24(1) ('In order to ensure prompt and effective action by the United Nations, its Members confer on the Security Council primary responsibility for the maintenance of international peace and security, and agree that in carrying out its duties under this responsibility the Security Council acts on their behalf.') See also UN Charter, art 39 ('The Security Council shall determine the existence of any threat to the peace, breach of the peace, or act of aggression and shall make recommendations, or decide what measures shall be taken in accordance with Articles 41 and 42, to maintain or restore international peace and security.')

71 *Nada v Switzerland* (n 65) para 174.

72 *Džinić v Croatia* (n 31) para 68.

73 ibid.

damage sustained should not be more extensive than that which is inevitable, if it is to be compatible with Article 1 of Protocol No. 1'.[74] After analysing whether the national court had struck a fair balance, the ECtHR concluded that the measures, although justifiable in principle, infringed Article 1 of Protocol 1 because they were executed and remained in force without the domestic authorities having determined whether the value of the seized assets corresponded with the potential value of a future order for confiscation.[75]

This principle ought to be relatively straightforward to apply in the ICC context: the value of frozen and/or seized assets ought to correspond with the expected value of a future fine, order for forfeiture or order to make reparations to victims. The ICC has yet to issue a fine or forfeiture order outside of proceedings involving offences against the administration of justice,[76] but it has issued a small number of orders for reparations. The sums ordered against convicted persons have been significant, despite the indigence of each of the accused: Thomas Lubanga Dyilo was found liable for $10 million,[77] Germain Katanga for $1 million,[78] and Ahmad Al Faqi Al Mahdi for €2.7 million.[79] These sums could provide useful yardsticks against which future requests for the freezing of assets could be measured in cases where the accused person is not deemed to be indigent.

As for UNSC-requested asset freezes, proportional application of such measures might be somewhat less concrete. This is because of the diverse purposes served by the freezing of assets in accordance with UNSC resolutions.[80] In such cases, it is not unreasonable to suggest that the State(s) acting at the request of the UNSC to give effect to the assets freeze ought to be afforded a wider margin of appreciation in their application of the measures because of the difficulties in quantifying their potential value.

---

74 ibid.

75 ibid paras 80-81.

76 *Prosecutor v Bemba Gombo and others* (Decision on Sentence pursuant to Article 76 of the Statute) ICC-01/05-01/13-2123-Corr (22 March 2017) 98-99 (imposing fines of €30,000 and €300,000 on Aimé Kilolo Musamba and Jean-Pierre Bemba Gombo, respectively). Both fines were subsequently confirmed in *Prosecutor v Bemba Gombo and others* (Decision Re-sentencing Mr Jean-Pierre Bemba Gombo, Mr Aimé Kilolo Musamba and Mr Jean-Jacques Mangenda Kabongo) ICC-01/05-01/13-2312 (17 September 2018) 50-51.

77 *Prosecutor v Lubanga Dyilo* (Corrected version of the "Decision Setting the Size of the Reparations Award for which Thomas Lubanga Dyilo is Liable") ICC-01/04-01/06-3379-Red-Corr-tENG (21 December 2017) 111. The sum was confirmed on appeal. See *Prosecutor v Lubanga Dyilo* (Judgment on the appeals against Trial Chamber II's 'Decision Setting the Size of the Reparations Award for which Thomas Lubanga Dyilo is Liable') ICC-01/04-01/06-3466-Red (18 July 2019).

78 *Prosecutor v Katanga* (Order for Reparations pursuant to Article 75 of the Statute) ICC-01/04-01/07-3728-tENG (24 March 2017) 118. The amount was confirmed on appeal. See *Prosecutor v Katanga* (Public redacted Judgment on the appeals against the order of Trial Chamber II of 24 March 2017 entitled "Order for Reparations pursuant to Article 75 of the Statute") ICC-01/04-01/07-3778-Red (9 March 2018).

79 *Prosecutor v Al Mahdi* (Reparations Order) ICC-01/12-01/15-236 (17 August 2017) 60.

80 See nn 15-18 and accompanying text.

The following section surveys another crucial aspect of the asset freezing process, namely the (mis)management of assets after they have been frozen and seized by the responsible domestic authorities, an issue of immediate practical relevance to the ICC.

7.2.1.2 Chaparro Álvarez and Lapo Íñiguez v. Ecuador

The right to the use and enjoyment of property was brought to the attention of the IACtHR in the case of *Chaparro Álvarez and Lapo Íñiguez v. Ecuador*.[81] This case arose as a result of the seizure and subsequent mismanagement by Ecuadorian authorities of a factory belonging to Mr Chaparro and a vehicle owned by Mr Lapo.[82] According to Ecuador, the seizure was performed because of the alleged involvement of the two individuals in narcotics trafficking offences.[83] In its judgment, the IACtHR elucidated the ambit of Article 21 of the ACHR (read together with Article 1(1)[84] and Article 2 of the ACHR).[85] Several of the principles articulated by the San José court are relevant to the practice of the ICC and UNSC as concerns the freezing of assets. It is these principles, that is to say (i) judicial supervision; (ii) management fees and the presumption of innocence; and (iii) prompt release, to which the chapter now turns.

Judicial supervision

At the outset, it is important to note that the IACtHR did not find the adoption of provisional (or, in its words, precautionary) asset freezing measures to inherently constitute a violation of Article 21 of the ACHR.[86] This said, the San José court stressed the potential for a violation of right to the use and enjoyment of property if the responsible domestic

81 *Case of Chaparro Álvarez and Lapo Íñiguez v. Ecuador* (Judgment of November 21, 2007) IACtHR Series C No 170 (21 November 2007).

82 ibid para 173.

83 ibid.

84 ACHR, art 1(1) provides as follows: 'The States Parties to this Convention undertake to respect the rights and freedoms recognized herein and to ensure to all persons subject to their jurisdiction the free and full exercise of those rights and freedoms, without any discrimination for reasons of race, color, sex, language, religion, political or other opinion, national or social origin, economic status, birth, or any other social condition.'

85 ACHR, art 2 provides as follows: 'Where the exercise of any of the rights or freedoms referred to in Article 1 is not already ensured by legislative or other provisions, the States Parties undertake to adopt, in accordance with their constitutional processes and the provisions of this Convention, such legislative or other measures as may be necessary to give effect to those rights or freedoms.'

86 *Case of Chaparro Álvarez and Lapo Íñiguez v. Ecuador* (n 81) para 187 ('The Court finds that the adoption of these measures does not constitute *per se* a violation of the right to property, if it is considered that they do not signify a transfer of the ownership of the right to legal title. In this regard, the property cannot be disposed of definitively and such disposal is restricted exclusively to its administration and conservation and to the respective acts of investigation and management of the evidence.')

authorities fail to ensure adequate judicial supervision of such measures in the following terms:

> these measures must be adopted and supervised by judicial officials, taking into account that, if the reasons that justified the precautionary measure cease to exist, the judge must assess the pertinence of maintaining the restriction, even before the proceedings are concluded. This point is extremely important, given that if the property ceases to fulfill a relevant role in continuing or promoting the investigation [as required by the pertinent Ecuadorian laws], the material precautionary measure must be lifted, because they run the risk of becoming an anticipated punishment. The latter would constitute a manifestly disproportionate restriction of the right to property.[87]

Management fees and the presumption of innocence

A second principle pronounced by the IACtHR in *Chaparro Álvarez and Lapo Íñiguez v. Ecuador* stems from the presumption of innocence, to which an accused is entitled not only under the ACHR,[88] but also under a range of international human rights instruments[89] and the statutes of ICTs,[90] including the Rome Statute.[91] In the view of the IACtHR, this presumption entitles an accused to protection from the application of measures that are disproportionate, including the requirement to pay fees incurred in the management of the assets while frozen at the behest of the State following an acquittal. In the words of the court in *Chaparro Álvarez and Lapo Íñiguez v. Ecuador*:

> [T]he Court emphasizes that material precautionary measures are adopted with regard to the property of a person who is presumed innocent; hence, these measures should not prejudice the accused disproportionately. The charges that a person whose case has been dismissed is required to pay, with regard to the property of which he was provisionally dispossessed, constitute a burden that is tantamount to a sanction. This requirement is disproportionate for those persons whose guilt has not been proved.[92]

87 ibid para 188.
88 ACHR, art 8(2).
89 See ECHR, art 6(2); ICCPR, art 14(2); Banjul Charter, art 7(1)(b); Arab Charter, art 7; UDHR, art 11(1).
90 See MICT Statute, art 19(3); SCSL Statute, art 17(3); STL Statute, art 16(3).
91 Rome Statute, art 66.
92 *Case of Chaparro Álvarez and Lapo Íñiguez v. Ecuador* (n 81) para 193.

Prompt release

A third principle expressed by the IACtHR concerns the length of time allowed between the end of proceedings against accused persons and the release of their frozen and/or seized assets before their right to the use and enjoyment of property is violated. In the case of *Chaparro Álvarez and Lapo Íñiguez v. Ecuador*, the IACtHR held that a one-year delay between the provisional stay of the proceedings against Mr Chaparro and the return of his property was too protracted. According to the IACtHR:

> [T]he property confiscated from Mr. Chaparro should have been returned when the reasons had disappeared that made the material precautionary measures necessary. … The Court finds that this [one-year] delay in complying with the order to return the property, which was no longer affected by a precautionary measure, aggravated Mr. Chaparro's situation when he was attempting to remedy, to some extent, the impediment to the use and enjoyment of his property, and this constitutes a violation of Article 21(1) of the Convention, in relation to Article 1(1) thereof, to his detriment.[93]

It is argued that, if asset freezing measures are subject to satisfactory judicial supervision in line with the first principle articulated by the IACtHR in this case, then the prompt release of assets at the conclusion of proceedings against the accused ought to follow as a consequence thereof. By the same token, it is not unreasonable to propose that the timely release of frozen assets after the proceedings against the accused person have concluded is less likely to take place in cases where the freezing measures are inadequately supervised by the responsible domestic authorities.

The principles that the IACtHR expressed in its discussion of Article 21 of the ACHR in *Chaparro Álvarez and Lapo Íñiguez v. Ecuador* are of particular import for the ICC, whose Pre-Trial Chamber II, in May 2020, rejected a claim for compensation and damages filed by Jean-Pierre Bemba Gombo.[94] In this filing, Mr Bemba claimed a total of €42.4 million from the ICC because of the alleged mismanagement of his assets frozen at the Court's request.[95] Indeed, Mr Bemba cited the IACtHR's conclusions in the case of *Chaparro Álvarez and Lapo Íñiguez v. Ecuador*, namely that 'property confiscated by the State … is placed in its custody; consequently, the State assumes a position of guarantor of its good

93 ibid paras 203-204.

94 *Situation in the Central African Republic* (Decision on Mr Bemba's claim for compensation and damages) ICC-01/05-01/08-3694 (18 May 2020) (*Bemba* Claim Decision). For analysis, see Chapter 8.

95 *Situation in the Central African Republic* (Public Redacted Version of "Mr. Bemba's claim for compensation and damages") ICC-01/05-01/08-3673-Red (11 March 2019) (*Bemba* Claim) paras 123-65.

use and conservation, particularly taking into account that precautionary measures are not of a punitive nature',[96] in support of his submission that the '[f]ailure to preserve the value of frozen property gives rise to a claim for damages'.[97] With the Pre-Trial Chamber having dismissed this component of his claim, Mr Bemba has since sought leave to appeal the decision.[98] In view of the ICC's obligation to apply and interpret its applicable law in a manner consistent with internationally recognised human rights,[99] it is the view of the present author that, if leave is granted, the Appeals Chamber ought to seriously consider the discussion of Article 21 of the ACHR by the IACtHR in its adjudicating Mr Bemba's appeal. Indeed, a strict application of the IACtHR's approach might require the ICC and/or the State(s) responsible for failing to preserve the value of Mr Bemba's assets while frozen to award him damages, if his claims are found to have merit. This argument finds further support in the fact that the findings of the ECtHR in *Džinić v Croatia* are congruent inasmuch as both human rights courts emphasise the threat posed to the right to the peaceful use and enjoyment of one's property by the protracted application of asset freezing measures. Without explicitly alleging a violation thereof, another right implicated[100] in Mr Bemba's claim is that to respect for private and family life. The following section addresses the constraints placed on the exercise of the asset freezing powers afforded to the ICC and UNSC under the Rome Statute and UN Charter, respectively, by this ECHR- and ACHR-protected right.

7.2.2 Right to respect for private and family life

Article 8 of the ECHR provides as follows:

> 1. Everyone has the right to respect for his private and family life, his home and his correspondence.
>
> 2. There shall be no interference by a public authority with the exercise of this right except such as is in accordance with the law and is necessary in a democratic society in the interests of national security, public safety or the

96 *Case of Chaparro Álvarez and Lapo Íñiguez v. Ecuador* (n 81) para 211.

97 *Bemba* Claim (n 94) para 136. In citing the case decided under the ACHR, Mr Bemba compares his situation to those of Mr Chaparro and Mr Lapo in that he alleges that the value of his assets significantly decreased while they were frozen. See also *Case of Chaparro Álvarez and Lapo Íñiguez v. Ecuador* (n 81) paras 211-14.

98 *Situation in the Central African Republic* (Request for leave to appeal the 'Decision on Mr Bemba's claim for compensation and damages') ICC-01/05-01/08-3695 (25 May 2020).

99 Rome Statute, art 21(3).

100 See *Bemba* Claim (n 94) paras 2, 89-106, 117.

> economic well-being of the country, for the prevention of disorder or crime, for the protection of health or morals, or for the protection of the rights and freedoms of others.[101]

Article 8 of the ECHR finds its equivalent provision in Article 11 of the ACHR, titled 'Right to Privacy'. This provision provides as follows:

> Everyone has the right to have his honor respected and his dignity recognized.
>
> No one may be the object of arbitrary or abusive interference with his private life, his family, his home, or his correspondence, or of unlawful attacks on his honor or reputation.
>
> Everyone has the right to the protection of the law against such interference or attacks.[102]

7.2.2.1 Nada v Switzerland

Article 8 of the ECHR, among other rights, was implicated in *Nada v Switzerland*.[103] This case concerned the domestic implementation of UNSC sanctions by Switzerland, leading to a ban on the applicant, an Italian and Egyptian national who lived in an Italian exclave surrounded by the Swiss canton of Ticino, from travelling through Swiss territory. At the same time, the measures agreed by the UNSC Sanctions Committee established by UNSC Resolution 1267 (1999),[104] later incorporated by Switzerland into its domestic law,[105] also led to the freezing of the applicant's assets.[106] The ECtHR recognised the potential impact of such measures on the applicant's right to respect for private and family life:

> [T]he Court considers that the applicant could not reasonably have been required to move from Campione d'Italia, where he had been living since 1970, to settle in another region of Italy, especially as it cannot be ruled out that, as

101 ECHR, art 8.

102 ACHR, art 11.

103 *Nada v Switzerland* (n 65).

104 UNSC Res 1267 (15 October 1999) UN Doc S/RES/1267. The UNSC extended the sanctions regime in UNSC Res 1333 (19 December 2000) UN Doc S/RES/1333.

105 On 2 October 2002, Switzerland passed the *Ordonnance instituant des mesures à l'encontre de personnes et entités liées à Oussama ben Laden, au groupe «Al-Qaïda» ou aux Taliban* (Ordinance on Measures against Persons and Organisations with Ties to Osama Bin Laden, the "Al-Qaida" Group or the Taliban). See *Nada v Switzerland* (n 65) paras 16, 66.

106 The applicant was added to the UNSC sanctions list on 9 November 2001. See *Nada v Switzerland* (n 65) para 21.

> a result of the freeze imposed by paragraph 1(c) of Resolution 1373 (2001) ..., he could no longer dispose freely of all his property and assets. Regardless of whether a request for authorisation to move house would have had any chance of success, it should be pointed out that the right to respect for one's home is protected by Article 8 of the Convention[.][107]

Referring to, among other factors, 'the duration of the measures imposed',[108] the ECtHR ultimately concluded that Switzerland's implementation of the UNSC sanctions had violated the applicant's Article 5 right.[109] The applicant brought his complaint to the Strasbourg court largely because of the impact of the UNSC-imposed travel ban on his ability to exercise his rights under Articles 5, 8 and 9 of the ECHR.[110] The ECtHR made no further findings with respect to the effects of the asset freeze on the applicant's Article 8 right to respect for private and family life. Nevertheless, the limited dictum from the Strasbourg court on the potential impact of asset freezing measures on the human right to respect for one's private and family life, which encompasses the right to respect for one's home, is significant not only for the UNSC, and States executing asset freezing measures requested thereby, but also for the ICC.

The ICC has requested States to freeze the assets of individuals, including real property. Pre-Trial Chamber I issued an arrest warrant for Mr Germain Katanga on 2 July 2007.[111] Four days later, the same Pre-Trial Chamber requested the national authorities of the DRC 'to take, in accordance with the procedures provided for in its national legislation, all necessary measures to identify, trace, freeze or seize the property and assets of Germain Katanga on its territory'.[112] Additionally, further to the Prosecutor's application for a

---

107 *Nada v Switzerland* (n 65) para 190.

108 ibid para 195. The ECtHR further found 'that the possibility of deciding how the relevant Security Council resolutions were to be implemented in the domestic legal order should have allowed some alleviation of the sanctions regime applicable to the applicant, having regard to [his specific situation], in order to avoid interference with his private and family life, without however circumventing the binding nature of the relevant resolutions or compliance with the sanctions provided for therein.' ibid. Reflecting on this approach, Erika de Wet argues that the 'presumption that the UNSC did not intend to deviate from human rights standards seems to be almost non-rebuttable, even where it would amount to a distortion of the text of a UNSC decision.' de Wet, 'From *Kadi* to *Nada*' (n 44) 806.

109 ibid para 199.

110 ibid para 3. The applicant also alleged a violation of Article 13 ECHR.

111 *Prosecutor v Katanga* (Warrant of Arrest for Germain Katanga) ICC-01/04-01/07-1-tENG (2 July 2007).

112 *Prosecutor v Katanga* (Request to the Democratic Republic of the Congo for the purpose of obtaining the identification, tracing, freezing and seizure of the property and assets of Germain Katanga) ICC-01/04-01/07-7-tENG (6 July 2007) para 3.

warrant of arrest for Katanga, Pre-Trial Chamber I issued another order on 5 November 2007,[113] in which it observed as follows:

> [I]n its application, the Prosecution informed the Chamber that Germain Katanga reportedly had two residences in Aveba at the time of the events ... and that he also [could have] be[en] expected to have retained at least some of the fruits of the crimes in which his combatants frequently engaged; that these assets potentially could be used to satisfy a reparation award, if such an award is entered; and that, moreover, Germain Katanga ha[d] the means to place his property and assets beyond the reach of the Court.[114]

The human rights infringed by the freezing of real property therefore has implications for the Court,[115] which must be prepared to justify any such infringement.[116]

7.2.2.2 The need for clear reasoning at the ICC

The ICC has explicitly referred to the law and practice of the ECtHR as regards the right to respect for private and family life under Article 8 of the ECHR in applying Article 21(3) of its constituent instrument to the execution of asset freezing measures. According to this provision, the Court must interpret and apply its sources of applicable law 'consistent with internationally recognized human rights'.[117] Albeit not in the context of asset freezing, in its application of this key provision, ICC Trial Chamber VII acknowledged '[t]he fact that international human rights law affords a right to privacy is beyond question and the

---

113 *Prosecutor v Katanga* (Order on the execution of the warrant of arrest against Germain Katanga) ICC-01/04-01/07-54-tENG (5 November 2007) (*Katanga* Order).

114 ibid 5.

115 In filings issued during the course of proceedings requesting to have an ICC-requested asset freeze lifted following his acquittal for crimes against humanity and war crimes, Jean-Pierre Bemba Gombo alleged that 'houses' belonging to him had been frozen at the request of the Court. See *Situation in the Central African Republic* (Public Redacted version of "Response to Redacted version of the Registry's Observations on Mr. Bemba's Request for Reclassification of Information relating to Mr Jean-Pierre Bemba Gombo's Assets") ICC-01/05-01/08-3657-Red (30 October 2018) para 4. See also *Situation in the Central African Republic* (Public Redacted Version of "Urgent request for partial reconsideration and associated orders") ICC-01/05-01/08-3663-Red (10 December 2018) paras 5-6, expressly making reference to Bemba's lack of contemporary 'knowledge of where [frozen] houses are located' and 'property in the DRC'.

116 Pre-Trial Chamber I offered such a justification in the same order in respect of the warrant for the arrest of Mr Katanga, noting that, 'for the purpose of awarding reparations to persons with victim status in a case, if property and assets are not identified, located and frozen or seized at the time of the execution of a cooperation request for arrest and surrender of the person, or very soon thereafter, it is likely that the subsequent efforts of the Chamber, the Prosecution or the victims participating in the case will be fruitless because existing technology makes it possible for a person to place most of his assets and moveable property beyond the Court's reach in only a few days.' Katanga Order (n 113) 5.

117 Rome Statute, art 21(3).

Chamber is duty-bound to respect this right pursuant to Article 21(3) of the Statute.'[118] In the ensuing paragraphs, Trial Chamber VII determined whether the violations alleged by Aimé Kilolo Musamba of his right to respect for private and family life were effected 'in accordance with the law',[119] having confirmed that infringements upon the exercise of this right may only occur without violating the ECHR under such circumstances.[120]

The same Trial Chamber, albeit with Judge Bertram Schmitt sitting as a Single Judge, affirmed this approach in response to a further filing by Kilolo regarding his bank account, which had been frozen by Belgium at the request of the Court.[121] Kilolo had alleged that the measure infringed his right to respect for private and family life because he was unable to provide for them financially.[122] After applying the ECtHR's criteria concerning the circumstances in which the right can be interfered with, Judge Schmitt rejected Kilolo's request that his account be unfrozen.[123] Consequently, in its limited (publicly-available) decisions on the application of asset freezing measures, the Court appears to have adopted and applied the ECtHR's criteria as determinative of whether the freezes were executed 'consistent with internationally recognized human rights' under Article 21(3) of the Rome Statute.[124]

118 *Prosecutor v Bemba Gombo and others* (Decision on Kilolo Defence Motion for Inadmissibility of Material) ICC-01/05-01/13-1257 (16 September 2015) (*Kilolo* Inadmissibility Decision) para 16, citing ICCPR, art 17; ECHR, art 8(1); ACHR, art 11; Arab Charter, art 21(1).

119 ibid paras 16-21. Trial Chamber VII also acknowledged that 'Interference with this right is subject to other requirements, such as the interference being "necessary in a democratic society in the interests of national security, public safety or the economic wellbeing of the country", but [stated that] there [was] no argument in the Request that Mr Kilolo's rights have been violated in these respects.' ibid fn 22.

120 ibid para 16, citing ECHR, art 8(2).

121 *Prosecutor v Bemba Gombo and others* (Decision on the 'Requête de la défense aux fins de levée du gel des avoirs de Monsieur Aimé Kilolo Musamba') ICC-01/05-01/13-1485-Red (17 November 2015) (*Kilolo* Lifting Decision) paras 21-23.

122 ibid para 21.

123 Judge Schmitt considered whether the freeze of Kilolo's bank account 'was taken in accordance with the law and for a legitimate aim'. Judge Schmitt also took into account whether it was 'proportionate vis-à-vis the legitimate aim pursued'. ibid para 22. For analysis of Judge Schmitt's application of the ECtHR's case law, see Chapter 5.

124 Rome Statute, art 21(3).

References to regional human rights jurisprudence, which, at the ICC, most often focus on decisions of the ECtHR,[125] although understandable and offering a number of benefits for the ICC's case law,[126] should be treated with caution.[127] As Annika Jones observes:

> The risk that reference to regional human rights jurisprudence could be used ... to the detriment of the accused ... highlights the importance of clear reasoning on the part of judges. To counter the risk of unfairness, it is important that judges demonstrate awareness of the different functions of the ICC and regional human rights courts in their reasoning, ensure compliance with the ICC's provisions on fair trial standards and provide a clear explanation of how human rights jurisprudence is being used[.][128]

Judge Schmitt could have more explicitly followed this final recommendation in deciding on the violations alleged by Mr Kilolo. Although the ECtHR's approach to balancing the application of protective measures with the right to the peaceful enjoyment of private and family life was plainly followed, and the multiple reasons provided by Judge Schmitt for his rejection of Kilolo's request were clearly articulated, a more thorough explanation of how the case law of the ECtHR (and, by reference, the IACtHR)[129] was used would have been beneficial to the parties in facilitating their understanding of the Court's reasoning. Adopting clear reasoning in this context could also serve to assist, in a similar manner, future parties to proceedings concerning the (un)freezing of assets. The reasons for relying upon the jurisprudence of a particular regional human rights court (for example, its

125 See Jones (n 7) 724 (analysing 'the Court's disproportionate number of references to the case law of the ECtHR vis-à-vis other international, regional and domestic mechanisms.') Jones notes that, during the proceedings in *Lubanga*, the 46 references made by the ICC to the case law of the ECtHR was 'almost double the number of references' made to that of the IACtHR (25). ibid. Jones justifies the ICC's preference as follows: '[t]he length of the ECtHR's operation and the quantity of relevant case law that it had produced explains the disproportionate number of references to the ECtHR vis-à-vis the IACtHR'. ibid 725.

126 See Jones (n 7) 704-06 (identifying benefits concerning the coherence of international law, the quality of the Court's case law and the perceived legitimacy of the Court).

127 See Jones (n 7) 706-08 (discussing the potential for the import of cultural bias and possible undesirable consequences for the rights of the accused); Volker Nerlich, 'Article 21 (3) of the ICC Statute: Identifying and Applying "Internationally Recognized Human Rights"' in Paolo Lobba and Triestino Mariniello (eds), *Judicial Dialogue on Human Rights: The Practice of International Criminal Tribunals* (2017) 84-85 (noting the case- and jurisdiction-specific nature of the ECtHR's case law).

128 Jones (n 7) 708.

129 See *Kilolo* Lifting Decision (n 121) fn 37, referring to 'further references to human rights case law [including that of the IACtHR] in related footnotes' in *Kilolo* Inadmissibility Decision (n 118) para 16.

expertise in international human rights issues),[130] ought therefore to be made clear,[131] not least 'to allow the defence to make effective challenges where the rights of the accused are at stake'.[132]

7.3 CONCLUSION

This chapter has sought to demonstrate that the freezing of individuals' assets necessarily infringes their fundamental human rights. Using the law and practice of the ECtHR and IACtHR as a lens through which to ascertain the human rights implications of asset freezing measures, the chapter shows that two specially-affected rights are the right to the peaceful enjoyment of one's possessions and the right to respect for one's private and family life, home and correspondence. The chapter has also demonstrated that the human rights repercussions of such measures have consequences for the ICC and UNSC, both of which have the power to request States to freeze the assets of individuals. These States are also impacted by the Strasbourg- and San José-based courts' findings because it is their national authorities who carry out the asset freezes requested by the ICC and UNSC. This is done in accordance with their respective domestic implementing legislation. Council of Europe States, whose members constitute the High Contracting Parties to the ECHR, and States Parties to the ACHR are particularly impacted. This is because their national implementation of ICC- or UNSC-requested asset freezes could form the subject of a challenge before the Strasbourg court, as in the case of *Nada v Switzerland*, or the IACtHR, respectively. It is not difficult to envisage a similar complaint being brought with respect to a freeze requested by the ICC. Indeed, the domestic execution of ICC-requested asset freezing measures has been challenged in the domestic courts of at least one Council of Europe Member State: Italy.[133]

---

130 See Julia Geneuss, 'Obstacles to Cross-fertilisation: The International Criminal Tribunals' 'Unique Context' and the Flexibility of the European Court of Human Rights' Case Law' (2015) 84 Nordic Journal of International Law 404, 425-26.

131 Julia Geneuss proposes a two-step approach in this context, as follows: 'Whenever faced with a human rights issue ICTs are obligated to consult ECtHR jurisprudence. And only after a thorough review can ICTs decide whether they are persuaded by the ECtHR's reasoning or whether they want to deviate from and re-interpret the human rights standard. ... In a second step, it is the *persuasiveness* of the ECtHR jurisprudence that matters. Here ICTs look at the contents of ECtHR case law and can decide whether and how they want to translate the ECtHR standard into their own context and whether the balance between, for example, fair trial and public interest must be different, because of the different context in which ICTs operate. However, ... ECtHR case law carries the weight of "directory authority" [it ought to be followed, but can be outweighed] and any deviation and differences in meaning must carefully be explained and justified.' ibid.

132 Jones (n 7) 708.

133 Corte di Appello di Roma (19 July 2012) Ordinanza N 4/12 RGIE (copy on file with author). Thanks to Dini Sejko for his assistance in finding this decision and translating it from Italian into English.

The chapter has shown that a strict application of the human rights principles identified in the case law of the ECtHR and IACtHR could have implications for the length of proceedings at, or at least the duration of asset freezing measures requested by, the ICC. As for the UNSC, which rarely imposes open-ended targeted financial sanctions, to strictly apply the principles developed in the jurisprudence of these two regional human rights courts would require that all asset freezes it imposes under Chapter VII of the UN Charter be time-limited. Other hurdles, namely that such measures be lawful, taken in accordance with a legitimate aim and proportionate should not pose too high a hurdle for States to overcome in executing ICC- and UNSC-requested asset freezes in their domestic legal orders. The same conclusion is applicable to the need for judicial supervision of such measures and the requirement that management fees not be charged to the individual who is subjected to the measures in question This is because of the wide margin of appreciation given to States when executing measures that infringe upon the rights under examination. As for prompt release, this principle has already proved problematic at the Court and could continue to do so if the division of labour between the ICC and the States responsible for freezing individuals' assets is not clarified by the Court in the course of adjudicating Jean-Pierre Bemba Gombo's claim for compensation and damages for *inter alia* the alleged mismanagement of his frozen assets.

In its limited (publicly-available) case law on the (continued) execution of asset freezing measures requested by the ICC, the Court has given weight to the case law of the ECtHR (and, to a noticeably lesser extent, that of the IACtHR) in determining the compatibility of such measures with 'internationally recognized human rights' in accordance with Article 21(3) of its constituent instrument. This practice, albeit justifiable in view of the authority of the Strasbourg and San José courts, nonetheless presents certain challenges, particularly in terms of the concerns raised about the lack of clear reasoning provided by the ICC when referring to the case law of regional human rights courts. Consequently, while advocating that both the ICC and its States Parties acting at its request ought to pay close attention to this case law with a view to respecting the human rights of those to whom asset freezing measures are applied, it is equally important that the reasons behind such reliance are clearly expressed to the parties. To adopt such an approach could serve to render the legal framework applicable to ICC-requested asset freezing measures more 'accessible and foreseeable'[134] and, in turn, more 'consistent with internationally recognized human rights'.

134 *Huvig v France* App no 11105/84 (ECtHR, 24 April 1990) para 26 ('The expression "in accordance with the law", within the meaning of Article 8 § 2 (art. 8-2), requires firstly that the impugned measure should have some basis in domestic law; it also refers to the quality of the law in question, requiring that it should be accessible to the person concerned, who must moreover be able to foresee its consequences for him, and compatible with the rule of law.') See also Sluiter (n 3) 466.

8 Managing the Frozen Assets of Accused Persons at the ICC*

The Fallout of the Bemba *Acquittal*

8.1 Introduction

The ICC is empowered by its constituent instrument to request its States Parties to identify, trace, freeze and seize the property and assets of accused persons, '[w]here a warrant of arrest or a summons has been issued'.[1] More precisely, Article 57(3)(e) of the ICC Statute authorizes pre-trial chambers to 'seek the cooperation of States pursuant to article 93, paragraph 1 (k), to take protective measures for the purpose of forfeiture, in particular for the ultimate benefit of victims.'[2] To the extent that such requests, or decisions discussing such requests, have been made publicly available, the ICC can be seen to have exercised this power in five cases involving persons accused of committing crimes under its jurisdiction since the entry into force of the ICC Statute. Such requests have been issued with respect to (i) Thomas Lubanga Dyilo;[3] (ii) Germain Katanga;[4] (iii) Jean-Pierre Bemba Gombo,[5] (iv) Francis Kirimi Muthaura, Uhuru Muigai Kenyatta and Mohammed Hussein

* An earlier version of this chapter was published as Daley J Birkett, 'Managing Frozen Assets at the International Criminal Court: The Fallout of the *Bemba* Acquittal' (2020) 18 Journal of International Criminal Justice 765-790.

1 Rome Statute, art 57(3)(e).

2 ibid. Rome Statute, art 93, which falls under Rome Statute, Part IX., titled 'International cooperation and judicial assistance', provides, in relevant part, as follows: '(1) States Parties shall, in accordance with the provisions of this Part and under procedures of national law, comply with requests by the Court to provide the following assistance in relation to investigations or prosecutions: ... (k) The identification, tracing and freezing or seizure of proceeds, property and assets and instrumentalities of crimes for the purpose of eventual forfeiture, without prejudice to the rights of bona fide third parties'. On the ICC's law and practice in the execution of 'protective measures', see Chapter 5.

3 See *Prosecutor v Lubanga Dyilo* (Request to the Democratic Republic of the Congo for the purpose of obtaining the identification, tracing, freezing and seizure of property and assets belonging to Mr. Thomas Lubanga Dyilo) ICC-01/04-01/06-22-tEN (9 March 2006); *Prosecutor v Lubanga Dyilo* (Request to States Parties to the Rome Statute for the Identification, Tracing and Freezing or Seizure of the Property and Assets of Mr Thomas Lubanga Dyilo) ICC-01/04-01/06-62-tEN (31 March 2006).

4 See *Prosecutor v Katanga* (Request to the Democratic Republic of the Congo for the purpose of obtaining the identification, tracing, freezing and seizure of the property and assets of Germain Katanga) ICC-01/04-01/07-7-tENG (6 July 2007)

5 See *Prosecutor v Bemba Gombo* (Decision et demande en vue d'obtenir l'identification, la localisation, le gel et la saisie des biens et avoirs adressées a la Republique portugaise) ICC-01/05-01/08-8 (27 May 2008) (*Bemba* Freezing Request).

Ali,[6] and (v) Jean-Pierre Bemba Gombo, Aimé Kilolo Musamba, Jean-Jacques Mangenda Kabongo, Fidèle Babala Wandu and Narcisse Arido.[7] Additionally, in November 2011, the ICC Prosecutor reported to the UNSC that the ICC had transmitted 'requests for assistance to Libya, State Parties, and five UN Security Council non-State Parties to identify, trace, seize and freeze all the personal assets belonging to [Saif Al-Islam Gaddafi and Abdullah Al-Senussi]'.[8]

The assets frozen by States pursuant to requests issued by the ICC under Article 57(3)(e) of the ICC Statute can be put to a number of uses during the course of proceedings and in the event of a conviction. These purposes include the payment of defence fees and, if the Prosecutor secures a conviction, the payment of fines, orders for forfeiture and reparations to victims.[9] But these assets cannot be used for the latter three purposes where the ICC acquits an accused person,[10] who ought to be able to regain control over the frozen assets. Therefore, regardless of whether the proceedings lead to a conviction or an acquittal, there is a clear interest in maintaining the value of the assets while they are frozen, for the benefit of the accused if he or she is acquitted or for the benefit of victims in the event of a conviction and consequent reparations order.

If not properly managed, frozen assets can lose value, thus thwarting the purposes behind the application of protective measures under Article 57(3)(e) of the ICC Statute. This

---

6 See *Prosecutor v Muthaura, Kenyatta and Ali* (Decision Ordering the Registrar to Prepare and Transmit a Request for Cooperation to the Republic of Kenya for the Purpose of Securing the Identification, Tracing and Freezing or Seizure of Property and Assets of Francis Kirimi Muthaura, Uhuru Muigai Kenyatta and Mohammed Hussein Ali) ICC-01/09-02/11-42 (5 April 2011).

7 See *Prosecutor v Bemba Gombo and others* (Warrant of arrest for Jean-Pierre Bemba Gombo, Aimé Kilolo Musamba, Jean-Jacques Mangenda Kabongo, Fidèle Babala Wandu and Narcisse Arido) ICC-01/05-01/13-1-tENG (20 November 2013) 17 ('requesting the States which will arrest the persons concerned, and any other relevant State which may be identified, to locate and freeze their assets').

8 ICC Prosecutor, 'Prosecutor's statement to the United Nations Security Council on the situation in Libya, pursuant to UNSCR 1970 (2011)' (New York, 2 November 2011) <https://www.legal-tools.org/doc/bil32o/> accessed 31 August 2020, para 13.

9 *Prosecutor v Bemba Gombo and others* (Decision on the 'Requête de la défense aux fins de levée du gel des avoirs de Monsieur Aimé Kilolo Musamba') ICC-01/05-01/13-1485-Red (17 November 2015) (*Kilolo* Lifting Decision) paras 17-20. For analysis, see Chapter 5; Carla Ferstman, 'Cooperation and the International Criminal Court: The Freezing, Seizing and Transfer of Assets for the Purpose of Reparations' in Olympia Bekou and Daley J Birkett (eds), *Cooperation and the International Criminal Court: Perspectives from Theory and Practice* (Brill Nijhoff 2016) 234-37 (analysing the *Lubanga* and *Kenyatta* cases).

10 Pursuant to Rome Statute, arts 75(2) and 77, the ICC can only order fines, forfeiture of property and assets and/or reparations directly against a convicted person. See also *Situation in the Central African Republic* (Final decision on the reparations proceedings) ICC-01/05-01/08-3653 (3 August 2018) para 3 ('The Chamber agrees with the submissions made that no reparations order can be made against Mr Bemba under Article 75 of the Statute. The Chamber must respect the limitations of this Court and recalls that it can only address compensation for harm suffered as a result of crimes when the person standing trial for his or her participation in those crimes has been found guilty.')

potential decrease in value is arguably a greater threat in the ICC Statute system than at the national level, where many State authorities possess similar powers to the ICC with respect to asset freezing.[11] This is because criminal proceedings on the international plane generally take significantly longer than those conducted at the domestic level.[12] The ICC acknowledges this prospective problem in a booklet published in 2017 on financial investigations and asset recovery: '[b]ecause assets are frozen during the entirety of ICC proceedings, their value could significantly decrease by the time they can be sold. Therefore, consultation with States at the very early stage is crucial to avoid the devaluation of assets frozen on behalf of the Court.'[13] But the ICC-issued booklet provides no guidance on what such bilateral consultations might involve.

This chapter examines the implications of prolonged asset freezes by the ICC through the lens of the proceedings in the *Prosecutor v. Jean-Pierre Bemba Gombo*. The *Bemba* case provides a suitable case study through which to conduct the present analysis because, at the time of his arrest, Bemba was in possession of a broad portfolio of assets, some of which were frozen by States at the request of the ICC in accordance with the procedure detailed in Article 57(3)(e) of the ICC Statute. The chapter demonstrates that gaps exist in the legal framework applicable to the management of assets under the ICC Statute system and suggests possible responses thereto at the domestic and international levels. In order to realize these aims, the chapter is subdivided into five parts. Part 2 elaborates the importance of the meticulous management of assets in view of the *Bemba* case, providing a procedural history of the case from his arrest in 2008 to his acquittal in 2018 as it pertains to the freezing of his assets. Part 3 turns to the procedures available under several States' national implementing legislation for the proper management of assets frozen or seized at the request of the ICC. Part 4 examines possible steps that could be taken at the international level to respond to certain issues identified in Part 2 as concerns the management of Bemba's assets. Finally, Part 5 offers some concluding remarks on the management of accused persons' frozen assets at the behest of the ICC in view of its first comprehensive experience thereof in the *Bemba* case, questioning *inter alia* whether sufficient use is being made of the provisions in the ICC Statute that provide for (urgent) consultations between States and the Court.

---

11 See Part 8.3.

12 For data, see Alette Smeulers, Barbora Hola and Tom van den Berg, 'Sixty-Five Years of International Criminal Justice: The Facts and Figures', 13 International Criminal Law Review (2013) 7, 16-18; Jean Galbraith, 'The Pace of International Criminal Justice', 31 Michigan Journal of International Law (2009) 79, 112-27. For further discussion of the length of proceedings at ICTs, see Alex Whiting, 'In International Criminal Prosecutions, Justice Delayed Can Be Justice Delivered', 50 Harvard International Law Journal (2009) 323, 323-30 (and footnotes thereto).

13 ICC, 'Financial investigations and recovery of assets' (ICC 2017) 13.

8.2 The *Bemba* Case

8.2.1 (Un)freezing Bemba's Assets

On 24 May 2008, Belgian authorities executed an arrest warrant by the ICC,[14] arresting Jean-Pierre Bemba Gombo near Brussels.[15] At the time of his arrest, Bemba was reported to be a 'millionaire',[16] in control of a 'large business empire'[17] and owning luxury assets in a number of States. These were reported to include a villa in the Algarve in southern Portugal,[18] and a private jet previously belonging to Mobutu Sese Seko, the former President of the DRC.[19] Indeed, Bemba was characterized by ICC Trial Chamber III as follows: 'clearly a man of considerable means, in the sense that he appears to "own", or to have a proprietary interest in, various kinds of property (e.g. buildings, cars, companies), and there are bank accounts held in his sole name, in a number of different countries.'[20] According to a claim for compensation filed by Mr Bemba, to which the author will return,[21] among the assets frozen by States following his arrest at the request of the Court were bank accounts and properties in Belgium, the DRC and Portugal, as well as a boat in the latter.[22]

Three days after Bemba was apprehended, taking into consideration arguments raised by the Prosecutor in his application for an arrest warrant for Bemba,[23] and observing Article

14 *Prosecutor v Bemba Gombo* (Warrant of Arrest for Jean-Pierre Bemba Gombo) ICC-01/05-01/08-1-tENG (23 May 2008); *Prosecutor v Bemba Gombo* (Decision to Unseal the Warrant of Arrest for Mr Jean - Pierre Bemba Gombo) ICC-01/05-01/08-5-tENG (24 May 2008).

15 Agence France-Presse, 'Congo Ex-Official Is Held in Belgium on War Crimes Charges' *The New York Times* (25 May 2008) <www.nytimes.com/2008/05/25/world/africa/25congo.html> accessed 31 August 2020.

16 ibid.

17 Marlise Simons, 'Jean-Pierre Bemba, Congolese politician, appears in Hague court' *The New York Times* (4 July 2008) <www.nytimes.com/2008/07/04/world/africa/04iht-05hague.14247286.html> accessed 31 August 2020.

18 See Bruno F Pires, 'Last stop Faro?' *Algarve 123* (15 March 2012) (copy on file with author). See also 'Written Question by Ana Maria Gomes (PSE) to the Commission, Subject: Jean-Pierre Bemba's residence in Portugal' (European Parliament, 3 June 2008) P-3176/08 ('According to the 26.5.2008 issue of the daily newspaper *Diário de Notícias* ... Bemba, former Vice-President of the CAR, principal political rival of President Kabila, and leader of the MLC, had been living since April 2007 in a luxurious refuge in the Quinta do Lago in Faro').

19 See Pires (n 18).

20 *Prosecutor v Bemba Gombo* (Redacted version of "Decision on legal assistance for the accused") ICC-01/05-01/08-567-Red (26 November 2009) (*Bemba* Assistance Decision) para 1.

21 See Part 8.2.2.

22 *Situation in the Central African Republic* (Public Redacted Version of "Mr. Bemba's claim for compensation and damages") ICC-01/05-01/08-3673-Red (11 March 2019) (*Bemba* Claim for Compensation and Damages) para 127. Mr Bemba also notes the freezing, 'apparently without judicial order', of aircraft and vehicles in the DRC and Portugal, a boat in the DRC and a property in Portugal. See para 128.

23 See *Bemba* Freezing Request (n 5) paras 1, 5. See also *Situation in the Central African Republic* (Prosecutor's Application for Warrant of Arrest under Article 58) ICC-01/05-01/08-26-Red (9 May 2008).

57(3)(e) and Article 93(1)(k) of the ICC Statute, among other provisions, Pre-Trial Chamber III called on 'the Republic of Portugal to take, in accordance with the procedures provided for in its domestic legislation, all necessary measures to identify, locate, freeze or seize the property and assets of Mr Jean-Pierre Bemba Gombo located on its territory, including his movable or immovable property, accounts or shares, subject to the rights of bona fide third parties'.[24] The ICC delivered similar requests to other States, which are not (yet) publicly available.[25] It has, however, been made evident in later filings that Belgium and Cape Verde each received such requests for cooperation from the ICC under Article 93(1)(k) of the ICC Statute. It is to these filings, in which Bemba brings the issue of the devaluation of his assets because of the ICC-requested freeze to the attention of the Court, that the present discussion now turns.

As a result of the execution of the freezing requests, Bemba was unable to access his property and assets in order to meet his defence expenses, among other costs. Trial Chamber III found that he consequently did not have 'sufficient means to pay for his defence'[26] and ordered the Registry '[t]o provide funding in the sum of €30,150 a month' to allow him to pay such fees.[27] On 8 June 2018, more than ten years after his arrest, the Appeals Chamber of the ICC reversed Bemba's conviction by ICC Trial Chamber III for crimes against humanity and war crimes,[28] acquitting him of all charges.[29] On 17 July 2018, Trial Chamber III issued an order instructing Bemba to repay the fees, totalling more than €1.8 million, which had been advanced to him by the Court to fund his defence expenses.[30] Bemba

24 See *Bemba* Freezing Request (n 5) Disposition ('demande à la République portugaise de prendre, conformément aux procédures prévues par sa législation nationale, toutes les mesures nécessaires afin d'identifier, localiser, geler ou saisir les biens et avoirs de M. Jean-Pierre Bemba Gombo qui se trouvent sur son territoire, y compris ses biens meubles ou immeubles, ses comptes bancaires ou ses parts sociales, sous réserve des droits des tiers de bonne foi') (author's translation).

25 *Bemba* Assistance Decision (n 20) para 10. The States to which requests were issued are redacted.

26 ibid para 105.

27 ibid para 111. This sum was increased in 2010 to €42,701 per month. See *Prosecutor v Bemba Gombo* (Redacted Version of Decision on the Defence Application for Review of the Registrar's Decision of 15 October 2010 on the Application for Adjustment of the Expenses and Fees of the Defence (ICC-01/05-01/08-1007-Conf)) ICC-01/05-01/08-1007-Red (7 December 2010) para 39. After the trial phase ended, the amount was reduced to €24,750 per month. See *Prosecutor v Bemba Gombo* (Order in relation to advanced legal assistance fees) ICC-01/05-01/08-3651-Red (17 July 2018) (*Bemba* Order for Repayment) fn 4.

28 *Prosecutor v Bemba Gombo* (Judgment pursuant to Article 74 of the Statute) ICC-01/05-01/08-3343 (21 March 2016).

29 *Prosecutor v Bemba Gombo* (Judgment on the appeal of Mr Jean-Pierre Bemba Gombo against Trial Chamber III's "Judgment pursuant to Article 74 of the Statute") ICC-01/05-01/08-3636-Red (8 June 2018).

30 *Bemba* Order for Repayment (n 27) para 7. The exact sum was €1,886,736.87.

subsequently filed an application before the same Trial Chamber,[31] requesting *inter alia* that: (i) the ICC reclassify all filings concerning his frozen assets so as to make them available to him and (ii) order the States in which assets belonging to him had been frozen to supply him with an account thereof.[32] In the application, Bemba argued that he required such an account because of the 'deterioration, depreciation or destruction [of his property] during its time in the custody of other states or institutions, whilst held on trust by them for its rightful owner.'[33] The application continues: '[t]he orders should be made expeditiously, to mitigate the losses Mr. Bemba continues to suffer as a result of the freezing of his assets.'[34] Importantly, Bemba argued that, following his acquittal, the statutory basis for the freeze ceased to exist and that, in order to repay money borrowed from the ICC's Registry for the partial payment of his legal fees, the freezing orders should be lifted.[35] Bemba also contended that, with the freezing orders having been given effect by States as a result of judicial decisions, a judicial decision was required 'to reverse the effects of those orders.'[36]

Trial Chamber III noted Bemba's application and ordered the Registry to file observations on the requests therein,[37] to which the Registry duly responded.[38] In its observations, the Registry opposed the application for the reason that, in its opinion, reclassifying the documents would have no impact on Bemba's capacity to repay the fees owed to the ICC.[39] The Registry further observed that, in the absence of a determination on the matter by the

31 *Situation in the Central African Republic* (Public Redacted Version of "Preliminary application for reclassification of filings, disclosure, accounts and partial unfreezing of Mr. Bemba's assets") ICC-01/05-01/08-3654-Red (30 October 2018) (*Bemba* Unfreezing Application).

32 ibid para 54. See also para 53 ('freezing another person's property creates fiduciary duties to account for it. It is not, nor was it, Mr Bemba's obligation to trace and identify his own property, nor to point out and protest about the continuing illegality involved in the freezing of his assets.')

33 ibid para 4.

34 ibid para 5.

35 ibid paras 25-37. Mr Bemba also observed that his contractual situation with the Registry concerning the fees advanced to him thereby had no bearing on the question of discharging the freezing orders and that there was no reason to doubt that his cooperation would be forthcoming in this regard. See ibid paras 38-44.

36 ibid para 1.

37 *Situation in the Central African Republic* (Public redacted version of "Decision on the Defence's preliminary application for reclassification of filings, disclosure, accounts and partial unfreezing of Mr Bemba's assets", 24 August 2018) ICC-01/05-01/08-3655-Red (16 November 2018). Trial Chamber III noted 'that the outstanding legal assistance debt is based on a contractual obligation between the Court and Mr Bemba, … [and] consider[ed] the Registry to be the competent body to conduct and arrange the repayment process in the way it sees fit, in consultation with Mr Bemba.' ibid para 9. The Trial Chamber therefore instructed Mr Bemba to 'direct further communication with respect to the repayment, if any, to the Registry'. ibid.

38 *Situation in the Central African Republic* (Public Redacted Version of "Registry's Observations on the Defence Request for Reclassification of Information relating to Mr Jean-Pierre Bemba Gombo's Assets", 3 September 2018) ICC-01/05-01/08-3656-Red2 (7 December 2018).

39 ibid paras 5-6.

Appeals Chamber, if the legal basis for the execution of the freezing requests ceased to exist, as Bemba had argued in his original application, 'the protective measures taken at the national level would be null and void'[40] and that reclassification would be of no import. Finally, the Registry noted that it had transferred more than €2.2 million to Mr Bemba, with over €2 million of this amount deriving from a cooperation request issued by the ICC to Cape Verde in 2014.[41] Bemba filed a response to the Registry's observations, in which he argued as follows:

> Those who take possession of other people's property, thereby hold that property on trust for that other person, the beneficiary or legal owner of the property. As trustees, they have duties to account for the property they have taken (which cannot be derogated), and to protect and preserve it until it is returned. Those basic and fundamental principles are reflected in the rules and protocols that apply to prosecuting authorities who take possession of property within the context of criminal proceedings. ... The same principles apply to all property effectively taken from Mr. Bemba .... Those who freeze and seize assets thereby become trustees of those assets for the lawful owner of them with all the ancillary fiduciary responsibilities to account for what has been seized and to preserve and protect it.[42]

Mr Bemba also observed that the ongoing freezing of his assets, including items of which the Registry was unaware,[43] had rendered his family members unable to exercise their rights over real property and to access bank accounts.[44] Mr Bemba also submitted that, with the Registry having conceded that the orders are without any legal basis and therefore 'null and void',[45] it ought to inform interested States thereof.[46] Further, Mr Bemba reiterated that the relationship between the value of his frozen property and the funds advanced to him by the ICC to finance his defence expenses has 'no bearing on the classification of

40 ibid para 7. The Registry also observed that consulting with all relevant States would be 'tremendously time-consuming'. ibid para 8.

41 ibid para 13. The exact amount that the ICC had transferred to Mr Bemba was €2,277,270.61, with €2,067,982 stemming from the May 2014 transfer from the Cape Verdean authorities to the Court.

42 *Situation in the Central African Republic* (Public Redacted version of "Response to Redacted version of the Registry's Observations on Mr. Bemba's Request for Reclassification of Information relating to Mr Jean-Pierre Bemba Gombo's Assets") ICC-01/05-01/08-3657-Red (30 October 2018) paras 1, 3 (footnotes omitted).

43 ibid para 8. Mr Bemba observed that the Registry's records were insufficient for him to identify which of his assets were frozen. ibid para 7. Mr Bemba further contended that he 'cannot be expected to trace his own assets ... It is the duty of the Court to undo what it has done.' ibid para 9.

44 ibid para 10.

45 ibid para 11.

46 ibid.

filings or the duty to account for his property.'[47] In its submissions filed in response to Mr Bemba's observations, the Registry restated that the Appeal Chamber made no pronouncement as regards the protective measures against Bemba's assets in its judgment acquitting Mr Bemba, nor did it order the Registry to alert States 'with pending cooperation requests' of the judgment.[48] Nonetheless, the Registry confirmed that it would inform the relevant States of the end of the proceedings in the cases[49] against Mr Bemba.[50] The Registry also sought guidance from Trial Chamber III as to whether such notification of Bemba's acquittal 'would mean that the protective measures taken on the basis of the Chamber's requests would be null and void'.[51] Mr Bemba filed a further response to the Registry's submissions on 8 October 2018,[52] in which he reiterated several of his earlier submissions. Of particular note for the purposes of the present analysis, Bemba submitted that the Registry's suggestion that his assets should remain frozen because of his contractual debt to the ICC is 'unfortunate, unfair and illegal'[53] and conflated the jurisdiction of Trial Chamber III, which is seized of the instant proceedings, and Trial Chamber VII, which ordered his fine for offences against the administration of justice.[54] Mr Bemba also contended that 'the impact of ongoing asset freeze 'is becoming cruel and inhumane and potentially interfering with his right to family life.'[55] Mr Bemba thus requested an expeditious resolution by the ICC.[56]

---

47 ibid para 17. See also *Bemba* Unfreezing Application (n 31) paras 38-41.

48 *Situation in the Central African Republic* (Public Redacted Version of "Registry's Submissions in relation to Protective Measures imposed on Mr Bemba's Assets", 21 September 2018) ICC-01/05-01/08-3658-Red2 (7 December 2018) (Registry Submissions) para 5.

49 In separate proceedings, Mr Bemba was convicted of offences against the administration of justice and fined €300,000. See *Prosecutor v Bemba Gombo and others* (Decision on Sentence pursuant to Article 76 of the Statute) ICC-01/05-01/13-2123-Corr (22 March 2017) 99. The fine was confirmed in *Prosecutor v Bemba Gombo and others* (Decision Re-sentencing Mr Jean-Pierre Bemba Gombo, Mr Aimé Kilolo Musamba and Mr Jean-Jacques Mangenda Kabongo) ICC-01/05-01/13-2312 (17 September 2018) 51.

50 Registry Submissions (n 48) para 8. According to the Registry, 'It is the Registry's understanding that the judicial authority that lies with a Chamber, pursuant to articles 57(3)(e) and 93(1)(k) of the Statute, to issue requests for cooperation to impose protective measures on assets at the domestic level necessarily also includes the authority to lift such protective measures. Unless otherwise instructed, the Registry understands its role in this context to be limited to the transmission of the requests for cooperation between the Chamber and the relevant states, in accordance with rule 176(2) of the Rules.' ibid 6.

51 Registry Submissions (n 48) para 9.

52 *Situation in the Central African Republic* (Public Redacted version of "Mr. Bemba's response to the "Redacted version of Registry's Submissions in relation to Protective Measures imposed on Mr Bemba's Assets"") ICC-01/05-01/08-3659-Red (30 October 2018).

53 ibid para 7. According to Mr Bemba, '[t]he frozen property and assets in question were frozen in order to preserve them so they could be used, in the event of a conviction, for a reparations process.' ibid.

54 ibid para 6.

55 ibid para 11.

56 ibid para 15 ('States and institutions continue to execute freezing orders imposed at the request of the ICC four months after Mr. Bemba's acquittal, amounting to an unlawful interference with his personal property, and the personal property of an unknown number of third parties. Mr. Bemba's original request for the reclassification of all material relevant to the freezing orders and an order to the relevant states for a full

Trial Chamber III issued its decision on 20 November 2018.[57] Having first confirmed that the ICC cooperation regime is structured such that 'the Court itself does not order the freezing or seizure of assets, but rather orders that cooperation requests be sent to States from them to do so',[58] Trial Chamber III found that 'the lifting of coercive measures, including the unfreezing of assets, must be done under domestic law.'[59] Trial Chamber III also emphasized that, in the aftermath of Bemba's acquittal by the Appeals Chamber, 'there is no longer any investigation or prosecution against [him] … and States are thus under no obligation to comply with *any* of the standing requests for cooperation.'[60] The Trial Chamber therefore confirmed that it would be for the Registry to inform interested States of the consequences of the acquittal, which, in turn, ought to lead to appropriate action by national authorities under domestic law.[61] Having dismissed Mr Bemba's application for the reclassification of documents,[62] Trial Chamber III confirmed that the repayment of his fine ought to be addressed by the Registry in consultation with Trial Chamber VII.[63] Trial Chamber III made no explicit findings as concerns the claims made by Mr Bemba regarding the depreciation of his assets and his right to family life.

On 10 December 2018, counsel for Mr Bemba filed a request to Trial Chamber III to partially reconsider its decision,[64] in which he argued *inter alia* that the relevant States had

accounting of seized and frozen property has now been pending for seven weeks. With every day that passes, the financial and economic loss resulting from the freezing of this property necessarily increases.')

57 *Situation in the Central African Republic* (Public redacted version of "Decision on Mr Bemba's preliminary application for reclassification of filings, disclosure, accounts, and partial unfreezing of Mr Bemba's assets and the Registry's Request for guidance", 18 October 2018) ICC-01/05-01/08-3660-Red2 (20 November 2018) (*Bemba* Unfreezing Decision).

58 ibid para 11.

59 ibid para 12. The Trial Chamber continued: 'an acquittal or other cessation of proceedings does not render the original cooperation requests nor the coercive measures invalid, null or void. The cooperation requests issued in this case remain, but cease to have effect in the sense that States are no longer required to comply with them, for instance by keeping any assets frozen. This, however, does not mean that assets are automatically released in the requested State. It is rather for the State to determine what action to take under domestic law as a result of the conclusion of its obligation to assist the Court through the freezing of assets.' ibid para 13.

60 ibid para 15.

61 ibid.

62 ibid paras 16-18. The Trial Chamber observed that it 'does not have the power to order States to, for instance, "provide a full accounting of the property frozen," as requested by [counsel for Mr Bemba]'. ibid para 18.

63 ibid para 21. Trial Chamber III added that 'the Court's legal framework does not prohibit the Registry from seeking States' *voluntary* cooperation in securing the repayment of the advanced legal assistance fees' (emphasis in original). ibid para 20. The Trial Chamber did, however, caution 'that States must at all times be made aware that the cooperation obligation under Article 86 of the Statute would not be applicable to such requests.' ibid.

64 *Situation in the Central African Republic* (Public Redacted Version of "Urgent request for partial reconsideration and associated orders") ICC-01/05-01/08-3663-Red (10 December 2018).

refused to respond to his requests as regards his frozen assets.[65] 'In Mr. Bemba's submission, especially given the urgency of the current situation, the effective *impasse* in the unfreezing of his assets, and the fact that almost five months have now lapsed since his acquittal',[66] Trial Chamber III ought to partially reconsider its decision and/or grant the relief sought in this request.[67] As of August 2020, there have been no further submissions concerning the frozen assets.

8.2.2 Bemba's Claim for Compensation and Damages

On 11 March 2019, counsel for Mr Bemba filed a claim for compensation and damages under Article 85 of the ICC Statute, which governs compensation to an arrested or convicted person.[68] Part of this claim pertains to his assets.[69] In short, Mr Bemba claims that the ICC acted negligently in seizing and freezing his assets, as well as in managing them after their freezing.[70] The total amount of damages sought by Mr Bemba is €42.4 million.[71] In his submission, after detailing the assets seized and/or frozen at the Court's request,[72] Bemba claims that frozen assets ought to be properly managed in order to avoid deterioration in their value[73] and that the ICC had a duty as concerns his assets.[74] Bemba further alleges that the Court was negligent in executing this duty,[75] that he has suffered loss as a consequence of the Court's negligence (or breach of fiduciary duty),[76] and that, for this reason, the ICC must provide him with a remedy.[77]

On 6 May 2019, the Prosecutor filed her response to Mr Bemba's claim for compensation and damages.[78] In her response, only a small part of which addresses the alleged loss to his seized or frozen assets,[79] the Prosecutor refutes Bemba's claim that the purported loss

65 ibid para 33. In his request, Mr Bemba's also provided 'with greater specificity the information and documents for which reclassification is being sought.' ibid para 32.
66 ibid para 2.
67 ibid.
68 Rome Statute, art 85.
69 *Bemba* Claim for Compensation and Damages (n 22) paras 123-65.
70 ibid para 6. See also ibid paras 123-65.
71 ibid para 125.
72 ibid paras 126-32.
73 ibid paras 133-38.
74 ibid paras 139-42.
75 ibid paras 143-50.
76 ibid paras 151-53.
77 ibid paras 154-65.
78 *Situation in the Central African Republic* (Public redacted version of "Prosecution's response to Mr Bemba's claim for compensation and damages", 6 May 2019) ICC-01/05-01/08-3680-Red (6 May 2019).
79 ibid paras 83-102. The Prosecutor confines the majority of her response to arguments concerning Mr Bemba's failure to discharge his burden under Rome Statute, art 85, the conduct of her office and that of

resulting from the seizure of his assets at the Court's request is sufficient to satisfy the criteria of Article 85 of the ICC Statute.[80] The Prosecutor also challenges Bemba's private law claim against the ICC for the allegedly negligent management of his assets.[81] Notably, the Prosecutor also contests Mr Bemba's understanding of the ICC cooperation regime as it concerns the freezing and seizure of assets.[82] In short, the Prosecutor endorses the opinion of Trial Chamber III as articulated in the proceedings concerning the unfreezing of Bemba's assets, namely that the Court transmits requests for cooperation to States, who then decide how to proceed in the execution and lifting of coercive measures pursuant to their respective domestic law.[83] According to the Prosecutor, '[in] this context, ... a demarcation of responsibility between the Court and States Parties is appropriate given that it is the States which are equipped with the necessary laws, regulations and mechanisms to carry out the freezing and seizure of assets.'[84]

On the same day, the Registry submitted its observations on Bemba's claim for compensation and damages.[85] Among other submissions:

> [t]he Registry observes that, notwithstanding that there may be follow-up to the execution of cooperation requests on freezing or seizure of assets, a duty to manage or 'fiduciary duty to preserve assets', is not supported by the Court's legal framework. The Defence appears to confound any such 'follow-up' on the execution of its cooperation requests with the states' responsibility in connection with the execution of these requests under their respective national laws.[86]

The Registry further emphasized its limited role as a facilitator in the execution of cooperation requests between the Court's judiciary and the requested State(s).[87] The Registry

Trial Chamber III, the role of the Legal Representative of Victims and the legality and propriety of his detention.

80 ibid para 84, arguing that Mr Bemba fails to demonstrate a 'grave and manifest miscarriage of justice', as required by Rome Statute, art 85(3) and that, absent such a determination, Bemba cannot rely on ICC RPE, r 175 as a ground upon which a claim for compensation can be founded. See also ibid paras 88-90.

81 ibid para 85, submitting that Mr Bemba's arguments as concerns a private law claim are beyond the scope of proceedings under Rome Statute, art 85 and ought to be dismissed *in limine*. See also ibid paras 96-102, contesting the private law nature of Mr Bemba's claim that the Court negligently managed his assets.

82 ibid paras 92-95.

83 ibid paras 92-93. See also *Bemba* Unfreezing Decision, *supra* note 57, at paras 11-12.

84 ibid para 94.

85 *Situation in the Central African Republic* (Public Redacted Version of the "Registry's Observations on the Defence Compensation Claim) ICC-01/05-01/08-3681-Red3 (6 May 2019) (Registry's Observations).

86 ibid para 15.

87 ibid paras 17-23. See also ICC RPE, r 176.

also stressed the dependence of the ICC on State authorities and their national implementing legislation in the context of the Rome Statute cooperation regime[88] and noted that the requested States were cognisant of their obligation to manage the assets they were asked to freeze or seize on behalf of the ICC in the instant case.[89] Notably, the Registry specified that the Portuguese authorities responsible for managing some of Bemba's frozen assets, including his Boeing 727-100 plane that was parked at Faro airport at the time of his arrest, have 'never consulted the Court under articles 96(2) or 100 of the Statute to explain any difficulties [they] may have encountered to manage the said assets located in Portugal once frozen or seized'.[90]

On 9 May 2019, at the request of counsel for Mr Bemba,[91] Pre-Trial Chamber II convened a hearing between the parties to the compensation proceedings, namely the Prosecutor and Mr Bemba.[92] Counsel for Mr Bemba emphasized the indiscriminate nature of the freezing orders implemented at the Court's request,[93] the decimation of his assets,[94] and the serious nature of freezing orders, noting the limited recourse made thereto by other ICTs.[95] In reply, the Office of the Prosecutor largely confined its submissions to disputing the legal basis of Bemba's claim, stressing that he had failed to satisfy the 'grave and manifest miscarriage of justice' criterion set forth in Article 85(3) of the ICC Statute.[96]

On 20 June 2019, Mr Bemba filed his reply to the responses submitted by the Prosecutor and the Registry to his claim for compensation,[97] in which he reiterates that his claim does indeed satisfy Article 85(3) of the ICC Statute,[98] that he is entitled to a resolution of his

---

88 ibid paras 27-30.

89 ibid paras 31-33.

90 ibid para 33.

91 See *Bemba* Claim for Compensation and Damages (n 22) para 169. For the order *inter alia* convening the hearing see *Situation in the Central African Republic* (Order on the conduct of the proceedings related to "Mr Bemba's claim for compensation and damages") ICC-01/05-01/08-3675 (14 March 2019).

92 *Situation in the Central African Republic* (Hearing on Mr Bemba's claim for compensation) ICC-01/05-01/08-T-376-ENG (9 May 2019) (Compensation Hearing).

93 ibid 6, line 11 ff.

94 ibid 10, line 8 ff.

95 ibid para 11, line 1 ff. The author disputes the argument by counsel for Mr Bemba that the ICTY, ICTR and SCSL did not request the freezing of the assets of those under their jurisdiction. The ICTY did so with respect to Slobodan Milošević, Milan Milutinović, Nikola Šainovic, Dragoljub Ojdanić and Vlajko Stojiljković; the ICTR Prosecutor did so with respect to Félicien Kabuga; and the SCSL did so with respect to Sam Hinga Norman. For a detailed discussion of these freezing requests, see Chapter 4.

96 Compensation Hearing (n 92) 18, line 4 ff.

97 *Situation in the Central African Republic* (Public Redacted Version of "Mr. Bemba's reply to the Prosecution Response to and Registry Submissions on "Mr. Bemba's claim for compensation and damages"") ICC-01/05-01/08-3687-Red (20 June 2019).

98 ibid paras 12-24.

private law claim,[99] and that the Registry mischaracterizes *inter alia* the value of his frozen assets and his ability to manage them.[100] Bemba also requests that the concerned States, namely Belgium, Portugal and the DRC, should be joined as participants to the proceedings, or invited to submit written observations thereon.[101] On 28 June 2019, the Prosecutor filed a redacted response to Bemba's reply.[102] As with the submissions made by her Office at the hearing, the Prosecutor's response was limited to repudiating Mr Bemba's arguments in support of his claim that he suffered 'a grave and manifest miscarriage of justice'.[103] Finally, on 25 July 2019, the Registry submitted its observations on Mr Bemba's reply.[104] Much of its observations as concerns specific assets are redacted.[105] This said, the Registry underscores that 'most of the assets claimed had either deteriorated before Mr Bemba's arrest or were not frozen or seized on behalf of the Court, or both.'[106] As for assets belonging to Mr Bemba that were or remain frozen and/or seized at the Court's request, the Registry claims that their management has been carried out in accordance with the procedures applicable thereto under the pertinent domestic legislation.[107] Lastly, the Registry opposes Bemba's request to invite the submissions of the States concerned.[108]

Pre-Trial Chamber II rendered its decision on Mr Bemba's claim for compensation and damages on 18 May 2020.[109] Consistent with the focus of most of the filings submitted throughout the litigation discussed in this chapter, much of the Pre-Trial Chamber's analysis focused on whether the claim at hand satisfied Article 85(3) of the ICC Statute,[110] with only a few paragraphs dedicated to Mr Bemba's claim that the ICC mismanaged his frozen assets.[111] In short, Pre-Trial Chamber II concluded that it had no jurisdiction over this component of Mr Bemba's request because the claim fell outside the scope of its mandate under Article 85 of the ICC Statute.[112] The Pre-Trial Chamber did, however,

99 ibid paras 25-26.
100 ibid paras 27-43.
101 ibid paras 44-46.
102 *Situation in the Central African Republic* (Public redacted version of "Prosecution's response to Mr Bemba's reply on compensation and damages", 26 June 2019) ICC-01/05-01/08-3690-Red (28 June 2019)
103 ibid paras 7-33.
104 *Situation in the Central African Republic* (Public Redacted Version of the "Registry's Observations on Mr Jean-Pierre Bemba Gombo's Lawyers' Reply ICC-01/05-01/08-3687-Conf") ICC-01/05-01/08- 3689-Red3 (25 July 2019).
105 ibid paras 23-41.
106 ibid para 42.
107 ibid.
108 ibid.
109 *Situation in the Central African Republic* (Decision on Mr Bemba's claim for compensation and damages) ICC-01/05-01/08-3694 (18 May 2020) (*Bemba* Claim Decision).
110 ibid paras 18-52.
111 ibid paras 53-64.
112 ibid para 61.

explicitly note that this decision was 'without prejudice to Mr Bemba's right to pursue other procedural remedies' in connection with this element of his claim.[113] Mr Bemba has since sought leave to appeal the Pre-Trial Chamber's decision under Article 82(1)(d) of the ICC Statute,[114] a request opposed by the Prosecutor in the most recent filing submitted in the context of this claim at the time the present book was completed.[115]

In reaching its decision, it is conceivable that Pre-Trial Chamber II might have found itself between a rock and a hard place. On the one hand, if it had found the Court to be at fault in managing Mr Bemba's assets, not only might he have been entitled to a large sum of money by way of compensation, but the accompanying reputational damage to the ICC could also have been significant. On the other hand, if the Pre-Trial Chamber had found that the blame for the diminished value of Mr Bemba's assets lay at the feet of the three states responsible for their freezing, this might have resulted in negative consequences for the Court's relationship with these states, thereby rendering cooperation less forthcoming in the future. In the end, by finding that the second component of Mr Bemba's claim fell beyond the scope of Article 85 of the ICC Statute, the Pre-Trial Chamber did neither, although it did appear to absolve the Registry of any fault in 'in acting as a channel of communication between the Court and the requested Three States'.[116] If Mr Bemba's application for leave to appeal succeeds, it is the hope of the present author that the Appeals Chamber is able to shed some much-needed further light on the division of labour between the Court and cooperating States as far as managing frozen assets is concerned. For example, although Pre-Trial Chamber II observed that 'the responsibility for the proper execution of a cooperation request emanating from the Court rests primarily with the requested States',[117] it is argued that the terms 'proper' and 'primarily' are both in need of elaboration, not least in view of the rights of the accused at stake in this process.

If clarification is not forthcoming on this front, whether because Mr Bemba's request for leave to appeal is not granted or if it succeeds but the Appeals Chamber reaches a similar conclusion to that of Pre-Trial Chamber II on the question of jurisdiction, then it is for the States Parties to the ICC Statute to act. In its decision on Mr Bemba's claim for compensation, the Pre-Trial Chamber laudably draws attention to the arguably excessive length of proceedings (and Mr Bemba's time in custodial detention) in the present case

113 ibid para 64.

114 *Situation in the Central African Republic* (Request for leave to appeal the 'Decision on Mr Bemba's claim for compensation and damages') ICC-01/05-01/08-3695 (25 May 2020).

115 *Situation in the Central African Republic* (Prosecution response to Mr Bemba's request for leave to appeal the 'Decision on Mr Bemba's claim for compensation and damages') ICC-01/05-01/08-3696 (1 June 2020).

116 *Bemba* Claim Decision (n 109) para 58.

117 ibid para 57.

and even intimates that the Court's constituent instrument, including but not limited to Article 85(3) of the ICC Statute, should be reviewed in order to better protect the rights afforded to accused persons therein.[118] If such a review is undertaken and, in the words of the Pre-Trial Chamber, 'if the Court's aim is to serve as a beacon at the forefront of all matters pertaining to individual human rights',[119] then surely the issue of who bears responsibility for the proper management of assets frozen at the ICC's request, and the modalities of their unfreezing after an acquittal, is also deserving of such attention.

In sum, Mr Bemba and the Registry, with whom Pre-Trial Chamber II would appear to agree,[120] interpret the Court's statutory framework as concerns the freezing of assets in different ways. Bemba is of the view that the ICC ought to retain a central role in the management of assets frozen at its request, while the Registry expresses the opinion that it is for the requested State(s) to discharge this responsibility in the Rome Statute system. There is no judicial guidance beyond the Pre-Trial Chamber's decision as concerns the management of assets frozen in accordance with requests for cooperation issued by the ICC. If Trial Chamber III's view of the ICC cooperation schema, namely that it is for domestic law to regulate the (un)freezing of assets frozen at the Court's request, also applies to their management, then it is domestic law that must be probed for direction as to how their value can be preserved during often lengthy proceedings.

8.3 DOMESTIC APPROACHES

The ICC Statute is clear that States ought to execute cooperation requests in accordance with procedures of their respective national laws.[121] ICC States Parties are therefore free to legislate as they deem appropriate to enable their domestic authorities to fulfil requests for cooperation transmitted thereto by the ICC. In other words, although Article 88 of the ICC Statute provides that 'States Parties shall ensure that there are procedures available under their national law for all of the forms of cooperation' specified under Part IX thereof,[122] the treaty provides no guidance as to what these procedures should entail. In the following section, it will be shown that there are procedures already available under certain States' domestic law that could offer guidance for other States in the management of assets seized and/or frozen at the Court's behest. Much of this legislation is analysed by the Open-ended Intergovernmental Working Group on Asset Recovery (hereinafter: IWG),

118 ibid paras 67-68.
119 ibid para 68.
120 ibid para 57, citing Registry's Observations (n 85) paras 1, 15, 22.
121 Rome Statute, art 93(1).
122 ibid art 88.

a subsidiary body of the Conference of the States Parties to the UN Convention against Corruption, in a 2017 study.[123] One of the aims of this study is to enable those responsible for managing seized and frozen assets 'to learn from the experiences of others and avoiding and/or managing some of the risks and challenges involved.'[124] Part 2 of the present chapter has identified some of the risks inherent to the Rome Statute framework for the management of assets frozen at the request of the Court. It is hoped that the legislation analysed in the following paragraphs might provide useful guidance for the mitigation of these risks in the execution of future requests for cooperation from States in the freezing of assets.

At this stage, it is important to elaborate the distinction between freezing and seizure of assets by States at the request of the ICC. First, it is noteworthy that the terms are not defined in the ICC Statute or the ICC RPE. Guidance can, however, be found in the UN Convention Against Corruption, which adopts the following definitions of the terms: '"Freezing" or "seizure" shall mean temporarily prohibiting the transfer, conversion, disposition or movement of property or temporarily assuming custody or control of property on the basis of an order issued by a court or other competent authority'.[125] The following section will discuss tools that could be of use to States during both the freezing and seizure phases of the asset recovery process, regardless of whether the legislation in question limits their application to one particular stage.

8.3.1 Third party management of seized or frozen assets

Pursuant to the legislation enacted by the UK to give effect to its obligation to cooperate with the ICC, among other aspects of the ICC Statute regime, applications for asset freezing ought to be made before the High Court 'in pursuance of a direction given by the Secretary of State under section 38'.[126] In turn, the High Court is empowered to appoint a receiver to manage the assets. According to Schedule 6, s. 5(4) International Criminal Court Act 2001: '[t]he powers conferred on a receiver ... shall be exercised with a view to securing that the property specified in the order is available for satisfying the forfeiture order or, as the case may be, any forfeiture order that may be made in the ICC proceedings in relation

123 Open-ended Intergovernmental Working Group on Asset Recovery, 'Study prepared by the Secretariat on effective management and disposal of seized and confiscated assets' (23 August 2017) UN Doc CAC/COSP/WG.2/2017/CRP.1 (IWG Study).

124 ibid 4.

125 UNCAC, art 2(f).

126 International Criminal Court Act 2001, sch 6, s 1. See also s 38. For analysis of this legislation, see Robert Cryer and Olympia Bekou, 'International Crimes and ICC Cooperation in England and Wales' (2007) 5 Journal of International Criminal Justice 441.

to which the order was made.'[127] In other words, the High Court may appoint a third party – the 'receiver' – to manage the frozen assets with a view to preventing their depreciation. Australia,[128] Kenya,[129] and New Zealand[130] adopt similar approaches in their respective national implementing legislation, albeit with the third party bearing different designations in each of the three common law jurisdictions.[131]

It ought to be noted that, despite possessing legislation to give effect to their obligation under Article 88 of the ICC Statute, none of the abovementioned States Parties include (future) orders for reparations among the grounds upon which orders to freeze or seize assets may be based. This can be contrasted with Ireland's national implementing legislation, the International Criminal Court Act 2006, which also provides for the appointment of a receiver with the power to take measures to preserve the value of assets.[132] In view of the consistent interpretation by the ICC of Article 57(3)(e) of the ICC Statute, namely that protective measures can be taken for the purpose of the enforcement of future reparations orders,[133] this ground ought to be explicitly listed by States in their domestic procedures facilitating the identification, tracing, freezing and seizure of assets on behalf of the Court. The Irish national implementing legislation clearly articulates the rationale behind the exercise of the powers of the High Court or a receiver in giving effect to Article 57(3)(e) of the ICC Statute, as follows:

127 International Criminal Court Act 2001, sch 6, s 5(4).

128 International Criminal Court Act 2002, s 82; Proceeds of Crime Act 2002, s 38.

129 International Crimes and International Criminal Court Act 2000, s 130; Criminal Proceeds (Recovery) Act 2009, s 80.

130 International Crimes Act 2008, sch 2, s 10 ff.

131 The third party is labelled 'the Official Trustee' in Australia, the 'Official Assignee' in New Zealand and the 'Public Trustee' in Kenya.

132 International Criminal Court Act 2006, s 38(4). ('... the High Court may make an order (in this Part referred to as a "freezing order") prohibiting any person from dealing with the property of the person to whom the request relates if the Court is satisfied — (i) that this section applies in relation to the property, and (ii) either — (I) that the International Criminal Court has imposed a fine, or made a *reparation* or forfeiture order, in the proceedings concerned, or (II) that there are reasonable grounds for believing that that Court may impose a fine, or make such an order, in those proceedings'.)

133 *Prosecutor v Lubanga Dyilo* (Decision on the Prosecutor's Application for a warrant of arrest, Article 58) ICC-01/04-01/06-1-Corr-Red (10 February 2006) para 134 ('The Chamber considers that in light of rule 99 of the Rules, the contextual interpretation of article 57 (3) (e) of the Statute makes clear that the Chamber may, pursuant to article 57 (3) (e) of the Statute, seek the cooperation of States Parties to take protective measures for the purpose of securing the enforcement of a future reparation award'); *Prosecutor v Kenyatta* (Decision on the implementation of the request to freeze assets) ICC-01/09-02/11-931 (8 July 2014) para 16; *Kilolo* Lifting Decision (n 9) paras 17-18; *Prosecutor v [Redacted]* (Judgment on the appeal of the Prosecutor against the decision of [REDACTED]) ICC-ACRed-01/16 (15 February 2016) para 63. For analysis, see Chapter 5; Ferstman (n 9) 234-37 (discussing the *Lubanga* and *Kenyatta* cases).

> [T]he powers shall be exercised with a view to—
>
> securing that the property covered by an order … is available to satisfy any order of the International Criminal Court imposing a fine or forfeiture or providing for reparation to, or in respect of, victims,
>
> in the case of realisable property held by a person to whom the defendant has directly or indirectly made a gift … , realising no more than the value for the time being of the gift,
>
> allowing any person, other than the defendant or the recipient of any such gift, to retain or recover the value of any property held by him or her.

In other words, third party management of assets seized or frozen at the request of the ICC is designed to protect the interests of victims and bona fide third parties. At the same time, even though not overtly noted in the foregoing provision, such procedures also enable third parties to take measures to preserve the value of assets in the interests of the accused person(s) in the event of an acquittal. In the view of the present author, this is a highly important yet ostensibly overlooked aspect of the protective measures process under Article 57(3)(e) of the ICC Statute.

8.3.2 *Use or Sale of Frozen Assets*

As well as the involvement of court-appointed third parties in the management of assets seized and/or frozen at the request of the ICC, certain States have also adopted (both legally binding and non-legally binding) instructions for those responsible for the management of such assets. For example, in the UK, s. 296(1) Proceeds of Crime Act states, in relevant part, as follows: '[i]f cash is detained … for more than 48 hours … , it is at the first opportunity to be paid into an interest-bearing account and held there; and the interest accruing on it is to be added to it on its forfeiture or release.'[134] In respect of depreciable assets, further guidance, in the form of a code of practice concerning the search, seizure and detention of property, provides:

> An appropriate officer should consider the proportionality of detention. This includes the calculation of the likely costs of storage and insurance as against the value of the property (particularly depreciating assets) in order to assess

134 Proceeds of Crime Act 2002, s 296(1).

> whether it is reasonable to continue to detain the property rather than seek a consent order for its sale or to take steps to release it. Conversely, this also includes calculating the value of the property against the likely amount to be found under any confiscation order – steps should be taken to release property should it exceed the probable value of such a future order.[135]

One issue raised by Bemba in his claim against the ICC for compensation and damages is the failure of those responsible for managing his frozen assets to earn an income from, or to sell, his aircraft.[136] It could be beneficial for the accused (should there be an acquittal) and victims (in the event of a conviction and consequent reparations order) for certain categories of assets to be actively utilized, or sold, rather than remaining frozen, and therefore unprofitable, if not lossmaking, for long periods of time. The IWG identifies a number of kinds of such assets.[137] These include perishable goods, 'rapidly depreciating' assets, property whose maintenance or storage costs are disproportionate to its value, and assets whose management needs expertise that is not readily available to the responsible authority.[138] Bemba's Boeing jet, as well as his other frozen vehicles, whether for use on land, air or sea, would appear to fall into the 'rapidly depreciating' category of assets. Additionally, in view of the costs incurred by parking at Faro airport, there would only have been a short window of time during which it would have been viable to contend that the storage costs of this asset were proportionate to its anticipated value. Other assets that could fall into one of the foregoing categories include live animals (such as racehorses), foodstuffs, fuel, building materials and hazardous substances.[139]

Certain ICC States Parties legislate for the interim use, or sale, of frozen assets in this manner. For example, Canada's Seized Property Management Act grants the Minister of Public Works and Government Services the following powers with respect to seized assets:

> ... to make an interlocutory sale of perishable or rapidly depreciating property;
>
> ... to destroy ... property that has little or no value; and
>
> ... to have property, other than real property or a conveyance, forfeited[.][140]

135 Home Office, 'Code of Practice Issued Under Section 47s of the Proceeds of Crime Act 2002: Search, Seizure and Detention of Property (England and Wales)' (January 2018) para 135.
136 *Bemba* Claim for Compensation and Damages (n 22) paras 129-32.
137 IWG Study (n 123) 21-24.
138 ibid 22-23.
139 ibid.
140 Seized Property Management Act 1993, s 7(2).

Similarly, in the Netherlands, the Public Prosecutor's Office is permitted to authorize the sale, destruction, disposal of or use for purposes other than investigative purposes of objects:

> which are not suitable for storage;
>
> whose storage costs are not in reasonable proportion to their value; [and]
>
> which are replaceable and whose value can be easily determined.[141]

According to the IWG, the Netherlands' dual-pronged approach of: (i) establishing a 'central registration system that allows for swift action to be taken when costs exceed the value of the asset' and (ii) adopting 'an aggressive strategy of selling off assets pre-confiscation' permitted the Dutch authorities to cut the costs of managing movable seized and confiscated assets from €23 million per year to €9 million per year.[142] Additionally, such an approach is in accordance with legislation enacted by the European Union[143] and non-binding principles adopted by the Organization of American States[144] and the G8 Group of States.[145] Without speculating as to the redacted content in the multiple documents filed in support of and in response to Bemba's claim for compensation and damages, it is sufficient to say that following such guidelines (or, in the case of EU Member States, applying the provisions of their legislation transposing the pertinent EU Directive

141 *Wetboek van Strafvordering* (Code of Criminal Procedure), art 117(2). See also Rome Statute, art 117(1).

142 IWG Study (n 123) 21.

143 ibid. See Directive 2014/42/EU of the European Parliament and of the Council of 3 April 2014 on the freezing and confiscation of instrumentalities and proceeds of crime in the European Union [2014] OJ L127/39, art 10 ('1. Member States shall take the necessary measures, for example by establishing centralised offices, a set of specialised offices or equivalent mechanisms, to ensure the adequate management of property frozen with a view to possible subsequent confiscation. 2. Member States shall ensure that the measures referred to in paragraph 1 include the possibility to sell or transfer property where necessary.')

144 ibid. See Organization of American States (OAS), *Asset Management Systems in Latin America and Best Practices Document on Management of Seized and Forfeited Assets* (OAS 2011) 17 ('There should be a law that regulates proceedings that, under conditions established in domestic legislation, allow the sale of perishable assets or assets that lose their value quickly, such as boats, airplanes, vehicles, animals and farms with crops. States should also evaluate the possibility of authorizing the advanced sale of assets that are too costly to maintain.')

145 ibid. See G8 Lyon/Roma Group, Criminal Legal Affairs Subgroup, 'Best Practices for the Administration of Seized Assets' (27 April 2005) 3 ('Legal proceedings should be possible to permit, under conditions laid down in national law, pre-judgment sale of assets pending the outcome of the confiscation/forfeiture proceeding for wasting assets that are perishable or rapidly declining in value, such as vessels, aircraft, cars, animals and farms with growing crops. States should further consider authorising pre-judgment sale of assets which are too burdensome to maintain. The resulting proceeds should be secured in accordance with national law (and the action notified to the court and other affected parties) pending a final determination of confiscation or forfeiture.')

into their respective domestic legal frameworks) ought to diminish the likelihood that further such claims might be brought before the Court in future. The following section briefly discusses possible steps that could be taken on the international plane to avoid or to remedy the mismanagement of assets frozen or seized at the request of the ICC.

8.4 International Responses

André Nollkaemper and Dov Jacobs term shared responsibility as 'ex post facto responsibility for contributions to injury', with a particular focus on 'situations where collaboration between two or more actors leads to harmful outcomes'.[146] Göran Sluiter further delineates this concept as it applies in the context of ICTs, arguing that, in the context of institutions, like the ICC, established to deliver international criminal justice, 'the emphasis lies on the prevention of harm', that is to say (serious) human rights violations.[147] Having analysed the problem of sharing responsibility between the (often multiple) relevant actors in three phases of international criminal proceedings, Sluiter concludes *inter alia* that a 'number of scenarios were insufficiently anticipated and regulated' when framing the ICC Statute and other sources of applicable law before the Court.[148] It is argued here that the modalities of and responsibility for managing assets frozen at the request of the ICC should be added to that list. Mismanaging such assets has the potential to (seriously) violate the human rights of the person whose assets are frozen as well as those of bona fide third parties.[149] The following paragraphs probe three provisions of the Rome Statute which could offer routes through which the risk of committing such violations might be mitigated.

8.4.1 *Utilising Article 96(3) of the ICC Statute*

Simply because Article 88 of the ICC Statute does not dictate a particular method that States Parties should follow in ensuring the availability of procedures under their domestic law for all forms of cooperation detailed in Part IX of the Court's constituent instrument, this is not to say that the ICC cannot request States to properly manage assets frozen or seized at its request. Article 93(1)(k) of the ICC Statute, read together with Article 93(1)(l)

146 André Nollkaemper and Dov Jacobs, 'Shared Responsibility in International Law: A Conceptual Framework', 34 Michigan Journal of International Law (2013) 359, 365.

147 Göran Sluiter, 'International Criminal Tribunals and their Relation to States' in André Nollkaemper and Ilias Plakokefalos (eds), *The Practice of Shared Responsibility in International Law* (CUP 2017) 215.

148 ibid 232.

149 Nollkaemper and Jacobs explicitly identify the example of 'infringing the rights of third parties' in describing what they mean by 'the term *responsibility*'. See Nollkaemper and Jacobs (n 146) 365.

and Article 96 of the ICC Statute, appear to provide a sound legal basis for such requests inasmuch as these provisions not only empower the ICC to request its States Parties to assist in freezing and seizing assets, but also with '[a]ny other type of assistance which is not prohibited by the law of the requested State, with a view to facilitating the investigation and prosecution of crimes' within its jurisdiction.[150] Should the requested State(s) face problems in executing the Court's demand(s) because of domestic law requirements, Article 96(3) of the ICC Statute provides for an avenue through which these obstacles could be surmounted, namely consultations between the concerned State(s) and the ICC.[151] A document issued by the UN Security Council Al-Qaida Sanctions Committee provides useful guidance in this context: 'Whatever ... body is responsible for regulating frozen assets should make reasonable efforts to do so in a manner that does not result in their undue deterioration, provided that this does not conflict with the overall intention behind the freezing action.[152] In the Rome Statute system, the body responsible for the daily administration of assets frozen at the request of the ICC is the pertinent authority (or authorities) within the requested State. But this state of affairs need not prevent the ICC, whose officials establish the intention(s) behind the freezing action, from acting in concert with the responsible domestic authorities to ensure that the aims(s) intended are not thwarted by misunderstandings and/or mismanagement.[153]

8.4.2 Lessons from Article 106 of the ICC Statute

Article 106 of the ICC Statute specifies how the enforcement of ICC-determined sentences and the conditions of imprisonment applicable thereto are overseen. Specifically, Article 106(1) of the ICC Statute provides that '[t]he enforcement of a sentence of imprisonment shall be subject to the supervision of the Court'.[154] It is argued that a similar arrangement could be particularly well suited to the management of assets frozen by States following receipt of a cooperation request from the Court. In other words, the ICC could play a more prominent role in supervising how frozen assets are managed after the responsible authorities of the requested State(s) have taken enforcement action pursuant to the procedures available under their respective national laws. Article 106(2) of the ICC Statute could also serve as a guideline in terms of clarifying the standards against which the State

150 Rome Statute, art 93(1)(l).
151 Rome Statute, art 96(3).
152 Security Council Committee pursuant to resolutions 1267 (1999) 1989 (2011) and 2253 (2015) concerning Islamic State in Iraq and the Levant (Da'esh), Al-Qaida and associated individuals, groups, undertakings and entities, 'Assets Freeze: Explanation of Terms' (24 February 2015) <https://www.un.org/securitycouncil/sites/www.un.org.securitycouncil/files/eot_assets_freeze_-_english.pdf> accessed 31 August 2020, para 11.
153 For examples, see *Bemba* Claim for Compensation and Damages (n 22) paras 147-49.
154 Rome Statute, art 106(1).

authorities' management of assets frozen at the Court's request ought to be held. The provision stipulates that the 'conditions of imprisonment shall be governed by the law of the State of enforcement and shall be consistent with widely accepted international treaty standards governing treatment of prisoners'.[155] The Rome Statute already provides that the freezing of assets in accordance with an ICC-issued cooperation request ought to be done under the pertinent provisions of national law.[156] As for international standards governing the management of frozen assets, it is acknowledged that widely accepted treaty standards might be more difficult to identify than those applicable to the treatment of prisoners. This said, the European Court of Human Rights and the Inter-American Courts of Human Rights have each developed principles relevant to the application of asset freezing measures, a number of which could be germane to the supervision of the management of assets frozen by States at the ICC's request.[157] The legislation analysed in the IWG Study and discussed in Part 3 could also offer a useful starting point for determining the standards applicable to managing such assets.

8.4.3 *Amending Article 85(3) of the ICC Statute?*

As Stuart Beresford has reasoned, 'in many criminal jurisdictions innocent persons who have been prosecuted ... may be compensated for the ... economic losses they have suffered as a direct result of the proceedings against them.'[158] Dave Michels has further observed that such compensation may be made available to those who are accused and subsequently acquitted in a number of national jurisdictions.[159] Compensation to acquitted accused also forms part of the Rome Statute, Article 85(3) of which reads: 'In exceptional circumstances, where the Court finds conclusive facts showing that there has been a grave and manifest miscarriage of justice, it may in its discretion award compensation, according to the criteria provided in the Rules of Procedure and Evidence, to a person who has been released from detention following a final decision of acquittal or a termination of the proceedings for

155 Rome Statute, art 106(2).

156 Rome Statute, art 93(1). See also Rome Statute, art 88.

157 *Džinić v Croatia* App no 38359/13 (ECtHR, 17 May 2016); *Case of Chaparro Álvarez and Lapo Íñiguez v. Ecuador* (Judgment of November 21, 2007) IACtHR Series C No 170 (21 November 2007). For analysis, see Chapter 7.

158 Stuart Beresford, 'Redressing the Wrongs of the International Justice System: Compensation for Persons Erroneously Detained, Prosecuted, or Convicted by the Ad Hoc Tribunals' (2002) 96 American Journal of International Law 628, 628.

159 See Johan David Michels, 'Compensating Acquitted Defendants for Detention before International Criminal Courts' (2010) 8 Journal of International Criminal Justice (2010) 407, 413 (listing Austria, Denmark, Germany, Iceland, Italy, Latvia, the Netherlands, Norway and Sweden as having procedures available for such compensation).

that reason.'[160] It has been convincingly shown elsewhere[161] that Mr Bemba's prospects of securing compensation under Article 85(3) of the ICC Statute are slim, not least because the provision makes no reference to the mismanagement of assets. Indeed, according to Kip Hale and Santiago Vargas Niño, to agree with Bemba's view that Rule 175 of the ICC RPE 'warrants compensation for damage, devaluation or destruction of property under Article 85(3) would stretch the "ordinary meaning" of these provisions to the point of breaking.'[162] Article 85(3) of the ICC Statute would therefore seem not to offer an especially suitable avenue for recourse for those alleging the mismanagement of their assets frozen at the Court's request. But the narrowness of this provision has been challenged in the academic literature, albeit outside the context of the management of frozen assets.

Dave Michels has proposed the addition of the following provision, among others,[163] to follow Article 85(3) of the ICC Statute: 'Compensation may be awarded by a Chamber, where it considers such compensation consistent with the interests of justice, to a person who has been released from detention following a final decision of acquittal.'[164] Róisín Mulgrew has made a similar plea for amendment of the provision, arguing in favour of the removal of the terms 'grave and manifest' and 'exceptional circumstances'.[165] These suggestions are not confined to academic debate, with the delegations to the 1998 Rome Conference expressing disagreement as to the breadth of this provision, as follows: '[t]here are delegations which believe that there should not be an unfettered right to compensation where a person is acquitted or released prior to the end of the Trial. ... Other delegations

---

160 Rome Statute, art 85(3). ICC RPE, rr 173-175 also form part of the system governing compensation to an arrested or convicted person, but remain subordinate to the Rome Statute.

161 See Kip Hale and Santiago Vargas Niño, 'Unexploded Legal Ordnance' (*Opinio Juris*, 10 April 2019) <http://opiniojuris.org/2019/04/10/unexploded-legal-ordnance/> accessed 31 August 2020; Kevin Jon Heller, 'Bim, Bam, Bem-Boom!' (*Opinio Juris*, 12 March 2019) <http://opiniojuris.org/2019/03/12/bim-bam-bemb-oom/> accessed 31 August 2020. On the high threshold required by Rome Statute, art 85(3), see *Prosecutor v Ngudjolo Chui* (Decision on the "Requête en indemnisation en application des dispositions de l'article 85(1) et (3) du Statut de Rome") ICC-01/04-02/12-301-tENG (16 December 2015) para 45; Salvatore Zappalà, 'Compensation to an Arrested or Convicted Person', in Antonio Cassese, Paola Gaeta and John RWD Jones (eds), *The Rome Statute of the International Criminal Court: A Commentary* (OUP 2002) 1583; Beresford (n 158) 643, discussing the burden of establishing 'a grave and manifest miscarriage of justice', albeit outside the context of the art 85(3) regime; Joris van Wijk and Barbora Holá, 'Acquittals in International Criminal Justice: Pyrrhic Victories?' (2017) 30 Leiden Journal of International Law 241, 257.

162 Hale and Vargas Niño (n 161). ICC RPE, r 175 provides as follows:' In establishing the amount of any compensation in conformity with article 85, paragraph 3, the Chamber designated under rule 173, sub-rule 1, shall take into consideration the consequences of the grave and manifest miscarriage of justice on the personal, family, social and professional situation of the person filing the request.'

163 Michels (n 159) 423.

164 ibid.

165 Róisín Mulgrew, 'The costs of suspicion: a critical analysis of the compensation scheme established by Article 85(3) of the Rome Statute' in Róisín Mulgrew and Denis Abels (eds), *Research Handbook on the International Penal System* (Edward Elgar 2016) 476-77.

considered this text to be too restrictive.'[166] There might therefore be some appetite for amending this provision, although it is acknowledged that few changes have been made to the treaty since its adoption in the Italian capital.

What, then, can be done to rectify this unfortunate situation? Hale and Vargas Niño argue that the ICC ought to use the occasion to 'consider cross-organ supervision over frozen assets and like matters, as well as developing methods to maintain transparent two-way communication with relevant State authorities.'[167] As proposed in the present chapter, the Rome Statute already contains a means through which the latter might be realized, namely Article 96(3) of the ICC Statute. It is also argued that the division of labour between the Court and requested States should be clarified as far as the management of seized and frozen assets is concerned. Is the involvement of the ICC limited to an oversight role after the cooperation request has been issued? Or ought the Court, through the Registry, play a more proactive role in the management of frozen assets in view of the various competing interests (which include those of the accused, bona fide third parties, potential victims and the prosecution) concerned in the protective measures process? It is the view of the present author that, at a minimum, the ICC must share responsibility with the requested States for the management of assets frozen pursuant to the Rome Statute.[168] As argued in the preceding paragraphs, the regime governing the supervision of the enforcement of ICC-determined sentences could serve as inspiration for establishing such a framework. If, like the International Criminal Tribunal for the former Yugoslavia, the ICC can be said to be 'like a giant without arms and legs ... [which] needs artificial limbs to walk and work',[169] the State authorities that act as those limbs are part of a wider body, which includes the Court.

8.5 Conclusion

In his claim for compensation and damages, Mr Bemba notes that he was acquitted on 8 June 2018 and advocates that, '[i]n a perfect world, the Appeals Chamber should have made orders relating to the freezing of his assets *eiusdem generis* to those sought herein.'[170] Clarity on the part of the Court in this regard could have avoided the need for further

166 'Working Paper on Article 84' (11 July 1998) UN Doc A/CONF.183/C.1/WGPM/L.74, fn 3. See also Hale and Vargas Niño (n 161); Mulgrew (n 165) 477.

167 Hale and Vargas Niño (n 161).

168 For a similar opinion, see Heller (n 161).

169 Antonio Cassese, 'On the Current Trends towards Criminal Prosecution and Punishment of Breaches of International Humanitarian Law' 9 *European Journal of International Law* (1998) 2, 13.

170 *Bemba* Unfreezing Application (n 31) para 51.

filings on behalf of Mr Bemba. In the absence of such orders, this chapter has sought to shed light on the fallout of the Bemba acquittal as far as his frozen assets are concerned. In so doing, it has been shown that lacunae exist in the legal framework applicable to the management of frozen assets under the Rome Statute system. At the very least, the filings issued in the aftermath of Mr Bemba's acquittal show that the division of labour between the (organs of) the Court and the States Parties to its constituent instrument could be made clearer in this crucial sphere of its operations.

The risk that assets will depreciate in value during the pre-trial, trial and appeal processes at the ICC and, indeed, at other ICTs, is arguably greater than at the domestic level because of the average length of these processes. This could render States' national legislation as concerns the freezing and management of assets less than ideally suited for application in response to requests for cooperation from the Court under the Rome Statute. This chapter has sought to identify procedures available under certain States' domestic law that might provide stimulation for those States in the process of adopting legislation allowing their national authorities to cooperate with the ICC. In adjudicating Mr Bemba's claim, Pre-Trial Chamber II expressed the view that the responsibility for discharging a cooperation request issued by the ICC lies chiefly with the recipient State(s). States should therefore ensure that their national implementing legislation allows their responsible domestic authorities to preserve the value of any frozen or seized assets throughout the routinely protracted proceedings at the international level. At the same time, there are avenues through which the ICC and the Assembly of States Parties to the Rome Statute could work to ameliorate the present state of affairs, namely by maximising the opportunity provided by Article 96(3) of the ICC Statute, by learning from the regime established by Article 106 of the ICC Statute, and by considering amendments to Article 85(3) of the ICC Statute.

Had Mr Bemba been convicted on appeal, it is entirely plausible that victims' representatives could have made similar representations to those filed by Bemba in the instant case, claiming instead that his frozen assets should have been better managed with a view to their being used to secure the enforcement of a reparations award against him. Equally, having been acquitted on appeal of all charges of crimes against humanity and war crimes levied against him by the ICC Prosecutor, Bemba ought to be put in a position resembling that which he occupied prior to his (arrest and) assets being frozen, minus any expenses incurred during proceedings. It is only by acting in concert that the ICC and its States Parties can ensure that the value of assets frozen pursuant to the Rome Statute is preserved, regardless of who the ultimate beneficiaries of adopting such an approach may be.

9 Conclusion

This study sought to answer the research question 'Are the asset freezing measures executed at the request of the ICC and UNSC consistent with the rights of the individuals against whom they are imposed?'. In order to respond to this question, Chapter 2 scrutinised the theoretical underpinnings for freezing individuals' assets in criminal law and non-criminal law contexts before situating ICC- and UNSC-requested asset freezing procedures in this framework. The conclusion reached at this stage was that both serve primarily preventive purposes (with some restitutive undertones), despite the differences between the two bodies' respective mandates. Chapter 3 continues the examination of the two bodies' asset freezing powers, but this chapter focuses on the practical situations in which the ICC and UNSC (could) have acted in concert. This chapter concludes that, though the bodies frequently act in similar situations (especially before, during, and after armed conflict) and share some of the same aims when asking States to freeze individuals' assets, their actions have rarely been coordinated in this sphere of their respective operations. The focus of Chapters 4 rests on ICTs' power to recover assets through ordering fines, forfeiture and reparations. This chapter concludes that, though most ICTs have been equipped with the power to recover (and, to this end, freeze) assets through one or more of the foregoing mechanisms, they have seldom utilised such procedures in practice. Chapter 5 turns to the law and practice of the ICC with respect to pre-trial protective measures for the purpose of forfeiture. After detailing the various competing rights and interests in the pre-trial asset freezing process, this chapter reaches the conclusion that the Court, by demonstrating a consistent approach in its case law, has thus far struck a fair balance between them. The focus shifts to the UNSC in Chapter 6, which assesses a series of (quasi-)legal protections available to individuals (and entities) subjected to targeted asset freezes imposed under the UN Charter. This chapter concludes that the foregoing protections vary widely between sanctions regimes and even the most robust procedures available in this context fall short of full judicial review. This stands in contrast to the protections available to individuals at the receiving end of ICC-requested asset freezes, who benefit from *inter alia* the right to appeal such measures.[1]

Chapter 7 returns to the approach taken in Chapters 2 and 3 inasmuch as it scrutinises the two bodies' asset freezing powers side-by-side. After arguing that both bodies are constrained by human rights when they request States, which are similarly constrained, to freeze individuals' assets, the chapter examines the principal rights implicated by the

1 See Part 5.2.3.

imposition of such coercive measures through the lens of the case law of the ECtHR and IACtHR. The chapter concludes that the ICC and UNSC ought to explicitly consider a number of principles identified therein, particularly in respect of the length of time for which asset freezing measures remain in force. Chapter 8 demonstrates the potential consequences of prolonged asset freezes, using the case of Jean Pierre Bemba Gombo as an illustration thereof. After detailing the procedural history of the case, which led to Mr Bemba seeking to claim damages from the ICC for the losses he alleged to have suffered, the chapter suggests potential responses at the domestic level and on the international plane through which similar situations might be alleviated in the future. This chapter shows that, though individuals subjected to ICC-requested asset freezes have a range of legal protections available to them after their assets are frozen, lacunae remain in the Rome Statute system, gaps which the preceding chapters demonstrated are also present in the UN Charter system.

Consequently, to conclusively respond to the research question posed at the outset of this book, it can be answered that the asset freezing measures executed at the request of the ICC and UNSC are largely consistent with the rights of the individuals against whom they are imposed, though certain problems remain as far as the protracted application of these procedures are concerned. In light of this conclusion, the following paragraphs detail two recommendations, designed to fit within the confines of ICC Statute and UN Charter as they stand at the time of writing, that could be considered by the two institutions in order to respond to the issues identified herein.

Immediately after dismissing Jean-Pierre Bemba Gombo's claim for damages resulting from the alleged mismanagement of his frozen assets, ICC Pre-Trial Chamber II turned to consider a set of issues under the heading 'Excessive Length of the Proceedings'.[2] At the outset of this discussion, the Pre-Trial Chamber declared itself 'receptive to Mr Bemba's submission to the effect that "[a] decade, to conclude a single accused case, with one form of liability, and events spanning a five-month period, is not reasonable".'[3] Can a similar argument be made in respect of UNSC-requested asset freezing measures? In the view of the present author, the answer to this question must be in the affirmative. For example, Muammar Gaddafi and several persons associated with his regime remain on a UNSC-appointed sanctions committee's list almost a decade after the death of the former

2 *Situation in the Central African Republic* (Decision on Mr Bemba's claim for compensation and damages) ICC-01/05-01/08-3694 (18 May 2020) paras 65-69.

3 ibid, citing *Situation in the Central African Republic* (Public Redacted Version of "Mr. Bemba's claim for compensation and damages") ICC-01/05-01/08-3673-Red (11 March 2019) paras 76-78.

Libyan leader and the ensuing fall of his administration.[4] This continued listing can hardly be said to be reasonable, at least not for the reasons provided on the sanctions committee's webpage.[5]

Chapter 4 demonstrated that the Court has interpreted its legal framework governing pre-trial asset freezing measures in a progressive and transparent manner. It also showed that the rights of those on the receiving end of such measures are protected through a number of safeguards. Still, the presence of these safeguards did not avert the situation examined in Chapter 8 with respect to Mr Bemba's assets. As for the UNSC, Chapter 5 identified a series of (quasi-)legal procedures available under certain UNSC targeted sanctions regimes that offer some form of protection to the individuals (and entities) against whom asset freezing measures (and indeed other sanctions) are imposed. But it was also argued that none of these measures represented full judicial review and that the legal protections available varied widely as between different sanctions regimes. Consequently, informed by the analysis of the case law of the ECtHR and IACtHR conducted in Chapter 7, especially as concerns the temporary, or provisional, nature of such measures as well as the need for judicial supervision thereof, the present author would recommend the following:

Recommendation 1: The ICC and UNSC ought to review asset freezing measures on a regular basis.

At the ICC, it is proposed that this could require the Prosecutor to submit a revised application for protective measures every year on or shortly prior to the anniversary of the date on which such measures were first imposed. For example, if the Pre-Trial Chamber asks States to freeze an accused person's assets on 1 January 2020, in order to ensure the continued application of these measures, the Prosecutor would need to request an extension of the freeze on or shortly before 1 January 2021, with the recipient of such a request to be determined according to the phase of proceedings. As with the Prosecutor's original application under Article 57(3)(e) of the Rome Statute, it is proposed that the chamber seised of the request pay 'due regard to the strength of the evidence and the rights of the parties concerned' in deciding whether to renew the measures.[6] Should the Pre-Trial Chamber ask States to implement asset freezing measures *sua sponte*, that is to say without responding to an application from the Prosecutor, then it would be for the same chamber

4 Security Council Committee Established Pursuant to Resolution 1970 (2011) concerning Libya, 'Narrative Summaries of Reasons for Listing' <https://www.un.org/securitycouncil/sanctions/1970/materials/summaries> accessed 31 August 2020.

5 See Chapter 7, nn 53-54 and accompanying text.

6 Rome Statute, art 57(3)(e).

(or another responsible chamber if at a later phase of proceedings) to renew the measures, again subject to the conditions detailed in Article 57(3)(e).

At the UNSC, this recommendation could require the relevant sanctions committee to review the list of individuals (and entities) subjected to asset freezing (and other coercive) measures on a regular basis. For example, the Security Council Committee pursuant to resolutions 1267 (1999) 1989 (2011) and 2253 (2015) concerning Islamic State in Iraq and the Levant (Da'esh), Al-Qaida and associated individuals, groups, undertakings and entities 'conducts an annual review of all names on the al-Qaida sanctions list that have not been reviewed in three or more years.'[7] Such a mechanism could be extended across all other sanctions regimes with a view to guaranteeing that asset freezing measures executed at the request of the UNSC are, in the words of the research question, more consistent with the rights of all individuals against whom they are imposed. As Feinäugle notes, only a modest number of sanctions committees currently conduct a similar, regular review.[8] In the alternative, UNSC resolutions establishing targeted sanctions regimes comprising asset freezing measures could include a sunset clause as standard.[9] Put otherwise, a 'commitment to review'[10] is insufficient to protect the rights of individuals subjected to asset freezing measures implemented at the behest of the UNSC. UN Member States discussed including such a provision in 2011,[11] but, as Boon shows in a 2017 empirical study, most UNSC resolutions establishing sanctions committees, including several resolutions issued since such discussions took place, do not typically contain such clauses.[12]

This recommendation could be accompanied by a further reform, namely the extension of the mandate of the Office of the Ombudsperson to cover all targeted sanctions regimes operating under the auspices of the UNSC. As with the inclusion of sunset clauses by default, equipping the Office of the Ombudsperson with a broader mandate has also been

7 Clemens A Feinäugle, 'UN Smart Sanctions and the UN Declaration on the Rule of Law' in Matthew Happold and Paul Eden (eds), *Economic Sanctions and International Law* (Hart Publishing 2016) 126, citing UNSC Res 1822 (30 June 2008) UN Doc S/RES/1822, para 13.

8 ibid 130, referring to Security Council Committee pursuant to resolution 751 (1992) concerning Somalia and Security Council Committee established pursuant to resolution 2206 (2015) concerning South Sudan. Feinäugle makes the additional observation that Security Council Committee established pursuant to resolution 1718 (2006) (concerning the Democratic People's Republic of Korea), among other UNSC-appointed committees, 'provide[s] for review but not on an established, regular basis.'

9 For a definition, see Kristen Boon, 'Timing Matters: Termination Policies for UN Sanctions' in Larissa van den Herik (ed), *Research Handbook on UN Sanctions and International Law* (Edward Elgar 2017) 240 ('Typically, a sunset clause will contain language that the measure "ceases to have effect unless it is reauthorized".')

10 ibid 239-42.

11 Feinäugle (n 7) 130.

12 Boon (n 9) 239-42; 255-62.

discussed at the UN level and in the academic literature,[13] but UN Member States would appear to remain divided as far as their support for expanding the Ombudsperson's mandate is concerned. It is notable that the ICC Prosecutor joined the then Ombudsperson (and later ICC Judge) Kimberly Prost in expressing support for making the Ombudsperson procedure available to individuals (and entities) listed by sanctions committees other than that established as regards Islamic State in Iraq and the Levant (Da'esh), Al-Qaida and associated individuals, groups, undertakings and entities.[14] According to a 2014 Press Release issued following a day of debate on ICC-UNSC cooperation subsequent to referrals of situations to the Court by the UN organ and due process considerations in the application of sanctions targeting individuals, the ICC Prosecutor, Fatou Bensouda:

> ... supported extending the Ombudsperson's mandate to all sanctions committees, as almost all of the sanctions regimes that overlapped with situations under investigation by the Court included individuals against whom arrest warrants had been issued.
>
> "There are important areas of convergence between the sanctions regimes and the work of the [ICC] as a whole, which would benefit from a single focal point to address them," she said .... The work of the Council and the Court could similarly benefit from a focal point, which could take the form of a working group for international tribunals.[15]

While the latter proposal might appear attractive from a prosecutorial perspective (insofar as UNSC-requested asset freezing measures have a much broader application),[16] it is rather less appealing when viewed through the eyes of individuals against whom asset freezing measures are imposed at the request of the two bodies. For example, to argue in favour of (customarily) listing individuals named on ICC-issued arrest warrants on UNSC sanctions committees' lists necessarily comprises support for subjecting those individuals to the less-than-robust review and de-listing processes analysed in Chapter 6. Effecting such a reform would therefore need to be coupled with additional measures in order to allay some of the concerns expressed about the legal protections available to individuals subjected to UNSC-requested asset freezes.

13 ibid 242, referring to UNSC 'Speakers Voice Diverging Views on Working Methods, Sanctions Regimes, in Security Council Open Debate' (23 October 2014) Press Release SC/11612 (Working Methods Press Release).
14 Working Methods Press Release (n 13).
15 ibid.
16 See Chapter 6.

Asset Freezing at the International Criminal Court and the United Nations Security Council

A related issue of relevance to the rights of individuals against whom asset freezing measures are imposed at the request of the ICC and the UNSC that has arisen in several chapters of this book is the risk posed by prolonged asset freezes to the *value* of the targeted assets. The case law analysed in Chapter 7 and the Bemba litigation examined in Chapter 8 constitute concrete examples of the impact of such measures on multiple rights. Of course, limiting the length of time for which assets can be frozen without explicit review can serve to mitigate some of this risk, but this step need not be taken in isolation. Alongside the ICC-specific recommendations put forward in the preceding chapter,[17] the present author would recommend the following:

Recommendation 2: The ICC and UNSC ought to take reasonable steps to preserve the value of frozen assets.

This recommendation was discussed in Chapter 8 in the context of examining certain States' approaches to asset freezing under their respective national laws. In this context, it was noted that a number of States provide for third party management of frozen assets in their domestic legal systems with a view to preserving the value of (or generating income from) the targeted property. But how might this recommendation be incorporated into the Rome Statute and UN Charter systems? In the former, the requirement could be satisfied through, for example, the competent organs explicitly asking the States to which the ICC sends requests for cooperation to take such steps under their respective domestic laws. This would appear to be the most likely path in light of the way in which the ICC has characterised the relationship between the Court and States in receipt of cooperation requests, namely that it is for national law to govern such matters.[18] Other options could include amending the Rome Statute to provide for more Court involvement in managing individuals' assets frozen by States at its request.[19] In contrast, the UN Charter would require no amendment to enable the UNSC to request States executing its asset freezing requests to take reasonable steps to protect the value of the targeted assets after taking coercive measures against them. The UNSC could simply add a clause to this effect to the operative paragraphs of the resolution in which it decides on the imposition (and renewal) of asset freezing measures. The case for including such a clause is made even stronger if the UNSC decides to express similar restitutive intentions to that discussed in Chapter 2, namely that 'assets frozen pursuant to … [Resolution 1970] shall at a later stage be made available to and for the benefit of the people of the Libyan Arab Jamahiriya'.[20]

17 See Part 8.4.

18 See Chapter 8.

19 ibid.

20 UNSC Res 1970 (16 February 2011) UN Doc S/RES/1970, para 18. The UNSC '[a]ffirm[ed] its determination' in this regard in UNSC Res 1973 (17 March 2011) UN Doc S/RES/1973, para 20. See Chapter 2.

Returning to the research question posed at the outset of this study, the foregoing analysis has shown that Court-requested asset freezes are largely consistent with the rights of the individuals against whom such measures are imposed. This said, protracted proceedings and the uncertain division of labour between the ICC and cooperating States in managing (and, following an acquittal, unfreezing) assets frozen at the request of the Court threaten to undermine the legal protections enshrined in the Rome Statute. As for the UNSC, the legal protections available to individuals targeted by asset freezes imposed under the UN Charter are not uniform. The asset freezing measures imposed by some UNSC-appointed sanctions committees are therefore more consistent with the listed individuals' rights than those requested by others. And neither constitutes judicial review akin to that available to those at the receiving end of ICC-requested coercive action. The measures detailed in the preceding paragraphs aim to offer suggestions as to how the two bodies might implement the asset freezing procedures at their respective disposal with a view to achieving greater consistency with the rights of those against whom they are imposed.

As this book has demonstrated, freezing individuals' assets contributes to the realisation of a number of purposes for which the ICC and the UNSC were established. At the same time, the employment of such measures inevitably restricts the exercise of multiple rights in accordance with which both bodies are bound to act. So as not to undermine the former, the latter ought to be given due consideration. It is the hope of the present author that the foregoing chapters have shed light on why and how this ought to be done.

Bibliography

Books

Alldridge P, *Money Laundering Law: Forfeiture, Confiscation, Civil Recovery, Criminal Laundering and Taxation of the Proceeds of Crime* (Hart Publishing 2003)

Ambos K, *Treatise on International Criminal Law*, vol III (OUP 2016)

Bass GJ, *Stay the Hand of Vengeance: The Politics of War Crimes Tribunals* (Princeton University Press 2000)

Boister N, *An Introduction to Transnational Criminal Law* (2nd edn, OUP 2018)

Bottigliero I, *Redress for Victims of Crimes Under International Law* (Springer 2014)

Broomhall B, *International Justice and the International Criminal Court: Between Sovereignty and the Rule of Law* (OUP 2003)

Cassella SD, *Asset Forfeiture Law in the United States* (JurisNet 2007)

de Wet E, *The Chapter VII Powers of the United Nations Security Council* (OUP 2004)

Evans C, *The Right to Reparation in International Law for Victims of Armed Conflict* (CUP 2012)

Gibbons ED, *Sanctions in Haiti: Human Rights and Democracy Under Assault* (Praeger 1999)

Heller KJ, *The Nuremberg Military Tribunals and the Origins of International Criminal Law* (OUP 2011)

Hervey T, Cryer R and Sokhi-Bulley B, *Research Methodologies in EU and International Law* (Hart Publishing 2011)

McCarthy C, *Reparations and Victim Support in the International Criminal Court* (CUP 2012

Orakhelashvili A, *Collective Security* (OUP 2011)

Organization of American States, *Asset Management Systems in Latin America and Best Practices Document on Management of Seized and Forfeited Assets* (Organization of American States 2011)

Schabas WA, *The International Criminal Court: A Commentary on the Rome Statute* (2nd edn, OUP 2016)

Schweigman D, *The Authority of the Security Council under Chapter VII of the UN Charter: Legal Limits and the Role of the International Court of Justice* (Kluwer Law International 2001)

Tzanakopoulos A, *Disobeying the Security Council: Countermeasures against Wrongful Sanctions* (OUP 2011)

Williams S, *Hybrid and Internationalised Criminal Tribunals: Selected Jurisdictional Issues* (Hart Publishing 2012)

Chapters in Edited Books

Abels D, 'Limiting the Objectives of the Enforcement of International Punishment' in Róisín Mulgrew and Denis Abels (eds), *Research Handbook on the International Penal System* (Edward Elgar 2016)

Ambos K, 'Command Responsibility and *Organisationsherrschaft*: Ways of Attributing International Crimes to the "Most Responsible"' in André Nollkaemper and Harmen van der Wilt (eds), *System Criminality in International Law* (CUP 2009)

Bentall P, 'United Nations targeted sanctions and other policy tools: diplomacy, legal, use of force' in Thomas J Biersteker, Sue E Eckert and Marcos Tourinho (eds), *Targeted Sanctions: The Impacts and Effectiveness of United Nations Action* (CUP 2016)

Berman F, 'The Relationship Between the International Criminal Court and the Security Council' in Herman von Hebel, Johan G Lammers and Jolien Schukking (eds), *Reflections on the International Criminal Court: Essays in Honour of Adriaan Bos* (TMC Asser Press 1999)

Biersteker TJ, Tourinho M and Eckert SE, 'Thinking about United Nations targeted sanctions' in Thomas J Biersteker, Sue E Eckert and Marcos Tourinho (eds) *Targeted Sanctions: The Impacts and Effectiveness of United Nations Actions* (CUP 2016)

Blanco Cordero I, 'Modern Forms of Confiscation and Protection of Third Parties' in Katalin Ligeti and Michele Simonato (eds), *Chasing Criminal Money: Challenges and Perspectives on Asset Recovery in the EU* (Hart Publishing 2017)

Boon K, 'Timing Matters: Termination Policies for UN Sanctions' in Larissa van den Herik (ed), *Research Handbook on UN Sanctions and International Law* (Edward Elgar 2017)

Cassella SD, 'Asset Forfeiture in the United States' in Simon NM Young (ed), *Civil Forfeiture of Criminal Property: Legal Measures for Targeting the Proceeds of Crime* (Edward Elgar 2009) 23

— — 'Civil Asset Recovery: The American Experience' in Jon Petter Rui and Ulrich Sieber (eds), *Non-Conviction-Based Confiscation in Europe: Possibilities and Limitations on Rules Enabling Confiscation without a Criminal Conviction* (Duncker & Humblot 2016)

Ciampi A, 'Security Council Targeted Sanctions and Human Rights' in Bardo Fassbender (ed), *Securing Human Rights? Achievements and Challenges of the UN Security Council* (OUP 2011)

Colonomos A and Armstrong A, 'German Reparations to Jews after World War II: A Turning Point in the History of Reparations' in Pablo de Greiff (ed), *The Handbook of Reparations* (OUP 2006)

Cortright D and Lopez GA, 'Introduction: Assessing Smart Sanctions: Lessons from the 1990s' in David Cortright and George A Lopez (eds), *Smart Sanctions: Targeting Economic Statecraft* (Rowman & Littlefield 2002)

de Brouwer A-M and Heikkilä M, 'Victim Issues: Participation, Protection, Reparation, and Assistance' in Göran Sluiter and others (eds), *International Criminal Procedure: Principles and Rules* (OUP 2013)

de Wet E, 'Human Rights Considerations and the Enforcement of Targeted Sanctions in Europe: The Emergence of Core Standards of Judicial Protection' in Bardo Fassbender (ed), *Securing Human Rights? Achievements and Challenges of the UN Security Council* (OUP 2011)

Devin J and Dashti-Gibson J, 'Sanctions in the Former Yugoslavia: Convoluted Goals and Complicated Consequences' in Thomas G Weiss and others (eds), *Political Gain and Civilian Pain: Humanitarian Impacts of Economic Sanctions* (Rowman & Littlefield 1998) 149

Eden P, 'United Nations Targeted Sanctions, Human Rights and the Office of the Ombudsperson' in Matthew Happold and Paul Eden (eds), *Economic Sanctions and International Law* (Hart Publishing 2016)

Feinäugle CA, 'UN Smart Sanctions and the UN Declaration on the Rule of Law' in Matthew Happold and Paul Eden (eds), *Economic Sanctions and International Law* (Hart Publishing 2016)

Ferstman C, 'Cooperation and the International Criminal Court: The Freezing, Seizing and Transfer of Assets for the Purpose of Reparations' in Olympia Bekou and Daley J Birkett (eds), *Cooperation and the International Criminal Court: Perspectives from Theory and Practice* (Brill Nijhoff 2016)

Furuya S, 'Victim Participation, Reparations and Reintegration as Historical Building Blocks of International Criminal Law' in Morten Bergsmo and others (eds), *Historical Origins of International Criminal Law: Volume 4* (Torkel Opsahl Academic EPublisher 2015)

Gowlland-Debbas V, 'Implementing Sanctions Resolutions in Domestic Law' in Vera Gowlland-Debbas (ed), *National Implementation of United Nations Sanctions: A Comparative Study* (Martinus Nijhoff 2004)

Guariglia F and Hochmayr G, 'Article 57' in Otto Triffterer and Kai Ambos (eds), *The Rome Statute of the International Criminal Court: A Commentary* (3rd edn, CH Beck/Hart Publishing/Nomos 2016)

Hall C and Jacobs DL, 'Article 55' in Otto Triffterer and Kai Ambos (eds), *The Rome Statute of the International Criminal Court: A Commentary* (3rd edn, CH Beck/Hart Publishing/Nomos 2016)

Happold M, 'Targeted Sanctions and Human Rights' in Matthew Happold and Paul Eden (eds), *Economic Sanctions and International Law* (Hart Publishing 2016)

Hoskins E, 'The Humanitarian Impacts of Economic Sanctions and War in Iraq' in Thomas G Weiss and others (eds), *Political Gain and Civilian Pain: Humanitarian Impacts of Economic Sanctions* (Rowman & Littlefield 1998)

Jorge G, 'Article 31: Freezing, Seizure, and Confiscation' in Cecily Rose, Michael Kubiciel and Oliver Landwehr (eds), *The United Nations Convention Against Corruption: A Commentary* (OUP 2019)

Mancini M, 'UN Sanctions Targeting Individuals and ICC Proceedings: How to Achieve a Mutually Reinforcing Interaction' in Natalino Ronzitti (ed), *Coercive Diplomacy, Sanctions and International Law* (Brill Nijhoff 2016)

Mueller GOW, 'Transnational Crime: Definitions and Concepts' in Phil Williams and Dimitri Vlassis (eds), *Combating Transnational Crime: Concepts, Activities and Responses* (Frank Cass 2001)

Mulgrew R, 'The costs of suspicion: a critical analysis of the compensation scheme established by Article 85(3) of the Rome Statute' in Róisín Mulgrew and Denis Abels (eds), *Research Handbook on the International Penal System* (Edward Elgar 2016)

Nerlich V, 'Article 21 (3) of the ICC Statute: Identifying and Applying "Internationally Recognized Human Rights"' in Paolo Lobba and Triestino Mariniello (eds), *Judicial Dialogue on Human Rights: The Practice of International Criminal Tribunals* (Brill Nijhoff 2017)

Panzavolta M and Flor R, 'A Necessary Evil? The Italian "Non-Criminal System" of Asset Forfeiture' in Jon Petter Rui and Ulrich Sieber (eds), *Non-Conviction-Based Confiscation in Europe: Possibilities and Limitations on Rules Enabling Confiscation without a Criminal Conviction* (Duncker & Humblot 2016)

Prost K, 'The Office of the Ombudsperson: A case for fair process' in Jeremy Farrall and Hilary Charlesworth (eds), *Strengthening the Rule of Law through the UN Security Council* (Routledge 2016)

Rastan R, 'Situation and case: defining the parameters' in Carsten Stahn and Mohamed M El Zeidy (eds), *The International Criminal Court and Complementarity: From Theory to Practice* (CUP 2011)

Roskam H, 'Crime-Based Targeted Sanctions: Promoting Respect for International Humanitarian Law by the Security Council' in Terry D Gill and others (eds), *Yearbook of International Humanitarian Law 2016* (TMC Asser Press 2018)

Rui JP, 'Introduction' in Jon Petter Rui and Ulrich Sieber (eds), *Non-Conviction-Based Confiscation in Europe: Possibilities and Limitations on Rules Enabling Confiscation without a Criminal Conviction* (Duncker & Humblot 2016)

Scheffer D, 'The Extraordinary Chambers in the Courts of Cambodia' in M Cherif Bassiouni (ed), *International Criminal Law Volume III: International Enforcement* (3rd edn, Martinus Nijhoff 2008)

Simons G, *The Scourging of Iraq: Sanctions, Law and Natural Justice* (Macmillan 1996)

Sluiter G, 'Human Rights Protection in the ICC Pre-Trial Phase' in Carsten Stahn and Göran Sluiter (eds), *The Emerging Practice of the International Criminal Court* (Martinus Nijhoff 2009)

—— 'International Criminal Tribunals and their Relation to States' in André Nollkaemper and Ilias Plakokefalos (eds), *The Practice of Shared Responsibility in International Law* (CUP 2017)

Smeulers A, 'Perpetrators of International Crimes: Towards a Typology' in Alette Smeulers and Roelof Haveman (eds), *Supranational Criminology: Towards a Criminology of International Crimes* (Intersentia 2008)

—— and Holá B, 'ICTY and the Culpability of Different Types of Perpetrators of International Crimes' in Alette Smeulers (ed), *Collective Violence and International Criminal Justice: An Interdisciplinary Approach* (Intersentia 2010)

Spörl C, 'Article 2: Use of Terms' in Cecily Rose, Michael Kubiciel and Oliver Landwehr (eds), *The United Nations Convention Against Corruption: A Commentary* (OUP 2019)

Stiel M and Stuckenberg C-F, 'Article 109: Enforcement of fines and forfeiture measures' in Klamberg M (ed), *Commentary on the Law of the International Criminal Court* (Torkel Opsahl Academic EPublisher 2017)

van den Herik L, 'The Individualisation of Enforcement in International Law: Exploring the Interplay between United Nations Targeted Sanctions and International Criminal

Proceedings' in Tiyanjana Maluwa, Max du Plessis and Dire Tladi (eds), *The Pursuit of a Brave New World in International Law: Essays in Honour of John Dugard* (Brill Nijhoff 2017)

van der Wilt H, 'Joint Criminal Enterprise and Functional Perpetration' in André Nollkaemper and Harmen van der Wilt (eds), *System Criminality in International Law* (CUP 2009)

Yee L, 'The International Criminal Court and The Security Council: Articles 13(b) and 16' in Roy S Lee (ed), *The International Criminal Court: The Making of the Rome Statute: Issues, Negotiations, Results* (Kluwer Law International 1999)

Young R, 'Fines and Forfeiture in International Criminal Justice' in Róisín Mulgew and Denis Abels (eds), *Research Handbook on the International Penal System* (Edward Elgar 2016)

Zaidi S, 'Humanitarian Effects of the Coup and Sanctions in Haiti' in Thomas G Weiss and others (eds), *Political Gain and Civilian Pain: Humanitarian Impacts of Economic Sanctions* (Rowman & Littlefield 1998)

Zappalà S, 'Compensation to an Arrested or Convicted Person', in Antonio Cassese, Paola Gaeta and John RWD Jones (eds), *The Rome Statute of the International Criminal Court: A Commentary* (OUP 2002)

— — 'Comparative Models and the Enduring Relevance of the Accusatorial – Inquisitorial Dichotomy' in Göran Sluiter and others (eds), *International Criminal Procedure: Principles and Rules* (OUP 2013)

Articles

'Developments in the Law: International Criminal Law' (2000) 114 Harvard Law Review 1943

Akhavan P, 'Beyond Impunity: Can International Criminal Justice Prevent Future Atrocities?' (2001) 95 American Journal of International Law 7

— — 'Are International Criminal Tribunals a Disincentive to Peace: Reconciling Judicial Romanticism with Political Realism' (2009) 31 Human Rights Quarterly 624

Ali MM and Shah IH, 'Sanctions and childhood mortality in Iraq' (2000) 355 The Lancet 1851

Akande D, 'The Legal Nature of Security Council Referrals to the ICC and its Impact on Al Bashir's Immunities' (2009) 7 Journal of International Criminal Justice 333

Arsanjani MH and Reisman WM, 'The Law-in-Action of the International Criminal Court' (2005) 99 American Journal of International Law 385

Banteka N, 'Mind the Gap: A Systematic Approach to the International Criminal Court's Arrest Warrants Enforcement Problem' (2016) 49 Cornell International Law Journal 521

Bassiouni MC, 'Justice and Peace: The Importance of Choosing Accountability over Realpolitik' (2003) 35 Case Western Reserve Journal of International Law 191

Bekou O, 'A Case for Review of Article 88, ICC Statute: Strengthening a Forgotten Provision' (2009) 12 New Criminal Law Review 468

Beresford S, 'Redressing the Wrongs of the International Justice System: Compensation for Persons Erroneously Detained, Prosecuted, or Convicted by the Ad Hoc Tribunals' (2002) 96 American Journal of International Law 628

Bergsmo M, 'Occasional Remarks on Certain State Concerns about the Jurisdictional Reach of the International Criminal Court, and Their Possible Implications for the Relationship between the Court and the Security Council' (2000) 69 Nordic Journal of International Law 87

Berman PS, 'An Anthropological Approach to Modern Forfeiture Law: The Symbolic Function of Legal Actions Against Objects' (1999) 11 Yale Journal of Law & the Humanities 1

Birkett DJ, 'Victims' Justice? Reparations and Asset Forfeiture at the Extraordinary African Chambers' (2019) 63 Journal of African Law 151

Blumenson E and Nilsen E, 'Policing for Profit: The Drug War's Hidden Economic Agenda' (1998) 65 University of Chicago Law Review

Bogart JH, 'Punishment and the Subordination of Law to Morality' (1987) 7 Oxford Journal of Legal Studies 421

Boister N, 'Transnational Criminal Law?' (2003) 14 European Journal of International Law 953

Boucht J, 'Extended Confiscation and the Proposed Directive on Freezing and Confiscation of Criminal Proceeds in the EU: On Striking a Balance between Efficiency, Fairness and Legal Certainty' (2013) 21 European Journal of Crime, Criminal Law and Criminal Justice 127

— — 'Civil Asset Forfeiture and the Presumption of Innocence under Article 6(2) ECHR' (2014) 5 New Journal of European Criminal Law 221

Cassese A, 'On the Current Trends towards Criminal Prosecution and Punishment of Breaches of International Humanitarian Law' (1998) 9 European Journal of International Law 2

— — 'The Statute of the International Criminal Court: Some Preliminary Reflections' (1999) 10 European Journal of International Law 144

Clark JN, 'Peace, Justice and the International Criminal Court: Limitations and Possibilities' (2011) 9 Journal of International Criminal Justice 521

Condorelli L and Ciampi A, 'Comments on the Security Council Referral of the Situation in Darfur to the ICC' (2005) 3 Journal of International Criminal Justice 590

Criddle EJ, 'Humanitarian Financial Intervention' (2013) 24 European Journal of International Law 583

Croquet NAJ, 'The International Criminal Court and the Treatment of Defence Rights: A Mirror of the European Court of Human Rights' Jurisprudence?' (2011) 11 Human Rights Law Review 91

Cross ME, 'Equipping the Specialist Chambers of Kosovo to Try Transnational Crimes: Remarks on Independence and Cooperation' (2016) 14 Journal of International Criminal Justice 73

Cryer R, 'Sudan, Resolution 1593, and International Criminal Justice' (2006) 19 Leiden Journal of International Law 195

— — and Bekou O, 'International Crimes and ICC Cooperation in England and Wales' (2007) 5 Journal of International Criminal Justice 441

Damaška M, 'What Is the Point of International Criminal Justice?' (2008) 83 Chicago-Kent Law Review 329

— — 'The International Criminal Court between Aspiration and Achievement' (2009) 14 UCLA Journal of International Law and Foreign Affairs 19

de Wet E, 'Human Rights Limitations to Economic Enforcement Measures Under Article 41 of the UN Charter and the Iraqi Sanctions Regime' (2001) 14 Leiden Journal of International Law 284

— — 'From *Kadi* to *Nada*: Judicial Techniques Favouring Human Rights over United Nations Security Council Sanctions' (2013) 12 Chinese Journal of International Law 787

Diab NI, 'Challenges in the Implementation of the Reparation Award against Hissein Habré: Can the Spell of Unenforceable Awards across the Globe be Broken?' (2018) 16 Journal of International Criminal Justice 141

Finkelstein J, 'The Goring Ox: Some Historical Perspectives on Deodands, Forfeitures, Wrongful Death and the Western Notion of Sovereignty' (1973) 46 Temple Law Quarterly 169

Fletcher GP and Ohlin JD, 'The ICC — Two Courts in One?', (2006) 4 Journal of International Criminal Justice 428

Ford S, 'Complexity and Efficiency at International Criminal Courts' (2014) 29 Emory International Law Review 1

Fried DJ, 'Rationalizing Criminal Forfeiture' (1988-1989) 79 Journal of Criminal Law & Criminology 328, 329

Gaeta P, 'Is the Practice of 'Self-Referrals' a Sound Start for the ICC?' (2004) 2 Journal of International Criminal Justice 949

— — 'Does President Al Bashir Enjoy Immunity from Arrest?' (2009) 7 Journal of International Criminal Justice 315

Galbraith J, 'The Pace of International Criminal Justice' (2009) 31 Michigan Journal of International Law 79

Galvis Martínez M, 'Forfeiture of Assets at the International Criminal Court: The Short Arm of International Criminal Justice' (2014) 12 Journal of International Criminal Justice 193

Geneuss J, 'Obstacles to Cross-fertilisation: The International Criminal Tribunals' 'Unique Context' and the Flexibility of the European Court of Human Rights' Case Law' (2015) 84 Nordic Journal of International Law 404

Ginsborg L and Scheinin M, 'You Can't Always Get What You Want: The Kadi II Conundrum and the Security Council 1267 Terrorist Sanctions Regime' (2011) 8 Essex Human Rights Review 7

Godinho J, 'When Worlds Collide: Enforcing United Nations Security Council Asset Freezes in the EU Legal Order' (2010) 16 European Law Journal

Goldsmith M and Linderman MJ, 'Asset Forfeiture and Third Party Rights: The Need for Further Law Reform' (1989) 5 Duke Law Journal 1254

Hendry J and King C, 'How far is too far? Theorising non-conviction-based asset forfeiture' (2015) 11 International Journal of Law in Context 398

Hutchinson T and Duncan N, 'Defining and Describing What We Do: Doctrinal Legal Research' (2012) 17(1) Deakin Law Review 83

Jones A, 'Insights Into an Emerging Relationship: Use of Human Rights Jurisprudence at the International Criminal Court' (2016) 16 Human Rights Law Review 701

Kendall S, 'Commodifying Global Justice: Economies of Accountability at the International Criminal Court' (2015) Journal of International Criminal Justice 113

Koller DS and Eckenfels-Garcia M, 'Using Targeted Sanctions to End Violations against Children in Armed Conflict' (2015) 33 Boston University International Law Journal 1

McCarthy C, 'Reparations under the Rome Statute of the International Criminal Court and Reparative Justice Theory' (2009) 3 International Journal of Transitional Justice 250

Michels JD, 'Compensating Acquitted Defendants for Detention before International Criminal Courts' (2010) 8 Journal of International Criminal Justice (2010) 407

Nollkaemper A and Jacobs D, 'Shared Responsibility in International Law: A Conceptual Framework', 34 Michigan Journal of International Law (2013) 359

King C, 'Civil Forfeiture and Article 6 of the ECHR: Due Process Implications for England & Wales and Ireland' (2014) 34 Legal Studies 371

Neuner M, 'The Security Council and the ICC: Assessing the First Ten Years of Coexistence' (2012) 18 New England Journal of International and Comparative Law 283

Noorda H, 'Preventive Deprivations of Liberty: Asset Freezes and Travel Bans' (2015) 9 Criminal Law and Philosophy 521

Nouwen SMH, 'Hybrid Courts: The Hybrid Category of a New Type of International Crimes Courts' (2006) 2 Utrecht Law Review 190

O'Connell ME, 'Debating the Law of Sanctions' (2002) 13 European Journal of International Law 63

Oette L, 'Peace and Justice, or Neither? The Repercussions of the Al-Bashir Case for International Criminal Justice in Africa and Beyond' (2010) 8 Journal of International Criminal Justice 345 (2010)

Ohlin JD, 'A Meta-Theory of International Criminal Procedure: Vindicating the Rule of Law' (2009) 14 UCLA Journal of International Law and Foreign Affairs 77

Orakhelashvili A, 'The Impact of Peremptory Norms on the Interpretation and Application of United Nations Security Council Resolutions' (2005) 16 European Journal of International Law 59

Pape RA, 'Why Economic Sanctions Do Not Work' (1997) 22 International Security 90

Prost K, 'A Reflection on Innovations in the Security Council: The International Tribunals, Counterterrorism, and the Office of the Ombudsperson' (2014) 46 Case Western Reserve Journal of International Law 465

Ramsden M and Hamilton T, 'Uniting Against Impunity: The UN General Assembly as a Catalyst for Action at the ICC' (2017) 66 International and Comparative Law Quarterly 893

Rastan R, 'Testing Co-operation: The International Criminal Court and National Authorities' (2008) 21 Leiden Journal of International Law 431

Robinson D, 'Inescapable Dyads: Why the International Criminal Court Cannot Win' (2015) 28 Leiden Journal of International Law 323

Rodman KA, 'Darfur and the Limits of Legal Deterrence' (2008) 30 Human Rights Quarterly 529

— — 'Is Peace in the Interests of Justice? The Case for Broad Prosecutorial Discretion at the International Criminal Court' (2009) 22 Leiden Journal of International Law 99

— — 'Justice as a Dialogue Between Law and Politics: Embedding the International Criminal Court within Conflict Management and Peacebuilding' (2014) 12 Journal of International Criminal Justice 437

Sarooshi D, 'Aspects of the Relationship between the International Criminal Court and the United Nations' (2001) 32 Netherlands Yearbook of International Law 27

Schabas WA, 'The Banality of International Justice' (2013) 11 Journal of International Criminal Justice 545

Scharf M, 'The Letter of the Law: The Scope of the International Legal Obligation to Prosecute Human Rights Crimes' (1996) 59 Law and Contemporary Problems 41

— — 'The Tools for Enforcing International Criminal Justice in the New Millennium: Lessons from the Yugoslavia Tribunal' (2000) 49 DePaul Law Review 925

Schrag M, 'Lessons Learned from ICTY Experience' (2004) 2 Journal of International Criminal Justice 427

Sejko D and Birkett DJ, 'When United Nations Sanctions Impact International Financial Governance: Lessons from the Libyan Sovereign Wealth Fund' (2018) 34 American University International Law Review 387

Simonato M, 'Extended Confiscation of Criminal Assets: Limits and Pitfalls of Minimum Harmonisation in the EU' (2016) 41 European Law Review 727

— — 'Confiscation and fundamental rights across criminal and non-criminal domains' (2017) 18 ERA Forum 365

Sluiter G, 'Obtaining Cooperation from Sudan – Where Is the Law?' (2008) 6 Journal of International Criminal Justice 871

Smeulers A, Hola B and van den Berg T, 'Sixty-Five Years of International Criminal Justice: The Facts and Figures' (2013) 13 International Criminal Law Review 7

Trumbull IV CP, 'The Victims of Victim Participation in International Criminal Proceedings' (2008) 29 Michigan Journal of International Law 777

van den Broek M, Hazelhorst M and de Zanger W, 'Asset Freezing: Smart Sanction or Criminal Charge?' (2011) 27 Utrecht Journal of International and European Law 18

Van den Wyngaert C, 'Victims before International Criminal Courts: Some Views and Concerns of an ICC Trial Judge' (2011) 44 Case Western Reserve Journal of International Law 475

van Sliedregt E, 'Editorial – International Criminal Law: Over-studied and Underachieving?' (2016) 29 Leiden Journal of International Law 1

van Wijk J and Holá B, 'Acquittals in International Criminal Justice: Pyrrhic Victories?' (2017) 30 Leiden Journal of International Law 241

Wartanian A, 'The ICC Prosecutor's Battlefield: Combating Atrocities While Fighting for States' Cooperation: Lessons from the U.N. Tribunals Applied to the Case of Uganda' (2005) 36 Georgetown Journal of International Law 1289

Weil S, 'The American Legal Response to the Problem of Holocaust Art' (1999) 4 Art, Antiquity and Law 285

Whittle D, 'The Limits of Legality and the United Nations Security Council: Applying the Extra-Legal Measures Model to Chapter VII Action' (2015) 26 European Journal of International Law 671

Whiting A, 'In International Criminal Prosecutions, Justice Delayed Can Be Justice Delivered', 50 Harvard International Law Journal (2009) 323

Wippman D, 'Atrocities, Deterrence, and the Limits of International Justice' (1999) 23 Fordham International Law Journal 473

Zappalà S, 'The Rights of Victims v. the Rights of the Accused' (2010) 8 Journal of International Criminal Justice 137

Zegveld L, 'Victims' Reparations Claims and International Criminal Courts: Incompatible Values?' (2010) 8 Journal of International Criminal Justice 79

Zhu W, 'On co-operation by states not party to the International Criminal Court' (2006) 88 International Review of the Red Cross 87

Newspaper Articles

Agence France-Presse, 'Congo Ex-Official Is Held in Belgium on War Crimes Charges' *The New York Times* (25 May 2008) <www.nytimes.com/2008/05/25/world/africa/25congo.html> accessed 31 August 2020

Owen Bowcott, 'Sudan president Omar al-Bashir leaves South Africa as court considers arrest' *The Guardian* (15 June 2015) <www.theguardian.com/world/2015/jun/15/south-africa-to-fight-omar-al-bashirs-arrest-warrant-sudan> accessed 31 August 2020

O'Brien F, 'High Court freezes €52m worth of Bitcoin seized by CAB' *Raidió Teilifís Éireann* (19 February 2020) <https://www.rte.ie/news/courts/2020/0219/1116299-bit-coin-clifton-collins/> accessed 31 August 2020

Pires BF, 'Last stop Faro?' *Algarve 123* (15 March 2012) (copy on file with author)

Simons M, 'Jean-Pierre Bemba, Congolese politician, appears in Hague court' *The New York Times* (4 July 2008) <www.nytimes.com/2008/07/04/world/africa/04iht-05hague.14247286.html> accessed 31 August 2020

Blog Posts

Hale K and Vargas Niño S, 'Unexploded Legal Ordnance' (*Opinio Juris*, 10 April 2019) <http://opiniojuris.org/2019/04/10/unexploded-legal-ordnance/> accessed 31 August 2020

Heller KJ, 'Bim, Bam, Bem-Boom!' (*Opinio Juris*, 12 March 2019) <http://opiniojuris.org/2019/03/12/bim-bam-bemb-oom/> accessed 31 August 2020

Litwin J, 'Smarter Sanctions: The Use of Targeted Asset Freezes and Travel Bans by the ICC to Effectuate Arrests' (*ICC Forum*, 13 March 2014) <www.iccforum.com/forum/permalink/93/4086> accessed 31 August 2020

Other Secondary Sources

FATF, 'International Standards on Combating Money Laundering and the Financing of Terrorism & Proliferation' (FATF 2012)

— — 'Financial Action Task Force – 30 Years' (FATF 2019)

G8 Lyon/Roma Group, Criminal Legal Affairs Subgroup, 'Best Practices for the Administration of Seized Assets' (27 April 2005)

Garfield R, 'Morbidity and Mortality Among Iraqi Children from 1990 Through 1998: Assessing the Impact of the Gulf War and Economic Sanctions' (Campaign Against Sanctions on Iraq (CASI), July 1999) <http://www.casi.org.uk/info/garfield/dr-garfield.html> accessed 31 August 2020

ICC, 'Financial investigations and recovery of assets' (ICC 2017)

ICC Prosecutor, 'Prosecutor's statement to the United Nations Security Council on the situation in Libya, pursuant to UNSCR 1970 (2011)' (New York, 2 November 2011) <https://www.legal-tools.org/doc/bil32o/> accessed 31 August 2020

Office of the US High Commissioner for Germany, 'Landsberg: A Documentary Report' (Office of the US High Commissioner for Germany 1951)

Swiss Federal Office of Justice, 'Taylor's accounts blocked as provisional measure: Legal assistance requested by Special Court for Sierra Leone' (Press Release, Bern, Switzerland,

23 June 2013) <https://www.bj.admin.ch/bj/en/home/aktuell/news/2003/2003-06-230.html> accessed 31 August 2020

Swiss Federal Office of Police, 'Décision de l'Office fédéral de la police dans l'affaire *Milosevic Slobodan* et autres' (23 June 1999) <www.admin.ch/opc/fr/federal-gazette/1999/4796.pdf> accessed 31 August 2020

www.ingramcontent.com/pod-product-compliance
Ingram Content Group UK Ltd.
Pitfield, Milton Keynes, MK11 3LW, UK
UKHW051118290926
15471UKWH00010B/1737

9 789462 361850